# Hearts and Collars

## Twenty Years in a Power Exchange Relationship

by Dan and dawn Williams

First Edition

First Printing, 2022

Layout and graphic design by Catherine Rogers

Editing and back matter by Elyria Little

Cover art © 2022 Janet Hardy

Author photo © 2018 kame bat

Interior artwork by Aether Studio, LLC

Williams, Dan and dawn.

Hearts and Collars: Twenty Years in a Power Exchange Relationship / Dan and dawn Williams. — 1st ed.

ISBN 9798818640198

1. Sex & Sexuality 2. Relationships—United States. I. Title. Hearts and Collars: Twenty Years in a Power Exchange Relationship

Library of Congress Control Number: 2022908629

Please refer to the author's website with any questions: www.eroticawakening.com

Printed in Box Elder, SD

United States of America

# *Dedication*

## *Dan says*

At an event not long ago, I noticed someone wandering around, trying to see if they fit in. Both awkward and shy, they had a look that they were worried that they might not be pretty enough or confident enough to fit in. Everyone else seemed busy, greeting old friends or having conversations or flirting, and this person seemed on the verge of heading to a corner to pull out their phone while they tried to figure out what to do next.

kame bat would have made a beeline toward that person, introduced herself, and just started talking about anything and everything. Then she would have helped the person move around and started to introduce them to others. I've seen her do that countless times. And it wasn't just for people who were attending for the first time or getting over that initial panic of being a new person in a new place. She would stay engaged until that person felt they were indeed 'enough' and that they belonged.

kame bat spent years in my collar because she needed to grow in a certain way that I could assist with. She then moved on, only to return to my collar a few years later because she wanted to. I was glad - even honored - to have her back.

She died in 2020. Her last act of service was to organize and throw a benefit for someone who was preparing for a title run.

This book is dedicated to you, bat. There are no more words.

*dawn says*

There are so many people I'd like to dedicate this book to. People who have supported us on this journey over the last two decades. From close friends to podcast listeners, poly partners to even our children. And as you can imagine, that list is long… I'm sitting here wondering if I can just mention a few names, but then I think of all the names that I wouldn't be mentioning that deserve space here, as well. So, I'm not going to start listing them for fear of leaving someone out. Many of you know who you are.

But, I will mention bat.

She showed up at a perfect time and brought rainbows to our life. To my life. Literally. I have pictures.

She embraced my friendship while in service to Dan, and even for those years that she wasn't collared, we supported each other in finding our deep strengths in this world… in service, in our relationships, and spiritually.

She was my friend, and I miss her. I miss everything about her. Her kindness. Her dedication. Her friendship. Her love.

*For kame bat*

# Table of Contents

# Introduction

## How This Book is Written

This book is co-authored by two people, Dan and dawn. As we wrote it, we kept our own voices. We have our own perspectives on various topics - that of the Leader and that of a follower. As we continue throughout the book, you'll see sections sub-headed with a "Dan says" or "dawn says" to represent who wrote each part. If you have listened to our podcast, Erotic Awakening, or seen us present on power exchange or other topics, we hope you'll be able to hear our voices in these writings; how we write is very similar to how we speak.

# A Bit of Background

## *Dan says*

Depending on how you look at things, you could say we started writing this book in March 2001. That might lead you to assume we are particularly slow writers but in actuality, we've published five other books between then and now. I say we started this in 2001 because that is when we started a full time power exchange relationship. During that time, we practiced a variety of tools, ideas, and concepts in working out exactly what it took to have a healthy, long term power exchange relationship.

Things have been going very well. We are happy, healthy, and still enjoying our roles and our power exchange. But as we approached the twentieth anniversary of the moment we started this journey, we decided to step back and take a deep look at our relationship. Not because we thought anything was broken - just the opposite, as we will both attest to this being the happiest we've ever been. Instead, it is a matter of cultivation. We wanted to make sure that not only was our relationship still as healthy as we perceived it to be, but also that it was growing. That we were growing. We realized that we have changed over the last twenty years, and we wanted to examine how this full time power exchange relationship still fed us.

The more we explored, the more we realized that we had learned a lot in the years since we last published a power exchange book. Since then (2011), we've presented over 300 classes at more than 150 different events; hosted over 500 episodes of our podcast on power exchange and other topics; run multiple power exchange events which ranged from the intimate formal ones to larger multi-day conferences.

Further, we have had a number of new experiences. Friends who live a similar lifestyle who taught us, as well as power exchange relationships in the form of collars that I put on people and brought into our pod. Those relationships at this time have all transitioned in a variety of ways - one of those people left my collar to go get married and have a very normal looking life. And on the opposite spectrum, another ended because someone in service to us died in a hospital bed while we sat with them, powerless.

It is these and many other experiences, lessons, and explorations that led us to write this collection you are reading now.

## A Collection

Within the following pages, we present a variety of stories, examples, and tools from the past twenty years of our lives. They range from concepts that have worked wonderfully well for us and others in our lives, as well as boneheaded mistakes that we hope you'll avoid making. We have brought them together here in a collection of our practical experience. Whether you are new to power exchange or have been around for some time, we believe you'll find a lot of value here.

There is neither desire nor expectations that you'll blindly accept anything in this book. Like going clothes shopping, try everything on. And if it doesn't fit, leave it on the rack.

## *dawn says*

As you'll notice, we write from our experience. There isn't any theory being offered here. This is our journey, our stories, our reflections, and the tools and lessons that we've discovered over the last two decades. By being vulnerable and sharing the good, the bad, and the ugly, we hope to help others in their quest for a healthy hierarchical relationship. We'd like to think that buried in our stories are nuggets of wisdom.

Regardless, welcome to this book! Welcome to this exploration! We hope you find it of value.

# Some Language

### *Dan says*

Within this book, we use a variety of language to describe the roles in power exchange. dawn and I have claimed (and earned) a few different titles that describe and help define our power exchange throughout the years - Dom/sub, Master/slave, Belum/belet. You may be using these same titles yourselves, or you may prefer others - Owner/property, Master/kajira, Lady/servant, Daddy/boi.

Most of the time in this book, I default to the terms Leader/follower just to keep it simple. Yet, sometimes it feels more authentic to use the terms we used at the time we are describing in the book, so you'll see that term instead.

To be honest, we've come to realize that for us, the term doesn't actually define the relationship. When dawn and I ran an event called Power eXchange Summit for several years, we brought all types of power exchange people together. The event had workshops, classes, peer sessions, and social interactions over a three day period. And what we found is that Leather Masters and Daddy doms nodded at the same things. Property and subs shared the same general challenges. Although the words we used to identify ourselves have value, we do not suggest that one label for power exchange is any better than another.

When dawn and I use titles, we use Belum and belet (Belum is after the name, so it is Daniel Belum and belet dawn), which is just another form of Leader and follower (more about those terms below). Whether you identify as a Domme or as a pet or any other power exchange type, this book and what it contains will be of value to you. When you read the term 'Leader' or 'follower' in these pages, you'll know if it is you.

Beyond that, here is a quick review of some definitions of words you might come across in this book that you may not be familiar with.

Note that we will continue with the common practice in power exchange culture of capitalizing the Leader role (Leader, Dom, Master, Owner) and not capitalizing the follower role (follower, submissive, property, slave). Further, as it is our habit, dawn's name is not capitalized. We find this of value in our relationship. Follow whatever protocol you are comfortable with in yours. We promise not to report you to the grammar police.

**Leader** - A person who is responsible for a power exchange relationship. It is a non-gender based term. The action of being a Leader and what it means to me and to you is far deeper than that one sentence. But a good half of this book is exploring those words (Leader, follower) so for now, we will leave it at that.

**follower** - A non-gender based term for the person responsible for the Leader. See above for thoughts on how broad this definition is - you'll see that dawn has written many pages on what it means to be a follower in the coming chapters.

**Master and slave** - A Leader and a follower in a power exchange relationship. Both are non-gender specific. Most commonly used in, but not exclusive to, Leather culture.

If you find the language Master and slave uncomfortable, then you need not use it, even within Leather culture. There are both Leather contests for Master and slave as well as some people who win those contests, then reject the terminology. The debate between 'tradition and these terms having no relation to non-consensual slavery of the past' and 'in this modern era it is just inappropriate to continue to use that language' will go on, I'm sure, for years to come. Give it some thought for yourself, perhaps listen to both sides, and make a choice based on what feels right for you.

**Authority Transfer Relationship** - An alternative terminology for power exchange relationship that is slowly becoming more popular.

**BDSM** - This is a catch-all acronym with several meanings, including Bondage/Discipline, Dominance/submission, and Sadism/masochism. Note that this book really doesn't have much BDSM or kinky sex in it. We enjoy that kind of play! But for us, power exchange is about how we live. BDSM has tops (people leading a scene, swinging a flogger for example), bottoms (people receiving a scene, getting spanked for example), and switches (people who enjoy both topping and bottoming).

**Dom/me** - "Dom" is a male dominant; "Domme" is a female dominant. Another label for power exchange Leaders, although often also used to reflect how someone plays as well. Sometimes people who are a top for a scene like to call themselves Doms but have no power beyond that scene, so when you hear this term outside this book realize it *could* be power exchange, or *could* be just play related.

**Submissive** - As with Dom/me, a submissive can either be a bottom, or a role in a power exchange relationship.

**Negotiation** - The process taken before starting a power exchange relationship. This is where discussion takes place on what each party needs, wants, or doesn't. You'll hear a lot about this in the following pages as well.

**House** - A group of people who view power exchange relationships in general in the same way, and thus create a group relationship. They may or may not live together and may not be in power exchange relationships with each other. When you find people who share similar views, ethics, and a like 'heart' regarding power exchange, they may come together in some form and create a House (also known as a Leather family or tribe).

**Consensual Non-consent** - If you do a web search of consensual non-consent, the first page of responses are about the BDSM version of this relating to sex. But as it pertains to power exchange, it is a style of relationship where the partners have very limited negotiation on what the relationship will actually look like and instead the

Leader just says 'this is what it will be, take it or leave it.' Depending on the people involved, this might reflect a great level of trust. Or it could mean that once the fantasy part of the relationship is over, you realize there isn't a lot left.

**Belum** (*benevolent Leader*) - Leads a power exchange relationship, including responsibility for the actions and words of those that follow. There is no title + name format. Instead, the formal term for those in service to use is simply Belum. If part of a name, it is positioned after the name (such as Daniel Belum). Sir is acceptable for simpler or more intimate situations. There is no suggestion of any title of any sort being required unless you are a follower of Belum.

**belet** (beloved servant, right hand of Belum) - follows Belum in a power exchange relationship. This term is a title (such as belet dawn) and is also hierarchical; there would never be more than one belet within the domain of a Belum. It is an earned title, never granted lightly, and bears the responsibility of being not only the servant of Belum, but also a reflection of the relationship itself. No limitations; thus, service is administrative, sexual, and an active extension of Belum's Leadership, and anything else desired by Belum.

The above terminology is just a sampling of power exchange language. Some parts of this book - particularly around concepts of power exchange and polyamory - will include additional terms.

# Different Flavors of Power Exchange

### *Dan says*

There are a variety of styles of power exchange - Dom/sub, Master/slave, Owner/property, Leather, Sir/boi, Victorian, Gorean, and on and on. We used to (and may again one day) run an event called Power eXchange Summit, bringing all of these relationship styles together for a three day conference of classes and workshops. One of the key takeaways for us personally was that although each style had some differences, when it comes down to it, they were all basically the same thing. You had a Leader, you had a follower, and they engaged in a non-egalitarian relationship. We covered some of this in the book's introduction. In the section below, we are going to talk about some of the categories that all these power exchange relationships fall into.

# Full Time and Part Time

## *Dan says*

When dawn goes out on a date with her long term boyfriend, I pretty much ignore her. I don't mean this in a negative way; instead it is more of a realization that she is off doing something that I don't have any attachment to. Whether they go to a Chinese restaurant or superhero movie, I have already pre-approved anything that might happen as long as she stays true to the fact that she is in my collar as she does them. In other words, holds herself to the standard I've set. So if she and her boyfriend go to an amusement park and ride the roller coaster, or a swing club and do a double penetration scene with some random guy? Ok. As she does these, is she being safe? Acting in a compassionate way when it is needed and avoiding drama? Showing up to places on time and prepared? Being honest with me in whatever adventures she gets up to (that I care to hear about), and checking in with me when plans change?

Some power exchange relationships are 24 hours a day, 7 days a week, no holidays. As you might guess from the above, dawn and I are in that category. She is never not my belet, never not under my collar. This does not mean I control her every action - who has time for that? But it means she is mine in the grocery store, at an event, or when she is on a 'girls night out.' There is never a situation where she is not responsible for acting in such a way that I would approve or that I expect of her.

Alternatively, some power exchange relationships are only power exchange at certain times or in certain situations. Perhaps when at an event, or in the bedroom, or when we are physically together. This works out very well for some people - perhaps I am dating a Dom, and when we are together I want to feel that power over me, but when our dates are over I am back to the rest of my life and don't need a Dom. Or when power exchange is more kink focused, we limit it to the bedroom. Or a situation where a Sir is already very busy but has limited time, so they create a limited time relationship.

Neither full time nor part time is better than the other. The only warning is that it can be very difficult to try to be both. Meaning, we are full time unless I say I want a break, then we go part time or not at all, and then later back to another state. I've never personally seen this work for a sustained relationship.

### *dawn says*

Basically, what I have to say is "do what works for you." As Dan said, he is Belum 24/7, always. Everything I do or don't do, he is in charge of and can change. This is our way.

And though I don't have other Doms per se, I do have dominant play partners. There is a limit both in time and deed as to where our power exchange moments begin and end, with Dan always at the top of the chain.

# Partial

## *Dan says*

As mentioned above, I have full authority over all aspects of dawn - how she serves me, what she eats, when she does the laundry, how often she orgasms. But I select to *not control* most of her life. It does not benefit the relationship for me to determine when she eats or what day the laundry happens. As long as those things happen - full bellies and clean clothes - I have no opinion on the how or the when.

Many of my past relationships have been *partial power exchange*. One collared submissive of mine was studying for her PhD. I had no interest in influencing that, nor would I have known where to start. So we negotiated that her school was off the table - out of my control.

Other areas where I have had relationship aspects negotiated off the table (either by our choice, my choice, or theirs) include child rearing, career, finances, existing relationships, and new relationships. I've had more than one relationship where I negotiated sex to be out of bounds. In one case, it was because the follower was both very new to sex as well as significantly younger. I decided that what they needed was discipline and structure, but not my dick. So I took sex out of our contract.

Partial power exchange is not by default any better or worse than full power exchange. It is situational; sometimes one makes more sense than the other. It acknowledges that we Leader types really are not all-knowing about all things. If I had a follower with diabetes, I would only require them to be educated about their disease. Beyond that, if they say 'It is time to eat' or 'I am not having ice cream,' then I have no say over that.

Common to both partial and part time power exchange for me, though, are some baselines. Regardless of how full or limited our relationship is, you can never be rude to me or my other partners, you can never be disrespectful, and you should never use the limits with an intent to manipulate our relationship.

### *dawn says*

As for Dan, he's explained a lot already. His relationship with a couple of his followers can be hard to explain. With one in particular, they were in a 24/7 power exchange relationship. It was known and could be seen. Yet there were limitations with what Dan had control of in her life. Specifically with this follower, finances, child rearing, and her career were under her control. But, even when she made decisions in those areas, she always thought about what would make Dan proud of her. How she dealt with people changed slightly to reflect who owned her. If she was confused about something, she would come to him for advice. So, though he didn't make decisions, he was definitely an influence over her choices. This is one way partial power exchange can work.

With another of his followers, the same areas weren't in his control: finances, children/family, and her career. This was absolute and she did not come to Dan for advice nor was he involved in any way with her choices. This is another way partial power exchange can work.

I have more examples, but each is going to be as different as the people involved. Again, these are consensual designer relationships that involve hierarchy. A Leader and a follower. Do what works for you.

## Co-op versus Military

### *Dan says*

Nearly everyone on some social media sites seem to believe that power exchange relationships are either about kink, or about long term loving connections. This is not so; some relationships I've been in have been primarily about me, or about service. At times, an emotional attachment isn't at all important to either one of us.

For the *Co-op* category of power exchange, I am going to include any relationship where the emotional wellbeing and happiness of the follower are a significant part of the picture.

For the rest, I'm going to designate that category as *Military*. Not that they are warlike or involve combat, but more as a general guidance of how the relationship works. If you prefer, think *Corporate*. But for now, let's stick with the military model.

Signing up to serve in the military (in times of peace) is an agreement. You agree to be in service for a set amount of time to gain certain benefits, including payment, training, and a host of others. In exchange, the military will teach you how to do certain things in a certain way, and then have expectations of you. If you don't follow through with those expectations, there is disciplinary action. How you feel about those things, or when they happen, or if they fulfill your heart song? That doesn't mean shit to the military. Do the thing, or pay the price.

When we talk about the Military style of power exchange, we are talking about a negotiated relationship that tends to have a specific goal or goals in mind. The relationship is likely to end once that goal is reached. An emotional attachment between the people is not as important. If such an attachment comes about, it is secondary and potentially accidental.

An example of this would be what I created with someone I called 'temp slave.' I had a need for a set amount of time for certain chores to be taken care of. They had a desire to learn Leather protocol and be introduced to the community. Our contract was just that - you get what you want, I get what I want, and I will be your Leader for a set amount of time. It is a great situation for both parties if they have a specific need or desire, and both can provide a path to it.

This is also a style very well suited for a few followers I know who prefer to avoid emotional power exchange at all. They prefer to be property, not partners.

### *dawn says*

These can be two different styles of power exchange (PE) relationships, but a relationship can also blend the two, as ours does.

We have friends that are completely a co-op couple. What I mean by co-op is that everything is discussed, and then the Leader makes a decision. There is no punishment involved in the relationship, and I don't think I would ever hear the Leader say 'no discussion, this is my decision.' I doubt I'd ever hear the Leader use 'da-quil,' or any other word that tells the follower to be quiet, like Dan does with me. This is great and totally works for them. Their relationship has lasted twenty years and is still going strong.

We have other friends that are military style. For the most part, decisions aren't discussed. The Leader makes a decision and tells the follower what is going to happen. The follower has rules and protocols, and punishment is usually part of the relationship style. These friends also have many years invested in their relationship.

For us, we are a blend. Dan and I discuss a lot of things, but not everything. There are times that Dan comes to me with a decision and the response he expects from me is 'Yes, Sir.' It's not time for my mouse tendencies with logistics and details. We have a punishment dynamic. And though it's been years since he's had to punish me, it's still on the table. This is what we agreed to and I like being held accountable. For me, I don't think I could do 24/7 military style. But, I don't think I could do 24/7 co-op style either. I need more of a firm hand, but with some input. That's what works for us. Again, designer relationships.

## Both Avoid Abuse

### *Dan says*

Be it co-op or military, if a power exchange relationship makes either the physical or mental health of that follower worse, then we are not talking about power exchange anymore. We are talking about abuse. You cannot say 'I treat a human like shit without understanding the impact it has on them, but it is ok because we are in power exchange.' Every category or style of power exchange relationships start with consensual negotiation.

# A Practical Guide to Writing Power Exchange Contracts

*A quick caveat about this section. First, it is presented as if the contract is for two people. Options for multiple relationships or polyamory are presented toward the end. Second, some power exchange relationships include a punishment dynamic, while others do not. We include mentions of that for those that do, but you don't have to include these if it doesn't make sense for you. We discuss punishment dynamics elsewhere in this book.*

# Part 1 - Why a Power Exchange Contract?

## *Dan says*

A power exchange contract is not, as naysayers will quickly point out, a legal document. It will not save you if the police come knocking on the door and want to know why someone is not allowed to use the furniture in your home, nor will it stand up in court if you are caught with a flogger and charged with domestic abuse. So why bother, people ask?

The value of the contract is that it will create a clear understanding of language and responsibilities for both of you. It provides guidance when shit hits the fan, or for more simple challenges. After all, these power exchange relationships we enter in are, for some of us, a new experience and not something we likely had role models in.

Quite simply, what a well written contract does - and does exceedingly well - is these four things:

1. It acts as a forum to negotiate what the relationship will look like.
2. It acts as a tool to improve understanding.
3. It makes a record of the tools you plan to be using.
4. It gives all parties a permission slip to be authentic.

Let's go more into these.

## Forum to negotiate what the relationship will look like

Power exchange contracts - whether Master/slave, Owner/property, or any other form - should be written as peers. Although at the point you are putting together a contract you are already starting to feel the power exchange vibe, for long term success, it is very valuable to approach this from a position as equals. How often do we see relationships begin with 'Not my thing, but I'll suck it up for them' or 'You may not want kids now but after a few years you'll change' or, the power exchange version, 'If this makes Sir happy, then so be it.'

'If this makes Sir happy' is likely ok down the road. But during this initial conversation, if you are planning for long term success, then stick to your authentic self. If you do not want kids and don't see it happening, state it. Sure, you might change in the future, but use this document to be clear about the you of the present moment. How this is verbalized in the contract will be addressed later in this section.

## It acts as a tool to improve understanding

Here are two definitions of a BDSM submissive

1 - "A submissive, frequently known as a sub, is a sexual participant who willingly gives up some or all of their control to a dominant partner." (www.kinkly.com)

2 - "One who gives over their rights, their desires, and themselves to another as a gift." (Urban Dictionary)

Which one of these is correct? Neither. Or if you prefer, both. The reality is that if you ask ten submissives what it is to be a submissive, some will say it is a bedroom activity, others will say it is 24/7 service, and... then you'll get 8 other definitions.

So, the contract will help you and your partner(s) all get on the same page as to what expectations, roles, duties, and more come with what you are trying to build. Believe it or not, the title doesn't define you. You define it. More about those titles appear in this section (and other parts) of the book.

## It makes a record of the tools you plan to be using

This document is your chance to help define any strategies you'll be using to communicate, as well as your expectations. The section on Porch Time in this book is a great example of this. Your contract should also include a guide to remind you of the path when things get rocky and/ or complacent. If you are unhappy, conflicted, or unsure, then you can refer to the part of the contract that would include some of the methods you are expected to engage in to assist in resolving those feelings.

## It gives all parties a permission slip to be authentic

Have you seen the TV show where the husband did something dumb, so he tried to hide it, but eventually his wife caught on and after a mild argument everything was ok again… until the next week? I'm not sure what show you are picturing but it could be any number of shows, as this is the plot of lots of them!

Personally I was taught that all relationships are equal partnerships and that it was like a democracy - each person had an equal vote. The relationship models I see on TV and in my own life not only didn't prepare me for power exchange, they actually actively went against it - that when one person has more power than the other, that it was likely abusive, and the follower was a doormat.

The contract is a great way to help create your power exchange as a designer relationship. It is used to help move your preconceived notions of what a relationship is supposed to look like, and helps you create from a blue sky. You get to decide what goes in, what stays out, and no expectations of 'this is what boyfriends do' or such has to exist.

And if you are in a punishment dynamic relationship, laying that out in writing - that physical punishment may be a tool that is used - is a great way to help you both get beyond the old programming and affirm that you are using punishment as teaching, instead of abuse.

## Part 2 - What is Included in a Power Exchange Contract?

### *Dan says*

Some of what goes in each contract is variable, depending on the situation. Not all power exchange relationships are full time, and not all of them are full authority transfer. Some are foundations for longterm relationships that include a romantic love aspect, while others are about training or achieving goals. So different contracts will focus on different aspects.

Yet, we believe some aspects should be common to any power exchange contract, such as terminology, situational tools around communication and punishment, timing until the end of the contract, (even if, in a romantic haze, you make that 'until the end of time,') and when things should be renegotiated.

Let's break down key aspects to include, and follow that with some examples.

**Vision Statement**

In my marriage contract, I'm not sure if it outlines the purpose or reason we got married. Was there anything more there than 'spend a life together in holy matrimony?' Well, my power exchange relationships are more focused than that. We include a statement of our roles, our responsibilities, our commitments to each other, and to ourselves.

**Terms**

Our contract terms not only include some logistics - when does the contract start and when, if it is designed to include that, does it end? If there is no ending date, then when do we renegotiate? Remember, not all contracts are intended to be for full time romantic loving power exchange. Some are shorter term, by desire of both parties, and have specific goals in mind. The Terms section is the beginning of those ideas. You might start with something like 'my property will serve me every hour of every day,' but then those ideas get explored and defined more clearly in a later section, such as Duties.

It should also begin to clearly start introducing concepts around punishment, discipline, and reward if those are part of your contract.

### Goals

This is the beauty of designer relationships - you get to set goals to strive towards! This doesn't mean goals like 'jog 3 miles a day' but more 'higher goals.' Things like growing as a family, or becoming healthier and happier than we are now. To come into our power as a Leader and follower.

### Needs and Wants

How great is this? We not only are moving into a relationship, but moving into one that is very clear in what we want to get from it. Sure, there are always surprises and bonuses in relationships we don't expect. But how often are we invited to really explore our needs and wants and put them on paper, to have them reviewed by another human being, and acknowledged and accepted? And it is a profound part of that power exchange. We usually visualize the Leader in these relationships to get what they want and need. But here, the follower also gets to say 'I will accept your lead and will even accept discipline if you require it - but you will provide for my needs as well, and will acknowledge the importance of my wants.'

### Duties

Here is where we are really starting to define some specific functions of each partner, and being very clear on the roles and responsibilities. We are making clear 'you will do this' or 'you are responsible for that' statements. This is actually my favorite part - it really helps to create a foundation grounded in reality for the dream of the relationship, and helps keep each part rooted in clarity. From something as simple as 'you will refer to me as sir' to 'you will make the bed' or 'you will ask permission to wear pants,' it starts to define that this is a relationship unlike many others.

And don't think this is all about the follower. The Leader starts to have responsibilities defined as well. Items like 'will recognize his follower's needs and will review them periodically,' and 'will continue to give his follower lessons and training and having them work on things that enhance who they are and their ability to serve.' It may well include clarifying whether the Leader is responsible for financial aspects of the relationships, living conditions, or even care of the follower.

**Limitations**

Limitations are not a bad thing. Not all contracts are 24/7 full time, but even those that are may include limitations. 'The Leader has no authority over' and 'The follower is not responsible for' may include a variety of areas where it doesn't make sense to transfer power, or there simply isn't any desire to do so. In any non-full time power exchange, I am likely to exclude any influence over the other person's biological family or children. A follower with a career or educational path already established may exclude any orders that conflict with those. This is the appropriate way to do things. One of my relationships was with a person working toward their doctorate. As I have never done that myself, why would I try to control their pursuit of it? I might influence motivation or time management, but I would not demand they take calculus over nanobiology.

### Disillusionment

As you are probably aware, power exchange relationships (and thus, contracts) are, in a way, an illusion. So are marriages. You might agree to 'until death do us part' but the truth is, either of you can walk at any time. And power exchange - even when our language is Master and slave, or property and Owner - is no different. That collar-wearing servant may one day reply to your demand that they kneel for you with a simple, 'Nah, I'm moving on' - and then stand up and walk out.

Personally, I would not have it any other way. It isn't the relationship language or terminology or a contract that binds us, it is the cement of consent. And either party can actually revoke that consent at any time. The only problem with this is that suddenly revoking consent can seriously impair the foundation of a power exchange relationship. This is where talking openly about the potential for disillusionment comes in.

It not only provides a way to cleanly and maturely end the relationship, but also to provide some steps along the way if a simple (or complex) renegotiation is what is needed instead.

## Part 2 Summary

### *dawn says*

Dan and I talk about contracts and the fact that we use one, but I don't know that we discuss much about how designing one was scary for us. We'd never created a deliberate relationship before. Of course, nowadays you read about them all the time in magazines, about how it's this 'new' concept. In the power exchange world, it's not so new. We already knew that we didn't want our relationship to be anything like what we'd had in the past - or that our parents had had, or even our friends. We were learning how to vocalize what it was we desired, needed, wanted.

The easy part was the rituals and protocols and mission statement. We worked on that together, as peers. It was important for us to do it this way, as I was already slipping into the 'whatever you'd like, Sir' attitude. That was not what either of us wanted. We were trying to build a solid foundation, and that required me to be honest with myself, and him.

It was the Needs, Wants, and Desires section that was scary. The scary part for me was two-fold: looking deep within myself to see who I was and what I wanted, and then sharing it - while also knowing that Dan had looked within himself and may have discovered that he wanted something completely different. Sure we had had discussions, over the year between our first interview and moving in together, and then over the next year as we tried out D/s 'lite' on weekends and in the bedroom. But now, we were looking deep inside and committing what we found to paper. We were writing down needs that were non-negotiable, and also sharing wants and desires.

This was a huge process for me. I'd never been good at looking at my feelings or figuring out who I was, or what I needed or wanted. My last relationship kind of happened by accident and then lasted for 14 years, because that's what you do.

We sat down and co-created the foundation of our hierarchical relationship. It was a long process because we both felt this contract was an important tool for keeping us on track when vanilla life seeps in. And how can it not? We don't have many role models. Media, family, friends, uninformed therapists... many don't understand or agree with anything outside an egalitarian style of relationship. Hell, even in the kink community, there are many that don't understand power exchange as anything but play, let alone a relationship style.

Something to keep in mind is that contracts aren't static. Each month we would go out to breakfast, and go over a section of the contract. If something seemed like it wasn't working, we'd talk about it, but at this point we were not peers. He'd want me to share my opinion, but then it was up to him whether it was updated in the contract or not.

We also had a little fun with the contract. Each year, we picked a theme to work with. The first year it was about building our foundation. The second year it was the year of high protocol. The third year was the slut year. And then we jokingly share that we liked the slut year so much, it became the theme of years four, five, and six, as well. Which is true.

After this long in the relationship, we don't renew our contract anymore, and our rituals and protocols are more fluid, changing as needed, but we do still have pieces that are firmly in place, like the disillusionment section. No one likes to think about breaking up while they are creating a relationship, but we felt it to be a very important addition to our contract.

The disillusionment section was first designed because of my abandonment and rejection issues. I didn't want him to finally come to the conclusion that I was too high-maintenance and just walk out, and I didn't want to be able to just take off the collar and be done. Emotions run high sometimes, especially while I was working on my healing path, and I needed some assurance that there would be warning if something like that was going to happen.

So, we came up with the separation process. It would start small, and slowly build up to the ending of the relationship, if it got that far. Before signing the contract we picked who would be our mediator if it got that far. She was/is a well respected elder in the Leather community, and was actually the one that suggested we add this part to the contract. She isn't biased towards either of us, so she would make a great mediator.

It is also understood that either party can invoke the disillusionment process if needed. Both parties have power in this situation, and need to remember that. When people ask who has the power in the relationship, our answer is, "the one who can walk away." So, each of us needs to be strong enough to walk away if it ever gets to that point.

We also have a section of our contract that automatically voids the relationship. These are the two items that I told my son when he asked me, "mom, is there anything Dan could do that would make you leave him?" I answered, "Why yes son, there are. If he uses drugs, including alcohol, or if he cheats on me - I'm out."

And it's still true to this day. Dan and I have talked about this. He wanted the drugs part put in there because he is a recovering alcoholic, and I can be a caretaker. It would not have been in my best interest to stay and try to help him if he relapsed. His last command in that situation has already been given. I am to clear out the bank account - if he hasn't already - and leave. And I'm the one that added in the part about cheating, though we both agreed to it. Dan and I are polyamorous. There is no reason to see someone without the other person's knowledge. For me, that's a huge break of trust. I can't serve someone I don't trust. And I can't live with secrets on my part. This is supposed to be a different type of relationship.

I am so glad that we put so much work into that document. That's how important our relationship was to us. Going back and re-reading the original contract gives me the warm fuzzies.

## Part 3 - Sample Contract

This is an example of an actual power exchange contract between two people who identified as Master and slave.

## Introduction

This contract is based on Trust, built with Love and Honesty.

This contract is intended as a guide to behavior and expectations for both parties. It is written as both an exact set of rules, and a tool to use to keep focused. It is written with the knowledge that we have lived a 24/7 life for a period of time now and recognize that which works in our relationship - a Master/slave bond that is rich in responsibility for each other, one's self, and others that touch our life. This contract is written specifically for this Master and slave, addressing their specific needs and desires. It may or may not have any bearing on anyone else.

A slave gives her self to her Master because she holds to a basic truth - that her Master will not harm her. He will push, punish, use, take, command, be unyielding, make her cry, and make her look deep within her soul. But not harm her. And she will find the freedom to become her true self.

A Master claims his slave because he holds this basic truth - that all the effort, energy, and attention will bring focus to his life and push him to move forward and grow. She is, without doubt in his mind, worth it. And he will find the freedom to become his true self.

## Terms

1. The terms of this contract are spelled out below. They are agreed to and are intended to outline a living arrangement that is safe, sane, and consensual between the two parties. The slave understands that she is going to be disciplined, punished, and pleasured in ways that are physical, mental, and emotional as need be. The slave understands that what others would view as abuse – such as spanking, the use of floggers and whips, and bondage - is used on her as a tool of training or an instrument for pleasure. The slave gives her Master via this contract complete consent to use those and other tools as he sees fit.

2. This contract will take effect from this day at the point it is signed and witnessed thereof. And as this is a growing, evolving relationship, the contract will be reviewed fully on the

anniversary date of its signing and adjusted accordingly.

3. This contract will be reviewed on a regular basis, to remind the slave and the Master of their duties and responsibilities.

4. Although many duties, needs, wants, and responsibilities are included in this contract, the Master and slave may negotiate changes to this contract before the one year period is up, but ONLY AT THE AGREEMENT OF THE Master.

## Goals

The goals of this relationship between a Master and a slave are a) for the family to grow as a whole, to be healthier and happier, b) the training of the slave to our mutual satisfaction via real-time experience, social groups, training sessions, books and training manuals, and any and all other resources that will help us achieve our goal, and c) continue to strive in areas of physical, spiritual, emotional, and the erotic. This will strengthen the Master and slave as individuals, and strengthen the bond of the relationship.

## Needs

It is recognized that the Master has these following needs. They are part of who I am today, part of what you need to accept to be with Me.

1. I need to be able to share how I feel and what I think without stopping to judge how it will be taken.
2. I need to find my sense of compassion, balanced with

acceptance that I have needs.

3. I need to find and maintain my sense of self.
4. I need my life to be more fun with you than when I was alone.
5. I need dawn to kneel in 'attend me' stance if she feels the need for attention. I need to be assured that if you need my attention you will not manipulate or trick me to get it.
6. I need dawn to hold nothing back from me, although she might take some time to reveal some things.
7. I need acceptance for who I am – Addict, emotional, Master, silly, at times self-absorbed even, and generally unusual.
8. I need sex acceptance. I have unusual tastes, and I have limitations. My desires flux in high and low bursts.
9. I need our relationship to have continued growth.
10. I need honest feedback when I'm instinctive.
11. I need to know that I do not have to constantly second-guess myself.
12. I need honesty – direct and immediate.
13. I need an emotional commitment.
14. I need to be heard.
15. I need you to enhance my life with social things, even to the point of pushing me.

It is recognized that the slave has these following needs. They are part of who I am today, part of what you need to accept to be with me.

1. I need to feel cherished.
2. I need you to be open and honest without worrying

about my feelings.

3. I need to grow as a person.
4. I need to be social.
5. I need to be needed. I don't want to just be another person in the house.
6. I need security and stability, both financial and emotional.
7. I need you to be able to talk to me when you need to. I need you to find others you can talk to, when you feel you can't talk to me.
8. I need you to be proud of me
9. I need me to be proud of me.
10. I need to be pushed/challenged.
11. I need U/us to be unconditionally honest.
12. I need the security of having to follow steps to get out of the relationship.
13. I need the freedom to search for my spiritual path.
14. I need to feel like I belong to a family unit.
15. I need the freedom to submit.
16. I need you to be strong within yourself.
17. I need you to realize what a gift my submission is.
18. I need you to tell me what you need from me.
19. I need you to realize that I NEED to submit to YOU.
20. I need to feel protected.
21. I need to feel feminine.
22. I need you to help me work on my insecurities.
23. I need your wisdom in my life.
24. I need you to hold me when I'm scared.
25. I need you to tell me when I'm not living up to your expectations.

26. I need you to hold me responsible for my duties and myself.
27. I need you to think of your/my/our wellbeing.
28. I need you to realize that this is where we belong.
29. I need to take time for myself sometimes.
30. I need to learn to be humble.
31. I need you to listen to my protest sometimes (kids could be around or something).
32. I need us to be secure enough in our relationship and ourselves so that we are not jealous.
33. I need help in breaking through these walls/insecurities that keep me from enjoying life.
34. I need you to remember that we complement each other. When you Dom me and I submit, harmony has been created.

## Wants

The Master has these wants.

1. I want my slave to be more aggressive with serving me. What can she come up with on her own?
2. I want enough free time.
3. I want nights away on occasion.
4. Balance with doing things regardless of kids (so that may mean we decide to do things apart).
5. Pushed toward personal growth.

The slave has these wants.

1. I want a ceremony of some kind.

2. I want free space to talk honestly.
3. I want to be shown off.
4. I want, when/if the time is right, a cock of Master's choosing.
5. I want to submit with other submissives.
6. I want to play with other Doms of Master's choice.
7. I want You to share with me Your innermost thoughts and fantasies.
8. I want to take care of Your house.
9. I want Your help around the house; it shows that we are part of a family.
10. I want to explore my sexuality with You.
11. I want to share my fantasies with You.
12. I want life with You to be fun and silly, but not forgetting the D/s side.
13. I want You to listen to my thoughts and ramblings.
14. I want to be around other D/s people, so that we may be ourselves.
15. I want to be trained on behavior.
16. I want to be punished when You believe I should be.
17. I want You to realize that I am a strong person that can make it on my own, but chooses to belong to You.
18. I want us to be able to take steps to ward off depression.
19. I want to be trained.
20. I want to be used.
21. I want to feel beautiful.
22. I want to embrace my Goddess side.
23. I want to embrace my slutty side.
24. I want to feel loved and respected while I'm exploring/embracing myself.

25. I want to marry You… but don't feel like I should admit to that.
26. I want us to take time for a ritual after work.

# Duties

## *A slave's duties*

My slave will attend Me in the following specific fashion. These rules of our household are valid for today, and may or may not be changed as Master wishes.

1. My slave will be aware of her Master, aware of His needs, desires, and wants at all times that they are together. Together is within the same building, so she will attend to Me whether we are in different rooms or separate parts of an establishment, unless instructed otherwise.
2. My slave is to wear her slave ring at all times. My slave will wear one of her collars that are pleasing to Me, unless instructed not to.
3. My slave will always be honest with her Master.
4. My coffee cup upon My awakening will be full with a vitamin near it. Further, fresh coffee will be available at all times.
5. My slave will not wear items in her hair without permission. I like her hair to be free and relaxed.

6. My slave will make the bed each morning and be assured that she does not have her stuff in My area of the bedroom.
7. My slave must ask permission to wear pants.
8. My slave will not wear makeup without her Master's permission, except for basic foundation.
9. My slave will attend Me as My slave in D/s households and places, practicing proper decorum (such as kneeling near Me).
10. My slave will use proper protocol when addressing Me in written fashion, always referring to Me in a capital letter and her self in lower case. In this way, she will be reminded of our relationship.
11. My slave will remember to make sure that her Master's seatbelt is fastened. This will remind her to stay focused on her Master.
12. My slave will look at her Master with a critical eye before I leave the house each day and will confirm that I am ready to present Myself with a clean shave, appropriate dress, and properly groomed. My appearance will be a reflection of My slave's devotion.
13. My slave will always treat her Master with proper respect and decorum in public. My slave will never argue with Master in public or show displeasure in His decisions.
14. My slave will never speak badly of her Master unless it is approved first. My slave will further not argue with Master unless first asking for and achieving a state of 'free space' where she can and is expected to speak freely without fear of reprisal.

15. My slave will not display anger inappropriately.
16. My slave will not do anything that she knows displeases her Master, with the intent to manipulate or control her Master.
17. My slave will, upon the command of 'attend Me,' come to her Master and kneel, with eyes down and hands behind her back, saying and doing nothing until instructed otherwise.
18. My slave will recognize her Master's needs and will review them periodically to make sure they are being met.
19. My slave will not leave her Master's presence unless she has asked permission and explained where she is going and why.
20. My slave will take her pleasure when and where her Master deems it to be, and in the amounts He deems is enough.
21. My slave will take her punishment, stay present for it, learn from it, and move forward.
22. My slave will use agreed upon 'safe words' to signify physical or mental limitations being exceeded. Her Master will then decide if He wishes to recognize those safe words and in what fashion. Each limitation will be addressed and either accepted or removed.
23. My slave will attend to the administrative task of running the family.
24. My slave will remember that at all times, including when playing with others, she still belongs to her Master.

## A Master's duties

The Master will attend to the following responsibilities within the relationship.

1. The Master will recognize His slave's needs and will review them periodically to make sure they are being met.
2. The Master will focus on His slave, being sure that she is being taken care of and treated like the prized and loved person that she is.
3. The Master will continue to give His slave lessons and training, having her work on things that enhance who she is and her ability to serve.
4. The Master will punish and discipline His slave as needed. He will not make excuses for not doing so, nor will He avoid this important duty. He will recognize that it is a duty of love, commitment, and growth.
5. The Master will make sure that His slave is being taken care of in matters of physical, emotional, mental, and spiritual health. He will push her to do what she needs to do to grow in these areas.
6. The Master will attend to and remember the importance of aftercare, especially after a heavy scene, seeing to the slave's physical and emotional well being.
7. The Master will write a set of guidelines for play that involves others, especially if playing with them more than once. This is for the protection and guidance of all involved.
8. The Master will be aware of the financial status of the family and will actively pursue the financial wellbeing

of the family.

9. The Master will be responsible for the family and take ultimate responsibility for the physical, emotional, mental, and spiritual health of the family.
10. The Master will recognize the difference between being responsible for His slave and the family and being powerless over results.
11. The Master will recognize His own limitations and seek help and guidance as needed.

## Rights

*The following rights are shared by both of us and may be called upon at any time without recrimination.*

1. Our relationship comes before all others. Therefore, if either party desires a return to monogamy to strengthen our foundation for a period of time, they will say such and it will happen.
2. If there is strife in the relationship, the options under Disillusionment may be called upon. If either party desires to call upon those items, they will say such and it will happen.
3. If either party requires immediate free space, they will say such and it will happen.

## Disillusionment

Be it known that prior to this contract being voided by either party, these steps must take place.

1. A letter to the partner, stating problems and intent
2. Little abort word
3. Mediation with predetermined person

Be it known that this contract shall become instantly and automatically null and void if either of the members of this contract:

1. Partake of the use of illegal drugs. For the Master, this is to include alcohol as well.
2. See other people outside of this relationship without the knowledge of the Master or the slave (commonly referred to as "cheating").

To void this contract is to void this relationship. To do so can not be done lightly and should be considered permanent. To void this relationship, the person shall clearly say "Abort" to the other party and physically tear this contract in two pieces.

# Communication

## *Dan says*

Recently, dawn and I have started a new habit of a 10 minute "planning session" early in the morning. The goal is a simple touch base that asks what are you doing today and are there any areas where we need to connect to accomplish something. For example, in our power exchange, finances are a joint effort, which we discuss elsewhere in the book. For those with a business background, yes, we are doing a daily 'stand up' meeting, and no, we don't literally stand up.

The reason we started this was because "I didn't know that" was being heard too often for two people who live together.

I'm sure you've heard more than once that communication is the key to any relationship. Power exchange relationships are no different. But there can be a challenge specific around these relationships in that sometimes our roles - be it Leader or follower - get in the way. We get stuck with thinking that a follower should not express frustration over certain things; that a Leader should not need to share about feeling unworthy or depressed. Although the logical mind will recognize that 'should feel' is a term that is problematic at best (you feel what you feel), we can get stuck in that mode.

Plus, communication takes time. Not just clock time, but time where we are engaged, paying attention, receptive to hearing and being listened to, too. This is how two or more people who live together can go throughout the day and still have moments of not communicating. Sure, you talk - what do you want for dinner, did anyone walk the dog - but there's more to healthy communication than simply talking.

So, we are going to talk about some tools for communication. If your goal is a long term power exchange relationship, this is likely one of the most important parts of this book. Don't think of these as a way to fix a problem; proper use of communication is a great way to prevent problems from arising.

But before we get into the tools, let's talk about how you process the world, so that you have a better chance of incorporating tools that work for your dynamic.

## How We Process the World

## Internal Vs External

### *Dan says*

I used to get really annoyed at the way dawn processes things. And she got equally annoyed at the way I processed. Because we did it so differently, and took different perspectives on what that processing was about.

Some people, like dawn, process thoughts and emotions out loud. It used to be that when dawn was processing something, I only heard about the first two sentences before I started to work out a strategy on how I was going to fix it. That is what many Leader types do - see a problem, plan a solution, implement the fix. Even when, in cases like this, I was trying to fix not only the wrong problem, but further, something that may not need to be fixed.

What dawn actually was doing was externally processing whatever challenge or emotion she was feeling, and we came to find out I didn't need to put on my tool belt and Leader Hat, I needed to just be quiet and let her go. Matter of fact, we realized I didn't actually have to pay attention at all, and I would often pick up my game controller and toss her an occasional 'uh huh' as she rambled on. Once she got through the tangle, though - she hit a spot of realization on what the issue actually was - then it was time to put down the controller, turn to face her, and pay attention. And find out if she wanted feedback on my part, or action, or if I ignored what she wanted and took on a Leader role and provided what I believed was the right thing to provide. That was the exception, to be honest. She got what she needed from my presence. But there were times where I would give her direction, for the good of the relationship.

Other people (like me) tend to process issues quietly in our heads, or perhaps in a journal. dawn took my quietness to be anger or ignoring her, or that she had done something wrong to cause this silence. (I don't fault her for this, the vanilla 'silent treatment' was a 'tool' in her previous relationship.) But as an internal processor, when I have some thought or emotion I need to work through, I do it slowly and in my head. Like a cow with cud, I would chew it and rechew it (I know, not a pretty picture) until I got to the point I was ready to act on it or share about it. And then I would.

I did have to learn, though, that it was of value to my followers to let them know that I was processing something. That way, they would not be worried that I had gotten silent or that something was wrong that I wasn't talking about. I was handling it, in my own manner.

Now, I will have to say that internal processing has its limits. It may well be that the thing I am working on gets moved from my head to a journal or to a friend's ear. There is a line between working something through in my gut and obsessing. I enjoy the saying "either talk it out or act it out" and find that to be true for some areas of my life.

Neither internal or external processing is better than the other. But it is very useful to know how the other person works.

## *dawn says*

As Dan shared, one of the challenges we had early on was not realizing that we processed things differently. There are probably a lot of different ways to process, but the main two are 'internal' and 'external' processing. Dan and I are very different and this caused a lot of issues at the beginning.

My head runs a mile a minute when it's chewing on something, and it tries to explain my feelings by putting it in a box that fits something else in the past. It takes me a while to get the feelings out of the past and into the present. And I can't do it alone in my head. I get stuck. So, I have to verbalize it. I have to hear myself think out loud. But this doesn't work if I'm by myself. I can't just pace and talk, or talk to the dog, or talk to the trees. Now, if I was sure the dog could actually understand me, it might work. I don't know why. I'm sure Dan would like it if I could figure out how to make these other options work.

I can remember one time when I was trying to explain something and I said, 'It's like spaghetti in my brain! I'm trying to pull the strands apart so that I can get to the nugget in the middle that is hiding from me.' Over time, I think he finally got to a place where he understood what I was trying to describe. I can remember how frustrating it was. Literally, my thoughts would be like a plate of spaghetti, the noodles all intertwined, no beginning, no ending, always feeling like I was starting in the middle and trying to find the ends.

I was sharing this with a friend, when she told me that she and her partner had come to an agreement. She had learned that she needed to process out loud, and from experience, it takes about half an hour for her to get through the nonsense and down to the real issue. So, her partner doesn't have to pay attention to her for the first half hour, she just needs him to be in the same room.

Bam! That's exactly what I needed. So, I brought it up to Dan to see if he'd be willing to do the same. Just be in the room while I paced and talked out loud. I didn't care if he was playing a video game, working on the computer, playing with the dog, whatever. He gave it a try and it worked! Such a relief!

Now I was able to get to the nugget, instead of having to stop before getting to that discovery because Dan wanted to fix the first thing I was talking about, which wasn't the real issue at all. If I'm complaining about the stove not working, he'd usually jump in to fix the stove. But, maybe the issue wasn't the stove at all, but my feeling of being out of control. Fixing the stove would fix the immediate surface problem, but not the underlying problem that we never discovered. That underlying problem is what I call 'my shadow' and if this shadow is discovered and worked with, it can reveal the unknown root of a lot of my responses to life. Luckily we figured out how to just let me talk and get to that emotional nugget. Progress in our communication skills!!!

With Dan, we learned with his internal processing style that it's easier for him if he's alone. In the past, he would walk away to chew on things, and it would trigger my abandonment and rejection issues. I would take it personally, figuring he was walking away because he was angry. We finally figured out, after discussing it, that this is what he needs to do for his processing style. It wasn't a cold shoulder, it wasn't him leaving the 'high-maintenance' relationship... and he would be back. That was huge! He would be back, and he wasn't punishing me by not talking out loud.

Though, oddly enough, over time we've learned how to do the opposite in our personal processing. There are times that I'll go into 'manual mode' to process things internally, before verbally vomiting what's in my head. And sometimes he'll process out loud, so that I can hear how he thinks. It helps me understand his decisions.

It's going to be a huge benefit if you can discover your processing styles and work with them.

## Introvert vs. Extrovert

### *dawn says*

Oddly enough, your communication style can differ based on whether you are an introvert or extrovert. What is the difference? Introverts recharge by being alone, and extroverts recharge by being around other people. This can affect how you communicate. Something to keep in mind: none of us are complete introverts or extroverts on the scale. In the middle is ambivert, and many of us lean closer to the middle, just on one side or the other of it.

Though I knew Dan and I were introverts, I didn't realize how much it affected our styles of communication until he started dating an extrovert. There were a lot of challenges happening, so we decided to write a Poly class on the differences between being an introvert and an extrovert. Oh my! Well, there was our answer to a lot that was going on.

As introverts who get overwhelmed when around a lot of people, we handle people and situations differently than extroverts. If you have a follower that is one, and you are the other, this could be challenging. Maybe the follower wants to dive into social situations, but the Leader would rather stay home. This is a challenge. Does the Leader suck it up? Or does the follower stay home? Or does the follower go to the event alone? Or do they go to the event together, but put care stations in place for the introverted partner? I've actually learned about some introverts doing this for weekend events. They know it's going to be taxing for them, so they figure out what they are going to need ahead of time to take care of themselves. For Dan and me, we take naps. We turn 'on' during a presentation, and we can make it through the 15 minutes after, chatting with attendees. Then we know we are going to crash and burn, so we schedule nice cozy naps.

Something else we've learned about introverts is that many of them might talk slower because they are thinking. For Dan, put that together with his internal processing, and you've got me, the external processor, jumping on his toes all the time. Yet, I get annoyed if I'm the one taking those pauses, and someone jumps into my paused moment. Hey! I was thinking and not done talking. If I'm interrupted more than twice, I stop trying. It's good to know this about yourself, and your partner.

So, introverts not only handle social situations differently than extroverts, we also handle communication differently than others. You'll need to figure out how you work. For me, like many introverts, I don't like to talk on the phone. When texting and email came along, it was huge for me. I can now think about what I want to say and answer when I'm able to, rather than being put on the spot with a phone call. Introverts don't like being put on the spot, especially in front of others. Public humiliation is generally not our thing, which is why Dan can use it as punishment with me.

What other differences are there between introverts and extroverts and how we communicate? I could add a huge list here, but I'm not sure that's as much of a benefit as knowing that there is a difference, and doing the research. See what resonates with you, and those in relationships with you.

I wish we had figured some of this out much earlier in our relationship. Different communication styles. What a concept! It should have been obvious. We are both smart people. But for a while, we were working off of what we learned in previous relationships and from what we saw with our parents. Clueless.

So, did it take you by surprise that Dan is an introvert? It does for most people. It just goes to show not to guess based on outward appearances. Dan is good at taking that breath and walking into a group of people. TaDa! Whereas I will arrive and skirt the edges of the crowd, unless we are in High Protocol and I'm following behind him. He will take control of his interaction with people and flit around saying 'hi' to everyone, moving on before the small talk begins. I will take control by finding a place to sit on the edge and inviting in other awkward people to have deep conversations with. Small talk is not our thing. And you'll notice that we are first in and usually first out of a social event. It's a way of managing our tendency of being overwhelmed by people.

## Communication Tools

### *dawn says*

Now that we've introduced some communication styles, let's talk about some tools that Dan and I have discovered and used over the years. These work for us.

## Daily Touch Base

### *Dan says*

As mentioned at the beginning of this chapter, dawn and I set time aside every morning to talk about our day. Through the years, we have done this in a variety of ways, but it ends up being the same basic experience. Early in the day, we sit together in recliners or on the porch with a hot beverage of choice, and spend a few minutes chatting. Initially we talk about logistics for the next day or two - who is going where, or what is scheduled. Any follow-ups on orders that I have given happen here as well. (Elsewhere in this book, I talk more about 'ask and acknowledge.')

But what normally happens from there is a generic conversation about what is happening in our lives. From 'did you see the email from,' to 'what are we doing for vacation this year,' this morning time spent together as the day starts helps avoid later hearing, "Did I forget to mention…?" but it also helps cultivate some simple connected time together. Sometimes, when we are on the porch and there is nothing left to talk about, we spend a few minutes in silence, hands reaching out to touch.

For long distance relationships, there is a modified version of this (see Hello Goodnight below). If you don't think you really have anything to talk about... then skip it, not a big deal. But for us, if nothing else, it is a moment to focus on each other and what we are doing, and be generally interested in each other.

## Good Morning Email

### *dawn says*

This 10 minute meeting probably happened because of Dan working from home. Before, when he went to work in the morning, we had a different way of keeping in touch. Even if we'd seen each other in the morning... me making his breakfast and lunch, setting out his clothes, getting him his vitamin... that doesn't mean we'd have time to chat about the day. So, after he left, the first thing I would do is sit down and write him an email. It would include what I had planned for the day, a boy/girl report, (this is what we called our dating report to each other, so we weren't surprised to hear about the other flirting with someone new later,) and other things that Dan found important to know about.

## Weekly Meetings Involving Nesting Partners

### *Dan says*

When dawn and I (very power exchange) bought a house and moved in with Karen, (not at all power exchange) we decided that we would participate in a household meeting every Sunday morning. Some of the below is planned (when and where) and some just evolved naturally (seating arrangement).

As a bit of background for this, it is important to note that Karen and I had a peer and vanilla romantic relationship. Karen understood power exchange but had no interest in it; her relationship with dawn was platonic friendship. She respected that dawn was my follower. But she did not interact with dawn in that role.

Each Sunday, we would all gather in a specific room and bring out the laptops and work out logistics. Who was traveling, are we planning any meals together, did the lawn need mowing, what color should we stain the fence, etc.

And though this meeting involved a non-power exchange partner, there were other aspects that we worked around as well. Such as, during this time, dawn was in a very light collar. Meaning, she was told to relax her 'follower' aspect and deal with Karen - and me - as a peer and fellow home owner. We didn't want these decisions to be made by just Karen and Dan - we all wanted dawn to have a voice in the creation and management of this shared living space. There were limits to this - at any point, we all recognized that I could override dawn and thus have 'two votes' to Karen's one. But over those five years, it never once happened.

Another interesting part was our seating arrangement. It organically ended up that we sat on the same curved sectional sofa, with me (Dan) in the middle, an equal distance from each other. We came to this place not as a combination of couples, or as a triad, but as three individuals.

When the scheduling was done and the conversations complete, we ended our ritual with a big Sunday breakfast.

## Hello Goodnight

### *Dan says*

For any relationship, but especially ones where you do not see the person daily, I issue a standard command that every morning when you wake up, you will send me a hello and tell me what you have planned for the day; every evening, you will send me a good night and let me know how the day went. Most commonly this is via text, occasionally email. If we are in each other's presence, then we do it verbally.

Now, we may well have many other conversations throughout the day - text exchanges, phone conversations, sexting perhaps (although I am not very good at sexting, as I tend to get busy and move on to other things). But regardless, these two 'bookends' are required, essential, and a source of discipline if they are not done.

It can be hard to stay connected when you don't live with someone. And long distance protocols and rituals are tricky to maintain. But this is your opportunity to always keep a minimal threshold to that communication.

## Develop Your Communication Tools

### *dawn says*

Find your own communication tool that works for you! We will talk about *porch time* in another spot, and a couple of other methods are sprinkled throughout this book. But, even if you don't use one of our tools, it's very important that you have one of your own. And, it would be best to develop it and agree on it before getting to a point where you'd regret not having it.

Let's face it, with most long term relationships, there will be issues. We are humans with different opinions, different ways of communicating, different personalities. So, what structures are you going to have in place when a follower doesn't feel heard? When a Master wants to stomp their feet and be seen? When there are unspeakables that need to be spoken? How are you going to handle it? How do you want your submissive to handle it? Maybe it's porch time, maybe it's an executive meeting, maybe it's something as simple as a "talking stick."

A *talking stick* is so very basic, but not commonly known. We've used this with the kids before, and with groups of people like my spiritual group. You literally have a stick, or if you are somewhere else, it can be anything you designate as the stick; a can, a salt shaker, whatever item you have close by. You sit across from each other and put the stick between you, within reaching distance of both. The first person picks up the stick and talks. They place the stick back in the middle and the other person picks it up and talks.

Only the person with the stick can speak, and they aren't allowed to hog it. This needs to be done in good faith. My kids liked knowing that they could talk and not have me talk over them. And by me putting the stick down when I was done talking, so that they could have their time for a rebuttal or such, they developed trust in the whole process. We were able to work out a lot of stuff this way. And when I used the talking stick in group situations, it helped keep the calm, because only one person could speak at a time.

Or maybe you both communicate better with the written word. Maybe develop a code word that means you'll both get on a messenger system and have the conversation that way. Don't pooh-pooh the idea. We know a power exchange couple that didn't want to say things that might upset the other person, but there were things that needed to be said. It was easier for them to say things when they couldn't see the other person's face. They would sit back to back in the same room and instant message each other during a specific time, expressly for sharing a frustration or a truth they had been holding on to because they didn't know how to express it. They tell the story with a laugh now, but it worked for them.

There are a lot of options to choose from. But, I can't stress the importance of picking one. You probably won't know if it works for you until you have to try it out, but try to pick one that matches your processing styles. And if it doesn't work, there are others to choose from. It would be awful if a relationship broke up because someone didn't know how to talk about something, or how to bring something up.

And… could it be that, when it comes down to it, this book is more about communication than anything else? That the real way that a power exchange relationship lasts for five or ten or twenty years is due to the ability to communicate effectively and efficiently? Perhaps. Regardless, for more about communication, see the chapters on Relationship Shorthand, Porch Time, Becoming a Leader, Grief, Contracts… and really, nearly everywhere else.

# Becoming a Leader

## *Dan says*

Some close friends of ours say 'my follower clears a path for me so that I can lead.' I'll leave it to dawn to talk about becoming a good follower. Here, we will talk about being a good Leader.

In my viewpoint, being the Leader - be it Belum, Dominant, Master, Owner, or any other title - is a tremendous responsibility. You are basically saying that you can run the life of yourself and another person more skillfully than the follower could alone. And that you have the right to do so. That is some cocky stuff.

So, this chapter is written from that perspective. It will challenge you to look in the mirror and be confident that you have that ability; that you see your failures and respond to them; and that you continue to grow and nurture your follower(s), your relationship(s), and yourself.

## Step One is You!

In case you were hoping step one was 'collar a hottie,' sorry to rain on that parade. It is valuable to address this step prior to looking for a relationship. If you are already in one, this is still well worth your energy to explore.

After all, the most important relationship in your life (according to the self-help books) is the one you cultivate with yourself. To be honest, I agree. What do you, as a Leader, bring to this relationship? This is where your self-confidence will start to be created. That honest appraisal of your good points; the discipline to address the areas that need it.

That self-appraisal, which will continue and be refined over and over again, will lead you to what you are going to need - knowledge, skill, confidence, experience, and instinct. But we are getting ahead of ourselves.

So, back to you. Let's create a quick, completely unscientific rating system. Are you a poor, good, or great Leader now? We will talk about defining it as well in a bit. But for now, stop thinking about it and just say (literally, out loud) what you believe - "I am a good Leader." "I am a poor Owner." "I am the greatest Dom evah." Now, if you really did say it out loud, is it true? And once you answer that, do it again, say it out loud and answer 'is it true?'

If you have self rated yourself as poor, as we move into the next section, you'll have a great chance to improve. The entire next section is about being a good Leader, so good for you, you are on the path! If you self-rated good, you can confirm it in the next section and feel more confident. And if you think you are great, then the next section should be a breeze. But, you'll likely pick up something of value on the way.

Let's come back to you, and the foundation that will create a great Leader. As mentioned before, you're going to need a number of components. Knowledge is one you are working on right now - reading a book on power exchange. This book will also include many skills. But this book is not enough.

Commit to yourself today that you will always be improving as a Leader in some way. You can make that simpler (but still the same) by committing to always improve. Be it the physical body, reading other books, (power exchange or otherwise,) getting involved in those conversations on social media sites, (without trying to win any arguments, just listening and hearing what people think, and asking yourself 'is that something that would benefit me?') watching a YouTube video on some random thing, the specifics of what you do don't matter. Find something that catches your attention and dig into it - for a day, for a week, or longer.

Confidence comes from successful experience. Successful experience leads to more confidence. Combined, this leads you to the instinct.

Confidence is trust in yourself, and belief in your abilities. An internal conviction that you are in the right place, you are good enough, you belong in the seat of power, and that mistakes you make, you can recover from without it knocking you out. But let's move on and talk about being a good Leader.

## Companions

When dawn and I first started, I was not a good Leader. It would be a stretch to even say I was a poor Leader. I was clueless and bumbling about. Although I had some theories and ideas, I had few examples in real life. And the fictional examples? They were hot and sexy but totally unrealistic. Way before Fifty Shades, there was The Claiming of Sleeping Beauty, The Marketplace, the Gor novels, and the Story of O. Great masturbation material for the most part, but not without value - they presented some aspects of power exchange that could be transmuted into real life. They were not guides so much as glimmers of potential.

So one of my first steps was to find some real life examples. Could this actually work in the real world? Today, I would have had a lot more options than I did twenty years ago. Before Fetlife, finding those events or groups took some digging. But I won't bore you with 'back in my day you had to walk uphill both ways' crap. Instead, check out your options. Finding local groups like MAsT (Masters and slaves together) in your area, or other power exchange gatherings. And if those are hard to come by, look for kink ones, where you'll likely find some crossover. Plus nowadays, you've got a few weekend conferences that focus on power exchange exclusively. Anon-Ms, Master slave conference, and Power Exchange Summit are a few. Of course, Fetlife groups are an option, but take them all with a grain of salt - or perhaps better said, take what you need and leave the rest. But I can not understate the value of having friends who are walking the same path. As we've often said, just being able to speak openly about being in a power exchange relationship with people who got it, and had similar challenges, was really powerful.

## Jump Around!

Now that you have some peers that will call you on your bullshit, I want to point you to some other parts of the book which you'll want to address next. The first thing I did and would recommend for you is to jump over to that section in the book regarding contracts and build one. Even if you have decided you will have a relationship with no contracts, build one anyway. Because this answers a key need: clarity. What does it really mean to lead? What is this power exchange relationship about? To you and to your followers, this answer is worth exploring.

And while you are at it, hop over to and read the part of the book about Styles of Power Exchange if you haven't already. I'll wait, and when you get back, we can start leading!

## Start Leading

A modern Buddhist teacher has a saying that "The point of a restaurant is not to read the menu; it is to try the food." So, time to try the food. Or, in the case of power exchange, you've gained that official acceptance of your ownership, you've put a collar on them, (or whatever your symbol or ritual is - and yes, this is another reference to the chapter on Rituals,) and away you go. So, now what?

Hopefully the exercise with the contract has already given you that foundation. But beyond that, here are some additional concepts to make you comfortable. We are moving toward being a good Leader.

*Undivided Attention* - We live in a multimedia world and we do not benefit from that. When you are talking to your follower, give them your undivided attention. And when they talk to you, demand the same. Laptops closed, TV muted or off, board game paused, pencils down. This will give your words more power; it will give you both a better chance of not just hearing each other, but actually listening. It makes your follower feel heard, which is a very powerful thing.

*Give Them Something To Do* - dawn and I are exceedingly busy. As a matter of fact, most of my followers have been busy people. From the one that was studying for their doctorate, to the one that wanted to become a nurse, to the one that always had four projects going. And I have made the mistake a number of times of thinking I was doing them a favor by not asking them for a service, especially if it was something I could do myself. Even my followers who would not consider themselves 'service based' liked serving me. It helped us stay connected, and reminded us of our relationship structure. So although dawn already has writing an article and preparing a Zoom class and making dinner on her to-do list, I need to remember to honor our relationship by asking for a service for me. And to acknowledge those services she provides.

*Honor the follower's vulnerability* - A very simple statement, but it carries a lot of depth. My followers are turning over their life to me (or at least parts of it) and that makes them very vulnerable. How can I honor that vulnerability? The obvious answer is to not take advantage of it. But beyond that, do I have a way to show my gratitude for it? Maybe it is as simple as saying so; maybe it is reflecting back to them what we have gained from that vulnerability.

*Master Owns The Collar* - In all my power exchange relationships, I present my follower a physical reminder of our bond, normally a collar, for them to wear and carry. You'll note I didn't say 'give them a collar' because I don't - I let them temporarily have one of mine. This is for a number of reasons. First, if the relationship ends, I am given the collar back. Depending on how things go, the collar may be given to another follower down the road, or retired. kame bat's collar still sits in my drawer at home; another collar was left in the woods to be found by someone new, and create a new chain of events.

This is, for me, a symbol that I own and am responsible for the relationship. Secondly, it acts as a reminder for the follower that we are in an 'at will' relationship. They can return the collar to symbolize they have finished with me being in charge (no matter the language you use - follower or slave - it is always a consensual relationship that can be ended by either member at any time). So this gives them a simple 'out.' 'Here is your collar, pal, I'm moving on.' When it comes to relationships ending, most collars have been returned ceremonially and with a shared honor and statement of completion. I've had one tossed at me with a 'fuck off' attitude. But they all help to create a sense of closure and completion. dawn is still the steward of a collar I gave her two decades back. To be honest, I hope she doesn't give it back any time soon.

*Recognize the Moment* - I give my followers a number of tasks and duties, but a lot of that is training. More on that in a moment. But as time goes by, they end up doing more service for me that I don't ask for. Meaning, the mindset starts to shift, and they begin to move into being a more instinctive follower. Yes, dawn makes dinner because I told her to, but adding fresh bread that I didn't ask for specifically and that she can't eat because she is following her feeling that it would be pleasing to me? It is great to just say 'thank you,' but you can do better than that. Stop what you are doing, look at them, give them your full and undivided attention, and acknowledge the anticipatory service they have provided. This is again a reminder that this is power exchange, and this is part of your exchange.

## Good Leader

Leaders, Owners, Masters and Mistresses, Doms and Dommes - they are a dime a dozen on social media sites. As you hang around, you'll see some people using the Leader language and maybe even judge them as clueless, arrogant, or just assholes. And in some cases, let's face it, you'd be right. But we are not here to judge anyone except ourselves. So let's look into the skills and actions required of a good Leader.

### *Training*

First off, there are schools you can send your follower off to that claim they will train them for you. I've backspaced over my less than generous thoughts on these, and will instead leave you with this thought - training isn't their job, it is yours. You need to teach your follower what you want, how you want it, when you want it, and then clarify it until you are receiving what you want. Even if what you want isn't that important. This is what good Leaders do. They set expectations, they are decisive, and they forge a follower into an extension of their will (more on that below). They set up a command structure, and then they give commands. And they never have to be loud about it, or abusive, or arrogant, because they are confident. They expect results. If the results are lacking, they do not get upset, they course correct and do it again.

So whether the training is something as simple as how to serve coffee or more complex, you drive the beginning and evaluate the end. Training how to serve me I can do on my own (or, in the case of a situation where I have an alpha follower, I train them, and they train everyone else). I have many skills that I know how to do, or how I want them, and thus I can provide that training directly. In some situations I may leave the training to them - I told one follower to learn how to twirl poi. They needed no further instruction and a few weeks later, showed me their new skill. Apparently YouTube has many tutorials.

Another follower I ordered to go learn everything needed to become clergy in a specific faith. I had no clue how to do that personally, so the actual command was 'find a school to teach you.' Then the next one was 'go to that school.' Now, I suggested earlier that you should not send your follower off to one of these 'slave schools,' but that doesn't mean you don't make use of resources. So if I want my follower to learn a skill that I am clueless about, then off to some education they go - either from a friend who knows, a mentor, or a class.

Now, to be honest, sometimes we train them to do things we don't actually care about one way or another.

This is where a good Leader can really shine. The follower I mentioned above, having them train as a clergy? That was something they wanted to achieve but didn't (yet) have the courage to accomplish. By listening and knowing them, I realized it was what they wanted, and gave them the push they needed. Go do it for me, I said, and with a smile they went and did so.

## *Forge Into an Extension of My Will*

When I want a coke, I can get up and walk over and get it. Not a problem at all. Alternatively, I can speak my desire and a coke appears in my hand. This small example is fine. But I'm really not into this power exchange thing for the five steps it saves me to the kitchen. Instead, I want to increase my influence and power by creating an extension of my will - that extension being my follower. So, when I want them to get me a coke, or get a fellow Leader a coke, or give them a blow job, or make a statement about appropriate power exchange, or cover a class I was going to teach at a conference, or any number of situations, my follower is acting in my stead, and doing so with an intimate knowledge of how I want things done. They are doing it as I would do it. Now, this doesn't make any of my followers mindless automatons. How dawn teaches a class or talks about a topic will always have her flair based on her experience. But the goal, the intent, the focus will be aligned with mine and how I want it. This is an extension of my will.

This is a double-edged sword, because it means that when I claim dawn as my follower, I claim her actions as mine as well. And that is necessary as I continue this forging process. Believe me, when dawn and I started, she did not reflect my approach in some arenas. If someone was an ass on some forum, she would call them out and if they countered, she would double down and crush them. This is not my way. So she was no longer allowed to do that. The first part of training in this is to stop doing it. Then, gain understanding why that is not my way and thus, not her way.

So I do believe that dawn (or any follower of mine) is a reflection of me. This is important because it means I need to stay engaged in that training, engaged in our power exchange dynamic, and alert to when we get out of sync. I want that level of commitment from us both that if she offends someone, it is as if I offended them, and I need to take responsibility for that.

> *Note: dawn giggled when she read the above section and suggested that what I was saying was that when she gave a blow job to someone, then it was actually me giving the blowjob. And in the case of when she blows me, does that mean I am blowing myself? I am leaving my words as they fell, and will let the reader make their own assumptions…*
>
> *Cheeky slave.*

A good Leader in my style of power exchange cherishes the emotional wellbeing of their follower. I want dawn to be happy and joyful and aware that her service to me brings us both pleasure and completeness. Thus, my ego is never threatened if dawn giggles when I am silly, or smiles when I do something unintentionally funny. Life is funny and fun and full of goofy mishaps, and we make a point of smiling and moving along. Just because I am a Leader does not mean I am infallible and unable to laugh at myself. I would not call dawn bratty… but she has her moments of goofing on me. We both take delight in that, because she knows the appropriate time and place for it. If I am giving her a command or correction, she knows it is time to be serious and attentive. But if we are chilling and watching TV while we eat ice cream and I can't find my glasses that are sitting on my head and she finds that humorous, well, heck, it is kinda funny. It is all about intent for me. Her humor is not to undercut or degrade - that would never be acceptable. And if she pushes a button that I am uncomfortable with, I simply tell her so, and we move on.

## *The Voice*

When my follower and I are in tune with each other, we can seamlessly interchange from random talk about grocery list, her laughing with me at my accidentally calling the dog by the wrong name (yes, that happened, the dog didn't mind), to me ordering her to take care of some task for me and receiving a 'Yes sir,' to us going right back to 'do you want corn or pineapple with the ham?' This is what we call 'the voice,' but really I think of it as our intimate dance that we have developed after becoming vulnerable and knowing each other.

## *Delegating*

The nice thing about all that attention to training and forging a follower into an extension of your will is that you can confidently delegate. 'Go do the thing' doesn't need to be explained in depth; they know you, they know your desires, and they go do it. And if they can't do it the way they think you would, they can make an educated guess and provide the best results they can. I don't have to say 'Contact Mistress Jan's submissive and compare calendars. Find a time and place where we can have coffee with them. I don't think Mistress Jan is into traveling a lot right now so find a place on their side of town. Of course, don't make it a Tuesday night 'cause I have gaming with Bob.' All I need to say is 'set up coffee with Mistress Jan,' I get a 'yes, Sir' in return, and it happens the way I would want it to happen.

## *Whoopsie-doodle!*

Do good Leaders make mistakes? No, they are all opportunities! Ok, to be honest, we do make mistakes. And depending on what they are, they can be a big deal. When you claim responsibility for the relationship, your mistakes impact more than just you. But the path between good and great Leaders is often about how we deal with these mistakes.

We are, regardless of time and experience and intention, human. And thus, prone to error. Bad judgment, poor timing, being accidentally inconsiderate, simply forgetting something important, or just having a shitty day and taking it out on someone who doesn't deserve it. It happens. Over time, it should happen less and less, but you'll never hit perfection. And if you are like me, who gets bored when things are too easy and wants to push the envelope, they will likely happen now and again. So what do we do about them?

## *Own Your Mistakes*

It is essential that you can inspire your follower to have confidence in you. And that often comes from clear goals, being decisive, and making decisions and having them followed through. And sometimes, those decisions are the wrong one. In that case, to maintain that confidence in you, you tell your follower clearly and without reservation that you fucked up, or whatever terminology you prefer to use. You own your mistake, then you verbalize what you are going to do to correct it, then you correct it. If applicable, you set up a plan to prevent this type of mistake from happening again.

You are not doing this for your follower so much as you are doing it for the relationship, which you are the steward of. And to be honest, you are doing it for yourself, because if you avoid the mistake or shirk off the responsibility for it, you'll either undermine your own confidence in yourself, or create an ego-based wall between yourself and reality. Neither is the quality of a good Leader.

## *Get Back on the Horse*

Did I make a mistake, or a series of mistakes, that caused significant harm to one of my followers? You'll excuse me if I am sparse on details here. I don't mind sharing, but I don't have the right to tell their story. But I had grave self doubts about the way I handled a situation. This responsibility for the relationship, when it goes sour, can be a heavy burden. To be honest, I beat myself up a lot over it.

You see, I had a pretty good track record for collaring

followers who had some personal challenges. We interacted and via our relationship, they ended up the better for it. This is not to suggest I am a great healer or guru - all I do is accept them where they are, and help them see they are more than they have been allowed to think they are. I've been proud to say that those in my collar have gained from that to some degree, some significantly.

And then this one person… it went very badly. Now, I understand logically that I am neither a medical nor psychological expert, and that sometimes shit is out of my control. Mentally I knew that, and realized things happened as they did regardless of what I did. But emotionally… I had a lot of 'If I only...' and 'Did I make it worse?'

The point is this - I had to 'get back on the horse' and start to be dawn's Belum again, to start taking a Leadership role in her life, and gain my confidence back. To bring my thinking mind and emotional mind in alignment - that I am no superman; but I am also not responsible for the wellbeing of all people all the time. I do my best, I avoid harm, my intent is good, my methodology is sound. I will own my mistakes… but I won't create self-recrimination where none is deserved.

## *Fears and Limitations*

If you want to be a great Leader, then you'll need to recognize if you have any fears around being a Leader, and then face them. And to be honest, you should have, if not fears, at least some cautious awareness. After all, you are signed up to be the person in charge, the place where 'the buck stops here,' the failure point for your relationship. And if you make a mistake, it might have some serious emotional or financial or even physical impacts!

So we as Leaders have to have the fortitude to look in the mirror, and course correct. We have to be unafraid to fail, but aware that we might.

And it isn't all just fear. Some of it is willingness to accept our limitations. Do you have enough spoons, as they say, to take on full time power exchange? Is it wiser to offer limited engagement only? And in those scenarios, when everything is offered, how do you know what parts to take on?

Sometimes my greatest challenge is knowing that I am not the right Leader for certain people. Sure, I can help with self esteem issues, and assist in building self confidence. But am I the right person for a follower who has an addiction issue, or a chemical imbalance, or cancer? I struggle with this. I believe everyone is worthy of love and affection and getting their needs filled. I need to know that sometimes, I am not the right one to provide it.

## *Failing at Trust*

When dawn and I first got started, she struggled with resistance. We both knew we wanted a power exchange relationship and that it was the right direction for us. But when it came to giving her an order, her fear would rear up and she'd start to dig her feet in. I recall in our talks that she wanted to work on body acceptance, and embracing her slutty self. So at a small house party, where it was an appropriate thing to do, I told her to take her shirt off, walk into the other room, and get me a drink. She first thought I was kidding, then reacted in anger, which was actually fear. I stayed neutral and unyielding, and she did as she was told.

So it can start with obeying the order because it is an order - talking yourself through it and forcing yourself along. But do this enough - and have it work out as the Leader said it would, being mutually beneficial, then trust begins to develop in you as a Leader.

Because this is power exchange, you can go out after work with the girls and grab a drink if that, as a Leader, is what you want to do. But while everyone else is calling spouses and saying they have to work late or traffic is bad, you are notifying your follower that you are going out for drinks. This is where trust is created. And when you say you will be home at 7 o'clock, you are home at that time. If you don't know when, say "I don't know." Consistently saying "This is what is going to happen" and that is how it happens - or if it doesn't happen, acknowledge that as your mistake, and do better next time.

But one of the most common ways to end a power exchange relationship (when you don't actually want to end it) is for a Leader to break trust. From something as simple as saying you will be at a place and not showing up until later, or not at all, to saying you will take care of something and not following through, to the more extreme having an extra relationship that you hide from your follower.

In this scenario, if you want to regain that trust, then it will take willingness to be vulnerable, non-manipulative, flexible, and owning the responsibility to do better.

In general, part one is doubling down on 'if you say it, do it.' And if you can't do it, communicate that. Part two is to live in a glass house for your follower. Meaning, share the email password and the phone lock, and if your follower wants to look through your messages… they get to, with no reservation from you. And you don't get to pipe up with 'still don't trust me, eh?' because, well, they probably don't.

Now, that does not mean they get to be disrespectful. Once the initial disappointment or pain is addressed, and some time goes by, we expect the lashing out to subside. We want to return things to normalcy, and normal power exchange should include respect.

Power exchange is a very vulnerable style of relationship and thus, the recovery from busted trust is a long road. We know a few people who have been successful.

## *Avoid Fucking It Up*

The subtle power exchange killers for a Leader to be aware of are complacency, lulls, and laziness. In reading this book, you might think power exchange is a lot of work, and you are right. So we, oh Leaders, get tired! We hit autopilot as decision fatigue sets in. But when the call for 'Captain to the bridge' comes and you don't show up… things start to drift.

When things are smooth and simple, it is a great time to take a break and catch your breath. Nothing wrong with that. But we use a viewpoint of 'minimum standard' to make sure we don't totally fall off. Our morning and evening rituals stay in place, ever reminding us of who we are. This makes it much easier to ramp up when need be. And if you've set a rule, you need to make sure it is followed. If you ignore it once, it is much easier to ignore it a second time. And your follower may well know you are ignoring it.

Doubt creeps in.

But the other side of this is that you may indeed need a break, and you should go ahead and take one. Now, how you do that is not to say "I need a break from power exchange, let's be peers for a week." Instead, what we say is "I am taking a day off to self focus," alerting my followers that I don't want to make any unnecessary decisions. I may stay home, I may go out.

And other times, my breaks are more significant. I put on a backpack and go hiking, perhaps even overnight, somewhere without cellphone service.

My followers are not dependent on me. They can get by just fine for a few hours or a few days without me. But when I re-engage, I make sure they are holding to the standards I require and still acting as an extension of me.

## Great Leader

Ok, the actual title of this section should be 'more difficult concepts to Master.' The skill on when to implement, or how, or the level of ego required, can make some of these a challenge. At least that was the case for me.

### *STFU and Kneel*

I am, as pointed out earlier, merely human. And sometimes dawn and other followers piss me off. Sometimes it is accidentally, the result of a bad day. Sometimes it is because I am not doing the maintenance in keeping everything on an even keel. And sometimes... my loving follower, who is also human, reverts to old ways and gives me some shit. But the short version of this is sometimes I get angry; and when I am angry, I cannot efficiently lead.

The first time I used the tool I'm about to talk about was in the woods, on some hiking trail. We were trying to figure out if we should walk to the end, or I should go back and get the truck and dawn walk it, or if we should just give up and both go home. I don't recall how the conversation got heated but it certainly did. I found myself loudly saying - ok, own it, I shouted - "Shut the fuck up and kneel!" as I squeezed a pair of sun glasses into pieces. dawn, an angry look in her face, complied.

This gave me time to catch my breath. I stayed quiet as I reviewed what the fuck had just happened and remembered my role in our relationship - to lead. The "STFU" command wasn't a punishment of any sort, nor was it intended to be. It was a 'time out' for both of us. Once I got my heart rate down and my mind in order, I talked about why I was so angry and I acknowledged her anger. I said we are not in a 'yell at each other' relationship so let's find another path. I apologized. I regained control of myself, of the situation, and gave dawn time to calm down as well. I stood her up, she apologized for her part in things, and I made a definitive decision - we would return to the truck and walk another day. Peace was restored.

This tool has come in handy since then, but instead of waiting until we are at the yelling stage, I speak it plainly beforehand. Or even just say 'kneel.' It works wonders for us both, to get past the years we had in non-power exchange relationships where yelling was part of the way things got done.

## *Iron Fist, Silk Glove*

Currently, dawn and I live full time in an RV. We show up at some spot and get set up for a few weeks, then move on to the next. There was one stop where, after three days, I decided it was time to go. Crummy spot, rotten wifi signal, depressing weather.

Now, I know dawn. She is a creature of habit and had already woken up and started to process her day and how she was going to go about it. I could have just said 'I am unhappy here, we are moving, make it so' or some such, and she would have complied. But it would have had an emotional impact. Instead, I said 'I am unhappy here, and our home has wheels. We are going to leave early, meaning today. I'll follow up with you on making this happen in five minutes.' This gave dawn the same command - we are moving - but presented it in a way that allowed her to process the emotional aspect and mentally adjust at her speed.

Don't be fooled to think that we, as compassionate beings, should always present our commands in the 'silk glove' way. The 'Iron Fist' is faster, more efficient, and is sometimes the best method. It can be of value to our follower to challenge them when we cut to the chase and give them very direct direction without room for improvisation. I want it this way, only this way, exactly this way, and anything less isn't good enough. For dawn, she will rise to the challenge. For kame bat, she always preferred Iron Fist - make it clear and make me push myself to be exact.

The challenge for you is to know when a follower needs the silk glove or the iron fist. Or you want it one way or the other, and being ok with the price they will pay for that.

## *Power Comes From I Don't Know*

Know what you know, and know what you don't know. We Leader types are not, as rumor might suggest, infallible and all knowing. Sometimes we are wise and sometimes we have no clue. The ego that cannot handle this is going to cause you trouble.

When I walk around some events, I've seen some Masters that appear to have all their shit together. The leather, the cap, everything polished and shiny, and the attitude of I am King Shit. Which is great; actually I've been that guy and it is kinda fun. But one such fellow was asked a question by his submissive and this Master did not know the answer. But instead of claiming it, he bullshitted the sub. The sub asked for clarification and the Domly Master seemed to feel challenged - in front of others no less - and lost it. His Mastery was maintained as a fragile illusion.

What I took from this was the power to say "I don't know" when I don't. And not be attached to that. There are a lot of things I don't know anything about, and owning that, speaking it, being one with it, gives me options. To either 'don't know, don't care' and go on about my day; to 'don't know but would like to' and learn something. Or 'don't know so I'll send my follower to go learn about it' so I know via an extension of myself.

Although when a follower asks me for guidance and I don't know, I respond with 'I don't know, but Master Zed is skilled in that' or 'I don't know, but seek the advice of your peers.' And I follow up with 'and tell me what you found out.' This allows me to maintain Leadership, even when I don't know all the things.

## *The Seat of Power*

There is a trick to balancing all this self-confidence and ego release and humility and successful Leadership. I am a Leader. A very good one. I've made mistakes and errors along the way, but overall, my track record and results speak for themselves. And at the same time, I am human, and prone to mistakes, and get angry sometimes, and can be selfish and lazy.

When I think about my Seat of Power, it is all these things, and it is knowing without a doubt that the true Dan, the self-actualized being, is a Leader in power exchange. This is where I shine, where I belong, where I can dance without thinking.

It's a daily challenge to know this while not letting it be a trap (too much ego to see mistakes) or an end point (I've reached my pinnacle); not allowing it to lead to arrogance. But when things start to slide, when dawn and I are having a conversation or trying to come up with a plan and I let too much slide into 'not what I think is best but tired of the conversation' or 'but I don't wanna' space, I remember my seat of power and where our best lives have come from these past 20 years. They have come from a wonderful partnership that has clear roles, and my role is to lead.

## *Flex*

I asked dawn to make me a cup of coffee. She did so. When she brought it over, I said to her to take it away because now I want tea instead. She looked at me questioningly and I said, "Flex."

A good Leader avoids arrogance at all times. They are not a dick just to be a dick. But then, there is the flex. The flex is when I, as a Leader, make my follower do something just because I can. It is a small reminder that we are indeed in a power exchange relationship and sometimes I get my way for no other reason than I want it. The flex is normally for small and unimportant things and it isn't meant to really do anything of great import or deeply enhance our relationship. It is just that gentle but solid way to say "Me Leader, you follower." A good flex often comes with a chuckle.

## *Make Me an Impossible Sandwich*

We were in a hotel in Chicago, our first time there, and once we were in our hotel room I said 'Go get me a roast beef sandwich.' Now, dawn has a few questions about this - from the hotel restaurant or from somewhere else? What if they didn't have roast beef? On white or rye or…

At least, I assume these are the questions she was going to ask, because I cut her off before any of them and said "Just go do it," and turned to my PC to do whatever I was working on.

Wallet in hand, she was out the door and, with some annoyance she told me later, set out to accomplish the task.

Another power exchange lesson I would suggest in the more challenging arena is when you give your follower an "impossible" task. You might be thinking that isn't fair or ever a good idea; that I am setting them up for failure. But the intent here is to make them stretch, to think, to improvise, to serve with intent instead of by the letter. I want a thing and I want you, based on our life so far together, your knowledge of me and my expectations for you, to accomplish this in the best way you can. They may become frustrated and angry or even self deprecating at such a task - they want, after all, to serve. So the result of the task should be acknowledged and appreciated, because the task was never that important. The willingness to try, to do their best, to have the courage to guess, and accept they might be more capable than they suspected, is the actual goal.

By the way, I ended up with a reuben, which was pretty tasty.

## *You Can Take a Break*

I get tired of being in charge sometimes. Specifically, I get tired of being the Leader. Being responsible for all the things all the time takes a lot of mental energy. It can get to a point where dawn asks, 'What would you like for dinner?' and I respond with an exasperated 'I don't care!'

The trick is to realize - before the tank gets too empty - that it is time to take a break. Now you might be thinking (like I did) that this idea would conflict with the idea that we are 24/7 and I am always in charge. The way to make this part of that is that you are making a decision - I have scheduled a day off, I am taking a day off, here are your marching orders for that day (which may include some task, or may be nothing at all), and now leave me alone.

For me, the effective break needs to be physical as well. We are not talking about the 'I'm playing a PC game and want to be involved in it' or 'I'm watching the last episode of some show so leave me be.' This is the dedicated significant recharge that happens every few months that I take to focus on me. Recently, that has been a long hike in the woods, including camping overnight, staying in a rented AirBnB, or spending a weekend with a non-power exchange partner. None of this is about dawn. Meaning I don't need a break from her. I need a break from the constant 'this relationship is your responsibility so think about everything.'

Never let anyone tell you that a Real Dominant doesn't need a break. Listen to yourself. You may be a great Leader, respected by peers and sought out by submissives from around the world… and yet, you are still only human.

# How To Be a Follower

### *dawn says*

Recently, I had someone tell me that I make being a slave/sub/follower look so easy. I blinked, not having a quick response. I had to think about that. I couldn't even get out a 'thank you' because at first I thought they were joking. But, looking at it, maybe it does look easy from the outside. It's definitely smoother than it was when we first got started.

There were a lot of lessons I had to learn to smooth out the path that I had decided to follow. A path that I was going to have to blaze on my own, because I didn't have any role models. I had a few friends that were on the same journey of power exchange that we found at about the time we got started, but no one with actual experience.

I really wanted to dive into this relationship and give it my best, but at the beginning my best wasn't that great. There were stumbling blocks to my submission that I had to overcome if I was going to help make this dynamic work. I talk about this a lot in the Survivor chapter of the book.

So, if it's rocky at the beginning, don't look at someone that's been doing this for 20 years and think that's who you are supposed to be at the moment. You'll have your own journey and hurdles to contend with. But, you can look at someone that's been doing this a long time, with a rocky start, and have hope that it does get easier.

The first skill that I had to learn was obedience. I thought it was submission, but in honesty, I'm not a very submissive person. In my young years I accomplished things through perseverance. I won awards for my artwork, my writing, and my science projects. I was the Leader of a couple of groups in high school and even in the lodge my parents belonged to, I became the youngest Leader in the state. In my experience, if I didn't lead the way on accomplishing what I wanted, it didn't get done. Then, I married right out of high school and ended up having to be in charge of that relationship to keep a roof over our heads. So, I'm not a submissive person. I wanted to be. I really wanted to be. But, the resistance that it caused was very hard on both of us. So, we decided to start with obedience.

## *Obedience, Trust, Faith*

Most Leaders that I know crave obedience. They want their follower to have enough trust in them to obey their orders. This doesn't work for all power exchange relationships, but it certainly does for ours. I need to trust, Dan needs to be trusted. Obedience feeds both of us.

When we were newbies, I can remember our first 'interview.' We were changing our relationship from one of friendship to one of Dom/sub. We are riding around in the car and Dan tells me to unbutton my shirt. What? What do you mean unbutton my shirt? Cars will see. He looks at me again and tells me to unbutton my shirt. On the verge of panic, I start to unbutton my shirt. We had talked about fantasies like this but I didn't know that I was actually ready to do it. I got about three buttons undone when he stopped me. It was a test to see if I'd obey him.

Not long after that, we were at a house party. We were in a separate room playing and he ordered me to go into the other room without my shirt on to fetch him a drink or something. I stumbled, not sure if I could do it. He said 'obey.' So, I did. Totally freaking out in my head. But, I obeyed and nothing bad happened. I was starting to trust him through these little practices.

Now, it's not like he was giving these orders at random. He had listened to my stories and my fantasies, knowing I wanted to get to the point where nudity wouldn't bother me. He knew that I wanted to obey and follow a strong Leader. So, he was starting out with small things, even though my head thought those were the biggest commands that could be given to someone. Boy was I wrong! But, by starting small and ramping up over time, trust and then faith was built, and I was able to do the bigger commands and the commands that don't have a lot of specifics given with them.

*(By the way, if you ever run for Master/slave title in the Leather world and you get a couple of specific judges, and they ask you what is the most important skill you offer as a slave? Obedience is the answer. Just thought I'd throw that in there.)*

It's through obedience that I can enjoy my submission

to Dan, even though I don't technically have a submissive personality. I've even been mistaken for a Dominant before, until Dan comes and stands beside me. My whole demeanor changes. I can lead. I don't want to lead. I'd much rather follow a strong Leader and be the extension of his will. I like seeing his dreams and making them happen. I like making his life easier.

## *Alignment of Will*

This is another skill that I've learned through the years that certainly makes our power exchange easier to navigate. I have a friend that calls it this. I used to call it something else, but I can't remember what it is. Let me 'splain.

There are times when I think I know the answer, and there are certainly times where I'd like to do things my way. Most of the time Dan will let me have a voice and share these wants or ideas. I feel like I'm giving service by throwing all the information on the table. He then takes that information and makes a decision. Sometimes I wonder how he came to that decision with the information I gave him. Well, just because I've given him information doesn't mean he has to make a decision based solely on what I've given him.

Let's say we are going to another state in the RV. I've figured out how long it's going to take us to get there and how many miles we should put in each day and where we should stop, all in service. I give Dan all these details. He decides that what I've come up with doesn't work for him and makes changes. Hell, he might even change the state. Ask me how I know.

It's my job to take that breath, and change my thinking.

Once I align my will to his, I don't have as many issues with resistance or thinking that my plan is better. Well, I might still think my plan is better, but it's now not an option, and I need to be ok with that. This is what I agreed to and just because his way is different, doesn't make it wrong. I've actually learned through the years that his way is usually more efficient. We just have different ways of looking at things. (See 'Hawk and Mouse' in a later section of the book for more on this.)

Alignment of Will can make obedience easier to follow through with. Dan mentioned a story about one of our walks in the woods, and not remembering what caused us both to get angry. Well, I remember, because it wasn't one of my prettier moments.

I was training for a half marathon. It was a lot of work, and I was trying to find pretty places to walk instead of just the sidewalk. I found a path and Dan decided to join me. We get into the woods and I'm blazing a path, trying to get my speed up. Dan says we should stop and turn around. My head is in 'charge ahead and get this accomplished mode' and as I'm striding, I'm trying to talk him out of going back. This is *my* walk, and I feel I should be in charge of it. Dan thinks differently and to get me to listen he yells, 'Kneel!' I gave him a look, which didn't go over well, but dropped to my knees there in the woods. I stayed quiet and waited for him to gather himself.

This was another moment of learning to trust him. I knew he wouldn't continue in anger. This was a moment for us to calm down. We both took that opportunity to do so. Breathing. I could feel the anger ground out of me. I was obeying and remembering who was in charge. He knew how important that half marathon was to me, and he wouldn't have stopped us if he hadn't thought that was the best. Once emotions were under control, he stated we were going back to the truck and at a normal pace. "Yes, Sir."

Later, he explained why he had to stop the walk. And he was right, it was the right thing to do. This was a hard experience, but it helped me develop more trust in him and our dynamic. He was able to resolve that issue of heated emotions without anger, assert his dominance, and lead. I was able to breathe through the moment, accept his dominance, and follow.

These are just small examples. In reality 'Alignment of Will' is much bigger than that. It is more about a cultivation of a shared vision. For me, this is about internalizing Dan's vision and turning it into 'our' vision. I surrender to his will. Not easily sometimes, and definitely not as a doormat. This is easy to do because I know that Dan's ego is not in charge. I'll double check with my inner-self every now and then to make sure that we are working with 'right action,' 'right speech,' 'graciousness,' etc. I like to make sure we are on the agreed-upon path. But, knowing that he has surrendered his ego, makes it much easier to surrender to his will.

## *Extension of His Will*

A reason to keep control of my control issues is because ultimately, I take pride in being an extension of his will. For this to happen, I need to surrender control, align my will with his, and obey. If he wants something, I like helping to make it happen. Whether it's getting him a cup of coffee, or helping him write a book, or create an event. I am an extension of his will. I help make things happen.

## *Reflection of Him*

Sometimes being an extension of his will means I have to do things his way even when he's not around. I need to know how he handles things, his desires, and what he expects out of me. He believes I am a reflection of him and his training, so I am. I do my best not to do anything to embarrass him. I'm respectful in public, which is easy to do. I have no interest in having a power struggle with him in general, let alone in public.

## *Playing the Game*

We just listened to a comedian joking about how husbands try to earn points with their wives so that when they earn enough points they can go play with their friends. I didn't find it funny. What he was describing was 'keeping score' and 'playing chess,' always looking at the next move as part of a game and a way to manipulate, instead of trying to work together as a team and figuring out how to communicate needs and wants.

Dan and I don't play games. He doesn't need to 'earn points' with me. He's in charge. If he wants to do something, he does it. It doesn't mean he might not discuss it with me first if he wants input, but I can't tell him 'no.' It's that simple.

And if I want to do something, I ask. I don't have to 'earn points' unless something is in place where I would earn points to earn a treat. But, it's something we are both aware is happening. There isn't room for manipulation in our relationship. We know our roles and we know how to communicate.

For me, life is so much simpler this way.

## Say what you mean and mean what you say, aka I'm going to take you at your word

This phrase can mean a couple different things, but the way I mean it here is basically to not play games, and tell the truth. This skill has been very important towards our growth. We've even taught friends and family that this is how we operate.

How does this work? If Dan asks me what's wrong and I say "nothing" in that tone of voice that says something is wrong, he might ask a second time to give me a chance to reconsider my answer and answer honestly. But, if I stick to my response and keep moping or slamming doors, he's allowed to walk away. This is basically because I've lied, and there are consequences for that. Usually he'll give me a third chance by saying, "ok, I'm going to take you at your word," pause, and wait for me to respond.

At this point, I take a breath, realize he's saying he's recognized something is wrong, but it's not his job to pull it out of me. It's my job to take responsibility for being truthful. Usually, I'll take a breath at this point and ask him if he has a moment for me to share what is going on, or that I'm working on something but don't want to bother him, etc. And that's usually what it comes down to for me.

I don't want to bother him with what is going on, or I'm so frustrated or angry at something and I don't want to admit to it, because I know he doesn't like me to respond to situations like that and I don't want to be a disappointment.

But, how can he Master me if he doesn't know what's going on? So, I might as well admit to it, even if it's saying, "I'm just so frustrated right now." If I don't say this, and still say 'nothing,' I'm poking holes in our foundation of trust.

Even one of my psychology professors joked that if a husband comes home and his wife is slamming cupboard doors, he asks her what's wrong, she says 'nothing' and he walks away, who is sleeping on the couch that night? Everyone shook their heads and spoke up that of course he is because he didn't read her body language and stick with it. I raised my hand. "Not in my house." We are expected to speak the truth. If we don't speak the truth, the other person can't be punished for it. That's pure manipulation and unfair to the other person. I refuse to play those games in a relationship that is supposed to be so important to me.

With family and friends, I might ask them if they need help with something. The answer is always no. I'll ask a second time, reminding them that I'm going to take them at their word. Not only am I going to take them at their word, I want them to take me at my word. That I would not be asking if they needed help, if I wasn't willing and able to offer it.

If they say 'no' and I butt in after that, in my world, that isn't consensual. If I've told someone no and they do so anyway, I'm not going to be happy about it. So, I give them the same consideration. There is no 'well you should have known that I was *saying* no but was *hinting* yes.' I don't work in that kind of world. I have no interest in playing games like that. "I said yes, but you should have known by my body language." Says who? That is pure guesswork that I'm likely to get wrong. I don't work well with that type of ambiguity. That's one of the reasons I work so well in a power dynamic. I don't like playing games. I don't like power struggles.

## *Perfection*

Believe it or not, perfection can be your enemy in the long run. Remember the quote of how life is about the journey? So is your relationship. I came into this relationship with past baggage of being a perfectionist, and it really caused issues. I punished myself more with my perceived failures than Dan ever felt the need to. I felt that I wouldn't be worth enough to be his submissive if I didn't get everything right the first time around. I abhorred the idea of being high maintenance.

So, I want others to be aware that "knowing" how to do this is very different from doing it. You can read all the books. You can go to all the conventions and attend all the classes. It's actually a great idea. But, until you put it into action, you aren't going to know what to expect. This is because each relationship is different. The combination of each Leader and follower with their different backgrounds and the experiences that they bring to the relationship is going to create a different dynamic. So, all you can do is take what you've learned and use it if it works, and create your own stuff if needed.

## *Seat of Power*

Come at this from your seat of power. What is your seat of power? For me, as I may have mentioned before, it's surrender and obedience. When I'm in that head space, and feeling instinctual in that head space without doubt in my heart, the relationship flows. Especially if Dan is also in his seat of power as a Leader. There will be stumbling blocks as we grow and evolve over time. Just remember to return to what works for you. What makes you happy? When Dan says 'dawn, fetch me a coffee,' and my response is 'Yes, Sir' without hesitation, because that's what's in my heart, that's my seat of power. Obedience, Trust, Faith, as I mentioned before, is a huge part of our foundation.

## *Surrender*

This idea works for some followers and not for others. Some believe that if they 'surrender' to their Leader, they lose their power. It's not true for me. I've surrendered to the Universe to lead me on my life path, knowing that it knows what I need more than I know what I need. And I've surrendered to Dan because his way of dealing with life is what I want to emulate and I know that he has my, his, and our best interest at heart. He is the Leader that I want to follow. I totally trust him, and that's what I need in my life. And with that, I'm totally empowered. Just because I've surrendered to him and our relationship, doesn't mean that I don't get to be a powerful person. It just means that I'm powerful, as his slave.

Keep in mind, that is for me. Some followers don't want to 'lose' their power, they want to follow. Others don't want to be powerful at all, at least in the way outsiders see power. They want to follow and submit. That is their world. Tell me what to do and how to do it is the whole of the law. This could involve surrender, or not. It's all good if it works for you and your dynamic.

## *Control Issues*

Was or is surrender always easy? For me, absolutely not. As I've talked about before, I have control issues. That's why following someone else is so powerful for me. I need to not be in control all the time. It's a learning experience about how not to let my fears control me. That's what my control issues are about: fear that someone will not put me first at least part of the time, fear that someone doesn't have my best interests at heart, fear that someone will purposefully harm me, fear in trusting anyone for any reason. I NEEDED to be a follower to have grown as a person as much as I have.

The trick is, I know it's healthier for me to be in a relationship where I'm not in control. Surrendering to the guidance of a balanced Leader and putting someone else first, trusting someone completely that deserves it, someone that takes that guidance and dominance seriously and takes care of us… is the best decision I've made for myself. That is my seat of power.

So, yes, I have control issues that made submitting a challenge on some days, especially at the beginning. Through experience and time, it's much easier to let go of wanting to hold onto the reins. Though, I still have my moments when I think my way is the right way. Luckily, Dan gives me space to express those ideas. He can pick apart the fear from the smart idea, and usually doesn't let the fear on my part win. Once I know it's in his capable hands, I can step back. I step back so that he can sit in his seat of power, which is to lead. Lead us and the relationship. That's when I can breathe and allow the tightness in my body to dissipate.

The times that I forget to let go… I physically and mentally don't feel good. I'm not living up to my side of the bargain. I'm not living up to what I agreed to. I'm not being my best self. I'm stepping on his toes and that makes the smooth rhythm of our dance falter. Self-talk goes a long way in this, and so does Dan's instinctive control of a situation.

## *"What would Master do?"*

Everything I do is with him in mind, or at least with his pride in mind. "What would Master do" or "What would Master have me do," is in my head a lot. And when I follow this path, life is much simpler.

I'm pretty sure I tell this story elsewhere in this book, but it bears repeating. When bat was first being exposed to power exchange as a relationship style, Dan had me take her to an event. On the drive there, there was a moment when I realized I needed Dan's answer to a question. I tried to contact him, but no answer. She wondered what I was going to do, since it needed to be taken care of in that moment. It couldn't wait for Dan to get back with me. So, I talked it out, out loud. "What would Master do?"

What would he do in this situation? And I worked it out. Then, I made a decision and took care of it. She was surprised that this was "allowed" in our relationship. I told her it had to be. Otherwise I'd be sitting on the side of the road waiting for his answer, and that didn't serve him and actually would make him look bad, as an answer was needed right away. She took that to heart in the years that she served him after that.

It's not only in these moments, but is an underlying theme with everything I do. Running a PTA meeting where someone loses their cool, how do I respond? "What would Master do?" Remember, I want to emulate him, so this is a good thought to have. Old dawn, dawn that wasn't happy being in charge, would have handled it in a very different way and caused a lot of backlash. That's not who I want to be, or how I want to handle situations. So, what would Master do? He'd not take things personally, use his words to calm someone down, and listen to them. This actually became a theme that bat and I talked about often over the years.

She even made a poster with Dan in a seat in our brains, and made bracelets to remind us... WWMD; "What Would Master Do?"

## *What do you bring to the table?*

After looking back at everything I've written, it feels like I'm saying that I'm in a power exchange relationship to grow as a person. That is partly true, but it's not all about that. Yes, I want to grow as a person. Yes, I want to emulate Dan's calmness, compassion, and graciousness, but there are also things that I bring to the table in this relationship. It was only after I realized this that my confidence in me and us blossomed.

I really thought I was bringing a broken person to the table. But Dan saw something different. He saw someone struggling with their identity, their healing process, and their resistance to allowing in the world… he was hoping to help with those parts, even if it just meant giving me safe space to figure things out.

A few of the things Dan saw in me I was able to discover for myself during the contract writing process. Others would take a few years for me to open myself up to. For instance, Dan saw a person of strength. I certainly didn't see that. But, when I would speak up and share how many ways I was weak, like my abusive past, leaving my husband, etc. He'd point out how they were strengths. I survived in spite of my childhood. I left a relationship that wasn't allowing me to grow into my true self. And then he'd point out things he had seen me accomplish over the years as friends, that I hadn't even thought of as strengths.

Dan saw a person of light. Sure, that light was trapped inside my shell of protection, but it was there nonetheless, and over time I let that side of myself out to experience the world. I have perseverance. I will fight for what I believe in.

Some of the skills I have that have served us well is that I'm focused, detail and task oriented, organized, and an overachiever. These are all valuable traits to bring into a relationship like ours. I am also a risk-averse experience junkie. Dan is a risk-accepting experience junkie. That's a great combination. I get to vocalize my fears of the risks, he gets to take them into consideration, make adjustments if needed, and then jump in with both feet if that is what he desires, knowing I'll be obedient, align my will with his, and then be an extension of his will, using my skills to make whatever it is happen. And we get to experience things that we might never have been able to experience with a different partner.

What do you bring to the table? This is the first question of the year that I've asked the sub roundtable I've facilitated for the last 10 years.

I like to have followers become aware that they absolutely bring something to the table in a power exchange relationship. Many followers concentrate so much on what the Master, Dom, or Leader provides a relationship that they forget their own skills and strengths.

Some of the items brought up have included organization, companionship, obedience, alignment of will, extension of will, a port in the storm, among others.

These skills and offerings should be thought about when negotiating the relationship. And keep in mind that you may not know everything you bring to the table. Ask friends what they see as your strengths. Ask your Leader, Master, or Dom what they see in you. And really listen.

Then, embrace what you bring. These are your strengths. This is part of learning the dance steps involved in your dance that is power exchange. If your Dom is smart, they will use these strengths to the advantage of the relationship.

## *Power Exchange is my kink*

So, all this cerebral stuff and growth and change and experience is great. It really is. But, I also find power exchange to be hot and sexy. Having someone that is strong enough and confident enough in themselves to dominate me, is steamy hot. There's just something about it, both in the relationship and in the sex. If he's horny, I'm a willing participant. He knows I find it hot for him to just bend me over and take me. I mean honestly, Dom/sub erotica and hot Leather sex erotica is what drew me into even wanting to try this style of relationship.

When we first got together, it was about the weekends of the kids being away and us being able to slip into our Dom/sub roles and having great sex. Him being in control in the bedroom really did it for me. Then, he had me make him a peanut butter sandwich during one of our weekends and I found that turned me on as well. What the hell?

Now I find scenes or sex that doesn't involve power exchange of some sort, even for just the time of the scene, does nothing for me. You can bend me over and spank me, but if you aren't also trying and succeeding at dominating me, it's going to fall flat. Make me want to do anything for you. I think some people call that primal. I'm not sure. I just know that Dan has 'it' and I want to do anything for him. A few others I play with have 'it' and I want to do anything for them during our scenes. Hot hot hot.

## *Alpha Slave*

In our world, alpha slave means me being in charge of another follower's training for Dan. Well, it's not Training with a big T - that's his job, but training with a little t. As in, if Dan tells the new person to get him a cup of coffee, they aren't to ask how he likes his coffee. They are to come to me. I teach them how he likes it, and how to serve it. If they are having problems processing something, Dan sends them to me for stuff that a follower peer can help with.

At first, I resisted this change in my status. I didn't have any interest in helping with training. Of course I would do it because he told me to, but… I like to do things and accomplish new things myself. It felt like I was going to be in charge of a person, and I didn't like that feeling at all.

And it felt like some of my options for service to him were being taken away, which felt like punishment. My brain knew it wasn't, but my heart felt differently. Now, instead of me serving his coffee, I was teaching someone else how to do it. I didn't get the satisfaction of being in his presence with something he desired, having that interaction, that connection as our eyes met. Feeling the energy shift as I handed him the cup of coffee. I feel shivers just thinking about it. Instead, I was in the kitchen having just taught a new person how to fix and serve the coffee and they were the ones taking it to him, in his dominant presence, feeling the zing of service and submission.

I finally explained this to Dan in a way where he heard me. His response was to explain to me that I would be doing this in his service and it would be a way of taking care of him. It would be little 't' training and would help grow me as a follower as well. Now that piqued my interest and totally shifted my thinking. It is a service to him. I even took a couple of his followers to their first events when he was busy elsewhere. That was a whole different experience. One that I grew from.

## *Power slave*

I'm not really sure what to call this part of who I am. I've heard it titled as 'power slave,' so I'll go with that wording until I find something else that fits. Huh, actually I have another title that fits; belet.

So, what is a power slave to me? I like to accomplish

things. I like to take care of Dan. I like to organize and take care of the things we do. I like to be in charge of groups and rituals, officiate weddings and funerals, help co-host the podcast, co-author books, and co-produce events. And I have even designed and facilitated my own successful event, Subs In Service Intensive, for over 8 years. I've authored my own book. I teach classes on my own. I do a lot. I love to do a lot. I love to be an extension of his will. It fulfills me.

I do want to throw out that this is not the only type of follower. Some followers and some Leaders do not want the follower to be involved in this much… stuff. Some want the main focus of the follower to be about serving or obeying the Leader. That's fine. You do you. Do what is fulfilling to you.

For all I know, Dan may get tired of me doing all the things, and change my role to someone that has a focus of only taking care of him. That would be a heck of a shift for us, but something new to learn. (I hope he doesn't read that line. Knowing Dan, he'd take that as a challenge to have me learn to do this very thing!)

## *Be my best me*

What does that mean? It was a hard lesson for me, but when it clicked, it relieved so much stress.

This means that I'm not perfect. Hard to believe, right? I'm not. Never have been. Never will be. So, instead of stressing over my lack of perfection, instead focus on being the best me that I can be in the moment, with the skills I have.

I used to get lost in thoughts like, "I know I shouldn't be feeling this way. If I was further along in my healing, or whatever, I wouldn't be feeling this way," or "If only…" Fill in the blank. I spent so much time stressing about how I hadn't reached perfection, that I wasn't being the best me at the moment.

My self-esteem was in the crapper because I hadn't figured out how to handle my emotions. I felt like I was being high maintenance in certain situations and I'd beat myself up over it. I was really rough on myself, which made it hard for Dan.

Over time, something clicked. It was something my daughter-in-law said, actually. I was stressed about everything. Why wasn't I better at handling jealousy? Why was I not able to handle specific situations? I knew how I *wanted* to feel. I knew how I *wanted* to be. I knew *who* I wanted to be. Yet, I was depressed and stressed out all the time because I hadn't figured out *how* to be that person yet. She told me, "Be ok with where you are now, in the moment. Look behind you and how far you've come. So what if you aren't where you want to be? It's a journey. Be the best *you* you can be today."

Well, that was a wake up moment. I was not being my current best self. I was letting the dissonance of who I was and who I wanted to be to crap all over my present moments. How can I serve, when all I can think about is who I'm NOT?

When she said that to me, in frustration I might add, I took a breath and it literally felt like something clicked in my brain. Be my best me. Each and every day. I could do that. I stood a little taller. I instantly felt more confident. I can be my best me for me and for Dan and for our relationship. The weight lifted. Or most of it did, anyway.

I can still fall back into that unhappy, dissonant state. But it's extremely rare, and when it happens I hear her voice. "Be the best *you* you can be today." Which doesn't mean, don't be depressed. It doesn't even mean don't be jealous, or whatever other emotion you want to put in there. It means that in spite of whatever is going on, be your best. If you spend your energy on lamenting that you aren't something else, not depressed, not jealous or whatever... you aren't being your best self.

## *Be confident*

Confidence is sexy. Well, we know it's sexy in a Leader, but did you know that some Leaders find it sexy in a follower as well? It doesn't mean anything except that you have faith in yourself as a person. For me, it helped to realize that Dan had faith in me, and had confidence in me to be his follower and to continue to do the work that I needed to do to be his follower. That means a lot. Who am I to argue when he believes in me? Well, I won't admit to it, but I did argue that very thing at the beginning. But his confidence in himself, in me, and in us, won the conversation.

In the first years of our power exchange, I can't say that I had much confidence. I was new to it all, I made mistakes, I was going through triggers as I healed. But we both continued with the journey. Things happened that layered together, slowly building my confidence. My daughter-in-law made that comment I mentioned above. Experience taught me that I had every right to feel confident in myself, Dan, and our relationship.

Honestly, the result of my lack of confidence was that I thought Dan would leave me. I thought about it all the time. About how I wasn't perfect, so why would he keep wanting to put in the work? Then one day it clicked. I'm not even sure how it clicked. Funny how that happens. I've had a couple of major thought changes (growth spurts?) over the last 20 years and I can't really tell you how they happened, just that they did. I didn't even realize it until I felt different, and looked back, and realized I had changed. Well, this click was realizing that if Dan ever decided to leave me, I'd be ok. I would grieve, but in the end, I'd be ok.

My confidence has soared and I personally feel like it's been a major shift in our journey. Dan forgets sometimes how much I've… changed? Grown? I'm not sure of the word to use. I forget myself some days, and fall into old habits. My best self is now 'new dawn' and she handles things differently. That person that I wanted to be and stressed out so much over? She's here, and it feels good.

Recently we were invited to visit a power exchange house. Not only are they 'aware' of power exchange, they live it in a formal way. Well, in the past I would have tried to talk Dan out of it. I would have so much anxiety over the idea of being on display. I would have expressed my fears of not being good enough or not understanding their protocols, etc. (This never worked, by the way. Dan likes the challenge.)

But, this time I still felt the same fears. I mean, with the pandemic it's been a couple years since we've been in a high protocol situation. The slave of the house had warned me that they were required to be naked at all times in the house and that they ate dinner sitting on the floor while the rest of the house sat at the table. Their question to me was if Dan would want me at the floor or at the table? I presented this question to Dan, and waited.

In the past I would have jumped right in with my fears. What if I wasn't graceful getting down, or up for that matter? What did they mean we had dinner on the floor? Dishes in hand? Dog food bowls? What about? What about? What about? That's 'old dawn.' 'New dawn' presented the question, felt the fear and doubts, and waited. This was my best self. This was my confident self. Regardless of my fears, I would follow his lead. I would obey. I gave him space without my rambling thoughts. He chose to have me not be naked, but to sit on the floor at dinner. My heart thumped. I said 'Yes, Sir,' and replied to the slave of the house his preference.

What a difference! It actually felt good to not jump in with my fears. How was he ever able to listen to his instinct in the past with me wanting him to hear all my concerns first? Instead, I held onto my confidence... my confidence that I wouldn't embarrass him, confidence that he'd challenge me AND look out for me, confidence in us and our power exchange. We would both be our best selves, and that's all we can possibly be. It turned out to be a pleasurable experience. I got to sit at his feet all evening. I got to feel submission and my role and... well, if you know what I'm trying to express, you know.

Keep in mind that If you have low self-esteem or a lack of self-confidence, it won't be an instant change overnight. Do the work, whatever that is for you. And in time, it will just happen. You probably won't be able to put your finger on the exact moment that it happened.

# How to help Master

Most of my writings are about how a submissive can help themselves, or how a Master can help a submissive, but there are ways we can help Masters as well. Let's cover a couple of these.

## *The Leader is Injured or Sick*

In my experience, most Leaders don't like to be sick, let alone having someone cluck over them like a mother hen when they are sick. They don't like to be powerless. So, how can we help them when they are injured or sick? Especially when, as a follower, we feel it is part of our service, our duty, to take care of them?

If the situation allows it, an easy way to resolve the power struggle that can happen during such a time, is to ask the Master how they would like to facilitate their healing. Instead of the follower stating that things are going to be done a certain way and then experiencing pushback by the Leader, have the Leader involved in creating a plan of expectations with caregiving. "How can we facilitate your healing?" and/or "How can I be of best service to you during your healing?" and/or "What are your expectations of me while you are healing?" This method puts the power back in the hands of the Leader. And it's a valid answer if they say, "I don't have an opinion" or "I'm too sick to care, just do what needs to be done."

## *Master is Emotionally Spiraling*

I talk a lot about my experience with emotionally spiraling and how Dan can help me, but he's also had his moments over the years. This one is harder for me to figure out the best way to help. If he has a broken wrist, there are things that can be done - change the wrappings, take him to the doctor, make sure it's elevated. But, when it's emotional, that's a challenge for me. Most Leaders don't want to be seen as vulnerable. They may not even realize they are spiraling. It's tricky.

What I've learned that can help in these situations is to ask Dan what story he is telling himself. I learned this from another submissive, and it works for us. Dan and I have done a lot of work with meditation and learning how to spot stories that we are telling ourselves based on past experience, not current situations. If I ask him what story he's telling himself, it makes him pause and then realize that he is living in a story, not the current reality. Or a story WITH the current reality. It's like a code for us. I'm lending him recognition that something is going on.

I've also been known to suggest that he journal about it, or I'll ask him if he's been meditating lately. These are not things that I can do for him. He has to want to do them himself. But, usually a gentle reminder that we have tools we know work will point him in the right direction.

## *Master Isn't Able to Lead*

For whatever reason, if Dan is in a situation where he isn't able to lead - maybe he's on pain meds from surgery, or he's having an emotional spiral… whatever the situation is, I know to keep on keeping on. As I've mentioned before, at this point I know what is expected of me, and if I have any questions I can just ask myself, 'what would Master do?"

I know of other couples where there is a standing order in case the Leader becomes incapacitated. He has a disorder that requires him to shut himself away from the world until it settles down. This could have left her stranded, but instead they prepped for these moments. They know they are going to happen. They don't know when. So, when it does happen, he doesn't have time to prepare for her each and every time. Instead, there is a standing order. She knows what is expected of her in taking care of him, their house, and herself. It works great for them to have a standing order.

## *Help Master Find His Seat of Power*

Believe it or not, not all Leaders come into these relationships full of confidence and know-how. Dan sure didn't. I was his first submissive. He was my first Dominant. We learned this dance together. He did a great job showing a face of confidence, and taking risks that proved fruitful for our dynamic. But, there were moments where I could feel a lack of faith in… himself? Our dynamic? These were few and far between, but I could still feel them. To me, it felt like part of my responsibility to help him out. If I was pushing and trying to get my way, mostly at the beginning, I could feel him wonder if it was worth the trouble.

Sometimes Leaders may wonder if power exchange is still desired in the relationship. Vanilla creeps in from all directions and sometimes it's easier to be peers than Leader/follower. Let them know that you are on board with getting back to your power exchange foundation, and that it is still important to you.

So I checked in with myself. What was I doing? Was it worth the resistance I was offering? If not, say 'Yes Sir' or whatever your positive response would be. Give them those moments of being right. Give them those confidence boosters. They need this to help them listen to their intuitive voice.

Let them know when something works. I've been known to thank Dan after he's punished me. Punishment doesn't feel good. I don't like it. But, I will thank him because it's what I asked for when we designed our relationship. It's not natural for him, so he needs to know that he's still on the right track, and it's a positive thing for our dynamic.

Feel the pieces you can contribute to to help your Leader find their seat of power. This relationship isn't just about developing the follower. It's not just the follower that can struggle with submitting. The Leader has their issues to overcome as well. I feel it's part of our responsibility to help them out, and let them know just how right it feels from our end.

## When a Follower is Sick

You think it's hard for a Leader to be sick? How about when a follower is sick, especially one who finds fulfillment in serving? I've had a few surgeries over the years, and when I get home, it's very hard for me to not try to rush my healing so that I can get back to taking care of Dan. I remember how frustrated he would get, constantly telling me to go back to bed.

Finally, he told me that I was not being a good servant. That it was his decision to take care of me so that I would heal quicker, and every time I tried to take care of him I was disobeying his desire. Well crap. Good point, Sir.

It helped to realize that it was his *decision* to take care of me. He even told me that he needed me to stay put and not serve him so that I wouldn't mess up my healing, which would get in the way of my service to him later. He went so far as to put a call out for a temp slave when I needed more help than he could give me because of his work schedule. That was a great experience for all of us. I could have made it difficult with thinking of how hard it was to have someone do my bidding, but Dan stressed that he needed the temp slave to take care of me, so that he could go back to work and know that I was taken care of. Done and done. I'm able to heal, and he knows I'm being taken care of when he's not able to be there.

# Collars and Tattoos

### *Dan says*

One of the nearly universally accepted symbols in the power exchange community is the collar. But without an understanding of what it represents, we end up with assumptions and empty gestures 'cause that is what I figured I was supposed to do.' When we talk about the power exchange collar - and to be clear, the below is about that, not a fashion statement except when pointed out - we have both the physical representation, but also a ritual that goes with it, and a commitment.

For dawn, there are two collars related to this conversation. Now, to be clear, she owns a few more than that, but those are hot and sexy 'goes with my corset' collars. They are accessories for fetish wear. Nothing wrong with that. But that is not what we are talking about here.

A vital part of this is to realize that collars are not just placed on followers. Instead it is a two step process (at least). There is the offering of a collar; there is the accepting of the collar. Let's talk about them in reverse.

## Accepting a Collar

Power exchange relationships kind of live in an illusion that we all perpetuate. Even those that practice what some would view as hard core consensual non-consent, with a naked slave bowing to every command, are actually in a consensual relationship that could be terminated at any moment. If not, they are unethical and abusive.

The collar is a symbol - and a powerful one - of commitment. But much like a wedding ring, which includes a commitment of 'til death do us part,' we all know the subtext to that is 'or until breaking up because of a variety of reasons leading to a divorce.' The collar, regardless of the powerful language around our power exchange relationships, is no different. Matter of fact, it is even easier, as it comes with no legal entanglement.

The only thing that keeps dawn in my service is dawn making that choice. No contract, no collar, no words of 'obey for all time' can keep her here against her will and her self-interest.

Now. With all that said, don't accept a collar if you're thinking you can ditch if things get uncomfortable. That will not serve the relationship, or you. This is what we call in the community as a 'velcro collar' - one that is worn until the hot fantasy fades or things get hard, and one party or the other calls it a day.

Accepting a collar should not be done lightly. Much like any other serious commitment, it should be thought out first. Commit to it for a time frame. For me, I would accept three months for specific training situations, but six months or a year and a day are more common. dawn accepted my collar for a year and a day, then did the same for an additional year, and again, and now it just is.

## Offering a Collar

Pretty much everything from above applies here as well. The offer of a collar should be time-based and be recognized as a commitment. Although you can end the relationship at any point, you likely should not just bolt when things get uncomfortable or hard.

You are offering not just a physical collar, but to be responsible for the person in that collar. Suddenly, you are the person who owns the decisions and failures of all the things. If the relationship goes south, or the person is not finding satisfactory fulfillment, you are likely culpable and need to address it. Now, I will say there are some mitigating circumstances that are out of anyone's control, but a good Leader doesn't look for those; instead they are willing to point the finger at themselves first.

## Who Owns the Collar?

You may have noticed in the above writing I wrote 'the collar dawn wears' instead of 'dawn's collar.' That is because I own all the collars. I did not give them to dawn; instead, what I offer is that she wears my collar. And if our relationship ends, the collars should be returned to me.

This is symbolic for us, as it clarifies not only who is in charge, but that the collar is worn at will. She is not a slave that has no choice in this matter. She can remove that collar at any time. This would never be done lightly, as it would be a symbol that it is time to move in a new direction. We talk about the appropriate way to terminate relationships elsewhere in this book.

That I own these collars also means that when a relationship ends, I get a collar back. When a new one starts, I recycle an existing collar. This is to impress upon the 'new' person that they carry the responsibility of not only being in service to me, but of carrying on a tradition of people who have been in service to me. This creates a sense of belonging to not only me, but to my entire power exchange lineage.

There are a few exceptions to collar ownership. Yarn collars, which I will explain in just a moment below, may or may not be given back, and they are not used again. Another exception was a relationship that needed to end and that the history of that collar was no longer for me. I carried the collar for a month in my pocket until one day I was walking through the woods and realized that I should just leave it there to… well, to whatever would become of it.

And the last exception is kame bat's collar. When she passed she was still in my service. It went from being my collar that she wore, to her collar that I now keep with me as a memento of sorts. No one else will ever wear that collar. Or, that is what I intend today.

More about who owns the collar and why I recycle them can be read about in the spiritual section of this book.

## The Yarn Collar

This, as the name implies, is a collar made of yarn. Yarn, by nature, is not going to last long. So I use these when the specific state of a relationship isn't going to last long. If the direction seems to be a desire to build a longterm power exchange relationship, then the yarn collar is worn to signify that we are testing the waters in a limited capacity, and we will make a yea or nay decision… well, in the time it takes yarn to break.

The yarn collar is also used in a situation where either party wants to test drive the power exchange dynamic. I, as a Leader, am not going to say 'is this ok' and 'are you ok to continue' a lot. I'll check in, but I'll also be in charge. What I will do is remind them that they have the power to end this at any time by simply reaching up and taking off the collar. Yarn is temporary, impermanent, and if removed, no harm done, as it was never intended to last. This gives the follower a sense of security and reminds them that they are able to opt out at any moment.

## The Day Collar

I am not the sort of person who finds it valuable to proclaim my power exchange relationships in non-power exchange situations. So I do not want dawn to wear her leather collar with an O ring on it to the grocery store. Instead, she wears a day collar, which is a necklace that she wears all the time - literally. It has the illusion of being just a necklace to everyone else, but we have clearly made it her 24/7 collar in our minds and hearts. Hers is a chain necklace with a heart on it, inscribed on the back with the date of the collaring ceremony.

We have a friend in a Leather household who wears a chain with a padlock on it all the time, even at work. Other friends wear stainless steel circular bands that have small screws on them that the Leader has the key to. In one case, this a very small hex wrench.

Kame bat wore her day collar on her ankle for a time, then we switched it up to a cable she wore on her wrist.

## The Event Collar

One day, while dawn and I were walking around a renaissance fair, we came across a leatherworker who was selling collars. Although not intended for kink wear, it had a great feel to it, an "O" ring for a leash, and some simple shiny bits added as well. The craftsman explained that he was new to working with leather and although this was very skillfully done, there was also a sense of his newness to working with the material as well. I purchased it, and it has served as the collar dawn wears to anything 'lifestyle friendly' for the past fifteen years.

Leather is one of the most commonly worn type of collar at events. Just peek into the vendor's hall, and you'll almost always see a selection of leather collars for sale. That said, many people prefer metal or other materials. Regardless of the material, the event collar proudly proclaims that the person wearing it is a follower.

## The Collaring

The collar, worn on the neck or wrist, made of leather or steel… none of that really means anything, without understanding the significance behind it.

In the chapter of the book about Rituals, we talk about the various collaring rituals I've been part of. Leaders, please go take a look at those as you think about putting a collar on someone. Because the decision should be a big deal. It should be celebrated and acknowledged as a special event, a significant event. For me, it is a commitment no less serious than when I married dawn. Not the part of marriage that says 'let's share finances until death do us part,' but the part that says "I am committing to you that I will be here, fully engaged, while we strive toward a mutually satisfactory experience."

## Wearing a Collar

### *dawn says*

When we were in our D/s 'lite' days - the days when we were trying out power exchange, but hadn't committed to a contract or collaring yet - Dan bought a piece of braided leather cord that would fit around my neck. When the kids were sent to their dad's for the weekend, Dan would call me by my codeword name and then place the leather cord around my neck. This was my first experience with the power of the collar.

When he wrapped it around my neck, a sense of peace

came over me. We'd have a little ritual that we still perform to this day when he puts the big heavy leather event collar on me. And I still feel the same way. I become centered, anchored. Breathing becomes deeper and the world falls away. There is only me and him… us. The creation of the 'us' is tangible. I mean, there is always the 'us,' but when he puts that collar on me, there is the US. People have told us that they can see it and feel it when they watch him put the collar around my neck, looking me in the eye as he checks the tightness. Nothing else matters. Just writing about it and remembering all those moments gives me goosebumps.

Not only a sense of peace, but submission to him, overtakes me. So much so that when we first started presenting and I'd be wearing the event collar because we were at an event, he'd have to take it off… carefully… so that I could do my part of the presentation. I say carefully because, if he'd taken it off without thought, it would have felt like punishment and I wouldn't have been able to present with him without some aftercare first to ground me.

It was a rock and a hard place at first, until we learned that he had to remove the collar with thought, focus, and gentleness. We even built a ritual that we performed before each presentation, so that we could connect in a different way after the collar was removed.

I learned over time to be able to present with the collar on, little by little. At first, we'd leave it on, and then at the end of the presentation he'd grab it, look me in the eye, and I'd fall back into my submissive space. Now, he doesn't need to do that, as we've graduated to another level in our relationship. I'm not sure I can explain what I mean by that, except that I'm more fluid with and without the event collar. Shifting focus is more of a mindset, instead of shifting with the physical collar.

It's kind of funny... Dan has suggested buying a new event collar, a fancier one. The first time he brought it up, I was stunned. Why replace a one-of-a-kind collar? I shook my head fiercely, feeling very protective of that piece of leather with its O ring and shiny bits. I'd like to keep this one, please. He was stunned that I wouldn't want a prettier collar. But, that one is special, I tried to explain. It's been around for so many years and was full of so much energy from all the events and dungeons and... all the yummy stuff. I wear this collar at events, during our title run, and even when I play with others. At this point, I consider it a magical item.

Of course, if Dan ever said that it was time to move to another one, I would. It's what I've agreed to with our relationship, but oh, how I would miss it! And as a Buddhist flavored person, I know that the leather and bits it is made with will one day fall apart, but until then, I hope Dan continues to consider it the event collar.

With the day collar, I absolutely feel naked and vulnerable without it. I don't feel *safe* without it. I'm not even sure how to explain that, except that the weight of the chain necklace reminds me that he is always with me. The only times I've taken it off have been during surgeries and medical procedures, of which I've had a few over the last twenty-odd years. I really don't like the feeling of taking it off and leaving it behind somewhere. And I hate to admit it, but I don't really feel complete without it.

With my wedding ring, I took it off one day because I'd lost a lot of weight and was afraid of losing it. So, I took it off and put it on a necklace that I remember to wear sometimes. Every once in a while my fingers feel naked, but it's not the same feeling as going without the day collar. The rings don't make me feel like I'm owned.

As with the event collar, I know this collar will one day break. I'm trying not to be so attached that it will break me when it breaks. Every time Dan grabs it now, I wonder if it's going to fall apart in his hands. By thinking about it now, and knowing it will happen one day because of its age, I won't be horrified and think it's some sort of sign. But, until that day, I enjoy the weight of it around my neck.

## Tattoo & Branding: The Collars That Can't Come Off

### *dawn says*

Though I don't usually recommend tattoos or markings to show ownership... they are hot! At the beginning of our relationship, I really wanted to be branded. I had read about the practice in a book, and it felt like it would be such a rush of a feeling. To be branded with his initials, permanently his. Claimed for all to see, for all to know. Oh, how I wanted this!

Dan did a lot of research on branding and came to understand that branding isn't so cut and dry. There are a lot of things to consider, and a lot of things that could go wrong, including how it heals. He would have no control over how it healed and what the final look of it would be after healing. So, he decided against it.

Instead, we did a tattoo of our initials on my upper right thigh. On the right, because when flagging hankies in the Leather world, the right side is the side you wear your hanky if you are submissive, or a bottom to the activity being flagged. So, the right side is the submissive side. It's a beautiful little tattoo that I designed and had been doodling for years.

A few people asked me how I could do our initials. What if we broke up? Well, if we broke up I could look at it a couple of ways. I could be heartbroken every time I saw it, or angry depending on what caused the breakup… or I could look at it and remember all the great times we had, and how I had grown as a person, and how I embraced my authentic self. That's how I wanted to look at it.

So, do I recommend tattoos now? I still don't. But, it's everyone's personal choice. I just hope they can look at it later with happiness, if anything happens to the relationship.

### *Dan says*

I really like my tattoo. I just have the one, a fair sized piece on my arm that includes some Buddhist symbology, a snow lion, and a mountain. Everyone told me that once I got one tattoo I'd want lots more, but… no, haven't felt that need yet.

I have another friend who has 'slave' tattooed on her upper thigh. She loves it very much, as dawn loves her 'D&d' tattoo.

Yet. As you read in the above, I've given a few collars to people and had them returned. Relationships often end.

So, if your tattoo can be a special way to commemorate a relationship without it requiring the relationship to last forever, then it makes more sense to get one.

Personally, if you want a tattoo that says 'me and Mistress forever' then I say go for it. If you are asking for my recommendation, make your tattoos about you, not about a certain situation in your life. But on the other hand, some people are happy with their tattoo of 'Git R Dun' so... you do you.

If you want to try branding, I'd recommend dry ice or violet wand branding. It is less likely to be permanent, but can be.

# High Protocol

### *Dan says*

Recently, I went on a social media site for kinky and power exchange people and asked the question "Is your relationship high protocol?" Some of the responses were yes, and some were no. But most of the responses were about an activity, not a relationship style. Let's back up a moment, though.

Defining High Protocol (or HP) power exchange is actually a bit tricky, as it seems to emphasize 'more.' More protocols, more rituals, more regimented. You might also phrase it as less relaxed, but that can be misleading. Some find comfort in the strict structure. And some simply enjoy it as a very clear, very well-defined, precise style.

A good way to help visualize HP would be for me to explain what would change in our life if dawn and I decided to go high protocol again - we'll come back to that 'again' in a moment.

The Dan and dawn HP would mean she would end

every sentence with 'Sir.' Thank you, Sir. I love you, Sir. What would you like for dinner, Sir? Right now, 'Sir' is heard often, but so is honey, or just 'I love you.'

Next, we'd brush off those protocols and rituals, and start to use them more often. dawn would not simply bring me a cup of coffee, but she would hand it to me in a prescribed manner. And if she failed, no matter by how much, I would reject it and have her make me a fresh cup. She would make the bed, and I would inspect the bed. When she was home, she would ask for her collar to be worn and I would place it on her. When it came time to take it off, she would never suggest that action. I would take it off her, or I would not.

Our podcast, where we currently co-host, would drastically change. Instead of a free-flowing conversation, she would wait for me to finish talking, never interrupting, and only speaking to respond to what I asked, or to emphasize what I said. She would never stand with hands on hips (parade rest only); she would always seek permission to do anything new or out of our normal pattern. If she wanted to offer a contradictory view, she would do so only after saying 'Sir, if I may have permission to speak?'

Now that I've written that out, I'm kinda turned on by the whole idea… but it also feels like I would lose a part of dawn that I cherish.

## As an Activity

We've done a lot of HP events, and those are a joy. All of the items I mentioned in the example above are in place. Also, my follower does not get to speak unless spoken to, she can't 'wander off,' and she should stay on high alert for any needs I may have.

HP Dinners are a great time. We build them thus. All the subs are in charge of preparing dinner, including shopping, table setting, and decoration. They are to keep quiet and stay in the kitchen unless called for (usually with a bell) except for one or two that are closer by, in case we have any desires. There is normally a theme, and the Dominants are all dressed up (no jeans or t-shirts allowed). The Dominants sit around drinking coffee, tea, or water and chatting while the submissives do all the work. They do not offer any feedback or thoughts - they are there to serve. Come dinner time, the Dominants sit around the table and are served, while our submissives stay quiet and out of the way.

From there, the rules for the event might be different from one event to the next. At some events, all submissives are just property of anyone in a dominant role. At others, only you can discipline or command your own submissive.

These events have been very valuable to us, not only as a learning and self growth environment, but in general as fun affairs.

## As a Style of Power Exchange

Some people live at this level of power exchange. We know a friend or two who find this is what resonates with them, and keeps them feeling connected. It is an intense and intimate way to be.

In our second year, we committed to being a high protocol couple for a full year. So, dawn would have her collar handy at all times, and we would emphasize our power exchange whenever we could. Every BDSM or lifestyle-friendly situation was a HP event for us, so out would come the leash and collar, and dawn would seek my permission to leave my side. When I had to use the facilities, I'd find a Dominant I respected and ask them to keep an eye on her, handing them the leash.

For us, that year of high protocol was great. But we retired from being full time HP after that year. We tend to move and grow pretty fast, and we felt that full time HP slowed us down a bit. I needed dawn to be self-actualized and self-sufficient. I needed to take time off and just be a goofy Dan sometimes.

But we do enjoy it, and we look forward to our next full Leather 'only speak when given permission' event.

### *dawn says*

Personally, I loved the year of high protocol. After spending the first year on building our hierarchical foundation, we slipped right into a High Protocol year naturally. It was challenging at some points, and thrilling during other times.

The year of high protocol started at the anniversary party of our first collaring. We had written the first contract to last a year and a day. Then, we signed a new contract for the 2nd year. It pretty much stayed the same, but we changed the focus of the year to be High Protocol, whereas the first year was about building our foundation.

There would be higher expectations on our interaction.

I would not talk unless spoken to, always standing a couple paces behind him to his left, eyes downcast, parade rest with my hands behind my back (after an elbow injury, that couple paces to the left changed to the right side so he wouldn't accidentally grab the hurt arm).

In those days, hugging in the community wasn't a thing, so I didn't have to worry about that, but my stance and focus on Dan would have given them a clue that hugging wasn't going to happen. What people did learn to do was to ask Dan for permission to speak with me if they were so inclined.

I loved that I didn't have to worry about people touching me without his permission. And he kept a close eye on me as his property. He took my safety and well-being very seriously. Not that he doesn't now, but I'm not as vulnerable now. I'm more capable of protecting myself and standing up for myself. Back then I was also at the beginning of my healing journey and was in a state of getting in contact with my vulnerable side as I opened myself up to Dan and my therapist. So, High Protocol was the perfect space for me to be.

As an introvert, I loved being quiet and in my own bubble. I loved that I didn't have to pay attention to anything but Dan and his needs. I was allowed to be hyper-focused and take care of him. I felt his connection to me, and if he did release me so that I could talk to others at a munch, I felt his eyes on me at all times. And if someone got out of hand, he would be there and would state firmly that I was his and I was to come with him.

I've mentioned that a couple of times now, that he was my protector. This is because at the beginning, we found ourselves in a swinging world or kink world that did not understand power exchange, or consent for that matter, and he had to step in a couple of times. In a couple of situations I found myself in, I had either frozen or came close to punching someone, which I was not allowed to do. We didn't expect others to know the rules of our protocol, but twenty years ago it was much different than it is now when it comes to consent.

If you read the survivor chapter, I talk a bit about getting a somatic counselor. It was because of a handsy fellow at a munch and another at a house party, that I sought out that kind of therapy. I was super glad Dan had rescued me, but knew he wouldn't be there all the time. And if we hadn't been in a HP year, he might not have even noticed what was going on.

A funny/not funny result of our HP year was that more than one person tried to hold an intervention for me. One person came to my house under the pretense of borrowing a computer. Once there, she got me outside to ask if everything was ok. I was totally confused. Of course everything was ok. But she was genuinely concerned. Even though she was in the Leather and kink communities, she had only seen power exchange of that level in scenes for limited time periods, never as a relationship style. I assured her I was ok.

Not long after that, a new friend who I had met at a drumming circle, who was not in the kink scene but had spent a lot of her adult life working on empowering women, took me out to tea. She wasn't aware of what power exchange was, let alone HP, and she was super concerned for me. It took me three hours and a lot of cups of tea to try to explain what I got out of this relationship. Finally, I got so frustrated that I blurted out, 'you are a feminist, right? And feminism is about being allowed to do what I want to do, right? Well, power exchange and high protocol makes me happy. I thrive in this dynamic and it's what I want to do.' ... She looked at me, processed that a little bit, and then threw her hands in the air. 'Well, if you'd said that to start with, we could have saved ourselves three hours.' She is now in the kink and power exchange community in a major way, with her own submissive in a loving PE relationship. They attend our HP events and have even hosted some of their own.

That year was an amazing experience and we still make sure to attend HP events to experience that thrill again.

# Rituals

### *Dan says*

There are a number of places in this book that already either include rituals, or refer to them. The chapters on collaring, contracts, relationship shorthand, and punishment all have aspects of ritual to them. This section delves into this topic in more depth, as well as giving many examples of rituals that we either have encountered or, more often, that we use.

You, by the way, have rituals you practice already; more than you might realize. From birthdays to weddings, Thanksgiving to Christmas, our lives are filled with rituals. Some of them are widely known; some are particular to certain families. In our home, I always put a can of cheap dollar store meat - spam, potted meat, sometimes anchovies - in everyone's Christmas stocking. It is a silly thing that even I would have a hard time remembering where it started, but it is my little thing. This is a form of ritual.

Rituals in the context of our power exchange

relationships can be as simple as a quick reconnection, a celebration of a milestone or commitment, or even a test that acknowledges the continued strength of the bond.

First, because I get asked this a lot and have to keep reminding myself, what is the difference between a ritual and a protocol? For me, I distinguish a protocol as being around a behavior that is practiced in a setting. We recently had dinner at a fellow power exchange person's home, and they let us know before we got there that their follower had a protocol of always being naked at home. They asked if dawn would need a chair and I said no, she will practice a protocol of sitting on the floor at my feet. Other protocols we practice include that dawn always walks in a certain spot (behind, to my right) at Leather events. We have friends who practice a protocol that the follower must always speak in third person, or never greets a Leader without permission.

A ritual on, on the other hand, is more about the action than the behavior. It might be observed often (when you hand me a drink, hold it in such a way, and make eye contact) or just on special occasions or as a ceremony (such as collarings).

Some rituals we do are intended to create connection or adjust my followers' mindset - one example of that is a simple 'belet, kneel' command that ends any conversation or other action and brings dawn to quietly sitting at my feet. Other rituals we do are a celebration, acknowledging that something special is happening. Let's get into some of them.

## The Collaring

Collarings in my view are significant events and should be treated as such. They should include a fair amount of forethought and dedication on the part of both parties. More is written about collarings elsewhere in the book, but let's look at the Collaring Ritual.

In a very broad view, you'll decide how it starts, what the middle (action) part looks like, and then how you will end it. Things to be considered are

- if you will have others there and, if so, in what capacity (active participants or just witnesses)
- the location (a play party might be too chaotic, but a side room at a conference might fit the bill; or perhaps the living room at home is a better reflection)
- the type and energy for the ritual you have in mind (more about this in a moment)
- will you as the Leader be fully creating it, or is it something co-created by both of you
- what can you do to personalize it - favorite color, materials, accessories, and other decorations to make the space you are doing this feel special

As mentioned, you'll want to set the type of collaring ritual you have in mind and the energy of it. Soft and romantic, or harsh and unyielding? Spiritual and inviting, or personal and intense?

The challenge here is it has to be yours, something that you create, and that feels inspired from within. To assist in giving you some starting points and examples, I'll share what my collarings look like below. Feel free to borrow anything you find valuable for your own collaring. And feel free to ignore them as well! They are not 'the right way' to do it, just my way. And further, I tend to lean more toward ordeal rituals, so it really may not fit you. Let me take a moment to explore what I mean by ordeal ritual before we get to the examples.

## The Ordeal Ritual

When I was younger, I came across a movie called 'A Man Called Horse.' Although I barely remember the movie, I clearly recall a scene where the star has (and willingly agrees) to be hung from his chest on flesh hooks to become a warrior of the tribe. The idea of including an ordeal as part of a ritual stuck with me as a way to give it power and substance. I have been through a few ordeal rituals myself; some were not my idea (as part of the military); some I signed up for, and some I created to put myself through.

All of them have been memorable, significant, and part of a transformation. This is in a way where I start to cross over to our spiritual power exchange part of the book, but let's set that aside for the moment, and get back to the collaring ritual.

I do want to quickly mention this. At an event in Arizona I had the chance to have flesh hooks placed into my chest and do an ordeal ritual around that. I have no regrets that I went ahead with it... but no interest in doing it again!

## My Collarings

The two examples of collaring ceremonies you'll see below are ordeal based. As mentioned, I am not saying all collarings should be ordeal based. Take what you need, and leave the rest.

For all the collarings I've done that are not dawn, one thing I have them do prior to it is to talk to dawn about the experience. Not so that they understand exactly what is going to happen (dawn doesn't know this, beyond a vague outline). But only that they are forewarned that it would be an experience; that it would likely be unpleasant, and that when they complete it, they would be able to say they have earned something.

One other thing I have them all do, prior to anything else starting, is to go to my home when I am not there and let themselves in. Then they will do three things - walk the dog, masturbate on my bed, and clean out the cat's litter box. The reason for this is it demonstrates *trust* (my dog is special to me), it demonstrates that sometimes my collar is *sexy* (and vulnerable), and sometimes it is about *cleaning up shit.*

The other preparation has taken place in the co-writing of a contract. See the chapter on contracts for more.

Ok, on to the examples.

## Collaring 1: House Slave

We used to have a play space in the city where we lived. For this collaring, we - me and many friends - had a play party there. The event theme was a collaring. Actually, in this case, it was a re-collaring of someone already in my collar, whose contract with me was expiring and we wanted to renew. At the beginning of the party, I took off her collar and proclaimed to everyone present that she was now an unowned slave of the house, and anyone could do anything they wanted with her. Someone who she barely knew immediately spoke up and told her to strip for her. Since she was no longer my slave, I turned and walked away...

Now, to be honest, that first person who spoke up? I set that up to be the first thing that happened. And I knew the people who were going to be there, and they knew us. So although it was indeed an ordeal, and significant, it had some measures to keep things from getting too crazy. This by the way was not only an ordeal for the follower, but for me as well! I had to let things go, not keep an eye on her (as was my nature), and hope that either on one hand she would not judge me too extreme by this stunt and back out... or that she really liked this freedom and would back out for that reason!

At the end of the night, back in the common room, I verbally and physically offered her the collar back. She accepted.

## Collaring 2 - The Room

For this one, I invited dawn (who identified as my slave at the time), a Master friend, and the soon-to-be-follower to a local space that dawn owned - a small studio where we did lifestyle classes. The relationship itself had started in a coffee shop with a scrap of paper where we explored via words and doodles what this could look like. Actually, mostly what I wrote were reasons I thought it would not work. I was wrong about that, but I digress.

So for this collaring ritual, when they showed up, I put a large blank paper up on the wall. Brought some markers, had a specific piece of music lined up, and a variety of BDSM toys (paddles, canes, floggers). I should not use the term 'toys' because they were not there for play. They were hand-picked with an eye toward hard and unpleasant - when used without warm-up.

From there, the potential follower showed up. They were instructed to strip and beg for my collar. I then put them through an ordeal - physical (the BDSM implements; don't think of this as a scene with warm-up, done for mutual enjoyment) and the emotional (will you embarrass me in front of other Masters? will you live up to your side of things? what right do you have to be mine? are you trying to usurp dawn's place?).

Was this cruel? I ask myself that on occasion as I write this, and again come to this view - when my collared followers talk about that experience, they have all said it was the right thing to break through any walls between us that remained.

After she was in tears and on the edge of not being able to take any more, I again asked if she really wanted my collar. She said yes and we went to the large paper and drew. We drew shapes and words and thoughts and all kinds of free flowing altered state impressions. We listened to her song that I had picked ("What the Soul Sings" by Massive Attack) and cried... and were deeply bonded.

# Foundational Rituals

## *dawn says*

Over the years, we've had so many rituals. They've changed over time simply because we've evolved. We don't do rituals just to have something to do, or because we've heard that we should have them in our dynamic. We see the power in ritual and come up with ones that are meaningful for us, modifying them when needed. These rituals include everything from how we start or end our day to the more intense ones like collarings.

## Greeting Ritual

Let's begin with our first greeting ritual. Before Dan and I moved in together, we had a greeting ritual for the weekends we spent together. I was to be kneeling in the living room at the appointed time, eyes down and my collar and leash in my hand in offering. He would come in, sit, and then state 'attend me.' That would be my cue to crawl to him, lay my collar and leash on his leg, help him remove his shoes and then present my neck for the collar. Once the collar was on, he'd snap the leash into place. I would then kneel on a pillow by his feet as he laid a hand on my head. We would then close our eyes and breathe together, to set the tone for the weekend.

After moving in together, this changed a bit. Instead of preparing for a weekend in Dom/sub mode, it was about prepping for our evening together as a family. Dan and I worked at the same company for the same department as peers, and on the same time schedule. So, we drove to and from work together as well. That's a huge chunk of the day not particularly in a power dynamic.

So, we'd come home from work, tell the kids to give us a few minutes, as they were wanting attention as soon as we walked in the door, like kids do. We'd go into the bedroom, strip, he'd sit on the edge of the bed and I'd kneel for him. We'd each recite a mantra that we had designed, or he would just place his hands around my neck, to set the intent and energy for the evening. It would create that powerful US that is a Leader and follower working in tandem.

## Drink Ritual

Our rituals can be modified during different situations as well. For us, when I serve his drink in front of family or such, it's very informal but still a ritual. We do not use honorifics in front of others, nor do I kneel. Instead, I bring him his drink, pause next to him, and wait for eye contact. Once the eye contact is made, I think 'Master' and with mindfulness hand him his drink. Or he nods and I set it in front of him.We keep the protocol as low key as possible. There are usually smiles and wiggly eyebrows involved, as we know we are being us but slipping under others' radars.

But, if we are in a high protocol situation the ritual may look a bit different, but not completely. The intent is still the same - mindful connection. It's the outer layer that will look different. I will bring him his drink, pause, wait to be acknowledged, state 'Your drink, Belum' or 'to quench your thirst Master'... kiss the rim with mindfulness, and then gaze in his eyes as I respectfully hand him his drink, totally present and in the moment. Sometimes he will have me kneel as I present his drink.

Currently, we don't find ourselves in too many situations around others. So, the drink ritual has changed quite a bit. Now, I'm expected to make his coffee before I go to bed, so that it's waiting for him when he gets up in the morning. It's in a thermos lidded cup, so it's warm when he wakes up. It's not the same, but it's what works for us. When we were able to visit a high protocol household recently, I was able to serve him an actual cup of coffee. Thank goodness I remembered the old expected protocol.

## Morning ritual

A lot of our rituals are based around leaving and arriving at the house, chores, and formal events. For example, when we lived in a house that was a distance from Dan's work, I was to get up a few minutes after him and prepare what he needed for the day. I packed his gym bag. I prepped a travel mug of coffee. I packed his lunch, with a daily surprise in it. I brought him his vitamins. He would be at his computer in the dining room and I'd bring them in. Flat in the palm of my hand I'd offer them to him, eyes downcast. He'd finish what he was doing and turn to face me. I'd raise my eyes and put the vitamins in his outstretched palm and hand him a glass of water. He'd finish with the vitamins, lightly stroke my palm or say something or just nod his head as he gave back the glass for me to carry away. When he was ready to walk out the door, I'd make sure he had everything he needed. That was our morning ritual.

After he left, I'd go make the bed. I only made the bed because he wanted me to. He knew I didn't like this chore, so he turned it into a ritual where my only thought was to be of him and how he would enjoy a nicely made bed to come home to in the evening.

## Bedtime rituals

This is another ritual that has changed over time. When we first moved in together, we'd play quietly (since the kids lived with us) for about 10 minutes. This was specifically to create a connection before sleeping.

We went through our ice cream phase where our evening ritual was to end the day with a bowl of ice cream and watch an episode of Scrubs, to wind down.

The next one, I had to admit when we ran for a Leather title and was asked if we had a nightly ritual. Dan nodded, giving me permission to share our monkey toe ritual. He usually goes to bed before I do, as he's an early riser. He would wear his socks to bed, call me in to cover him up and take off his socks. I'd grab his socks, and then he'd proceed to keep me from being able to pull them off by grabbing them with his toes. This usually ended up with us laughing until he released the socks. I'd throw them into the hamper and then cover him up. Since moving into the RV, we don't really have a bedtime ritual. I'm sure that will change as we settle into a routine of some sort.

## Other Rituals

## Boot Ritual

This ritual is specific to his Leather boots. When we go to Leather events and sometimes kink events, Dan has a pair of leather boots that he wears. I help him put them on and take them off. It's a special ritual. Of course, he doesn't NEED help. It's a ritual that puts us both into a deeper headspace for the occasion. I kneel or sit if my back is hurting me. I make sure his boots are clean and shiny and then loosen the laces. He slides his feet in. I push them on and tie the laces, making sure they aren't too loose or too tight. There is no talking. It's all about the leather, the boot, and the power dynamic.

At the end of the evening, it's the same in reverse with a little extra. I sit before him, unlace his boots, pulling them off one by one and setting them aside. Then, I place each foot in my lap and massage them. He likes this for a little bit and then he's done. I take off his socks and set them aside. He helps me to my feet and if I'm still wearing the event collar, he will then take it off so that we can go to bed. Once he goes into the bedroom to get out of his event clothes, I put his socks in the hamper and wipe down his boots and put them away. No talking. Mindful of every moment.

## Football Ritual

This one is probably a little strange, but totally worked for us. Dan used to like watching football… a lot.

I know enough about football to hold my own, but wasn't as interested in it as he was. On Sundays, Dan would spend all day watching football, but I'd want some attention, especially on the weekends that the kids were with their dad. Dan got creative and came up with a ritual that fulfilled both of our needs. He turned me into a footstool. Before the game started, I would make sure he had all his snacks and drinks. Then, as the opening started for the first game, I'd get on all fours and make myself available for his feet. I'd get the physical contact I needed, and the bonus of being humiliated as he used me as a simple piece of furniture. And stools don't talk, so he'd be able to focus on the game. Win/win for both of us.

## How Do You Design Rituals?

### *dawn says*

This is a question we get asked a lot. We can only tell you stories of rituals that we've used over the years. For your rituals, you'll need to find what speaks to your heart. Maybe your Leader doesn't like eye contact. Maybe they want a coaster each time you serve them. Maybe he has a special glass. Maybe she wants you to kiss her feet when she walks in the door. There are so many options.

What do you want to accomplish with yours? What is the purpose? Answering those questions will help you create personal, meaningful rituals. Then, get a little creative.

## *Dan says*

Many of the rituals I've come up with were to defeat lack of attention or automation. Such as 'when you hand me a drink, the handle will face this way, you hold it like this, and we will make eye contact.' Creating those moments in your life where you can be fully present, and avoiding situations where meaning is lost to repetition.

One of the rituals I've created most recently started with this issue - I go to bed before dawn. Sure, I will say good night and kiss her, but that felt like it was becoming just a routine. So I decided that from now on, after that, she would come to the bedroom and 'tuck me in' - straighten out the bed sheet, cover my feet, and also help the dog (who has very stubby little legs) get in bed as well. If I am ready to go to sleep, this is all it is. If I am feeling goofy, I take her blankets or hide mine so when she comes in it is more of a production to get me all set.

So when you design your rituals, it starts with what (I want more connection at this time of night), how (come to bed and make sure I am covered up), and style (fun, solemn, intense).

# Spirituality and Power Exchange

***Dan says***

## Spirituality? Do You Mean Like Religion?

It is easy to explain physical actions. The arm lifts, moves toward a cup, the hand closes and then lifts, and you feel the cold water from the cup. Describing the mental part or the emotional parts of power exchange isn't overly complex either. Here is some concept for us to define and see if we can come to mutual understanding.

The spiritual aspect is where it gets really complex. If you have a religion you align with, you may have a definition of spiritual from there. If you don't have a religion, or only loosely attach to it, then your definition is something that you've come up with via any number of influences.

In short, I can share a general definition of spirituality.

It is "the quality of being concerned with the human spirit or soul as opposed to material or physical things," according to the Oxford Dictionary, 2020. Further, I can give you *my* definition of spirituality, and I will, below.

But I can't give you *your* definition. You may be very spiritual, but it has nothing to do with power exchange; or your power exchange may be the only place you express it.

Alternatively, your spirituality is part of everything in your life; or you take a pass on the whole thing, as it has nothing for you. Most likely, you have some combination of these that fits you.

For me, there are things I *know*, things I *believe*, and things I *feel*. Some are demonstrable and obvious. If I drop a pen, it is going to fall to the ground. I am nearly 100% sure that it is due to gravity. So I call that something I *know*. Spirituality dances around what I *believe* and what I *feel*. When we talk about spiritual objects below, for example, I have no empirical evidence to support what I am saying. I do have my experience, and my feelings, and that is actually all I need.

The below is Power Exchange Spirituality for Dan & dawn. Your experience may vary.

# Skunk Medicine

## *Dan says*

As we mention elsewhere in this and other writings, surrounding yourself with like-minded people can be a great boon for power exchange relationships. This works even better when it is consistently the same people, so you can get to know them, relax, and become a bit more vulnerable when things don't go well. Your people are there to give you a pat on the back when they do go well - both are important.

This view led us to create a small group of like minded people, which we called House Metta. If you attend Leather events, you'll see people walking around in leather vests, many of them with insignia on the back, proclaiming them to be part of House of Delgatto or House Black. Often these insignia would include icons that were meant to represent what the house believed was important - a bear, perhaps for strength, or an eagle, or a tiger. Our House Metta had a vest and patches like that as well - but our power totem animal was... a skunk.

Skunk, from a Shamanic perspective, works like this. Skunk is about respect and reputation. We, as part of our 'skunk medicine,' were secure, easy going, and confident. As they respect themselves, others normally respect us right back. And do you know who is attracted to skunks? Other skunks. And who is repelled by skunks? Well, not skunks.

Terminology like Master might mean a whole lot of different things, depending on who you talk to. It could mean someone involved in a Leather full time power exchange to one person, and 'I want to get my dick sucked when I want to, and not have to do anything cause I claimed a title' to another... it can be easy to misunderstand or misinterpret titles like that. But we never had to recruit or kick anyone out.

People that fit with us naturally showed up. People that had significantly different views on what power exchange was about either didn't try to join us, or if they did, quickly found the door and moved on.

## The Illusion of All These Titles

There is a Buddhist saying: "If you meet the Buddha on the road, kill him." Now, as with many Buddhist sayings, there are a number of ways to interpret this. One is 'avoid being so attached to what you think you are, or should be, that you lose sight of who you are.'

And sticking with Buddhism for a moment, the Heart Sutra says "Form is no other than emptiness, Emptiness no other than form. Form is only emptiness, Emptiness only form."

Both of these are concepts that I struggled to understand for years, and I may or may not be anywhere near having a skillful view. But let's skip all of that for a moment and talk about this.

We have all these great titles; Leader, follower, Owner. We attach ourselves to them. Before dawn could call herself slave, before I could call myself Master when we used those titles, they were earned - we earned the right to use them at all. That was important to me, as the power exchange version of those words had history and tradition. But you know what? In our previous book on power exchange (which included Master and slave in the subtitle) we pointed out that in the computer world, years back, "Master" and "slave" were used to refer to primary and secondary hard disk drives. The terms are also used in other industries. Of course, the terminology is also used to describe a period of time when one group of people degraded and disregarded another group of people in a really horrible way. So, which of these is right?

Now, back to our Heart Sutra. The word 'Master' itself is empty. It has no power. It is we, the person who hears it, that gives it power and attaches good/bad, right/wrong, evil, pride, or nothing to it. I can prove that like so - walk up to someone who doesn't speak English and ask them if you are a good Master. They will look at you blankly. Find a translator, and suddenly that person has a strong opinion about what you asked.

You, though, do understand the language the book is printed in, and you likely have an emotional attachment to this word and others, perhaps very weak or very strong. And that is perfectly ok by the way. I am not saying 'words don't have power.' They do. Look at all the catchphrases and sound bites we get each election cycle. And look at words that inspire and convey hope and courage.

Your attachment to words and how you perceive the translation of them is how you'll pick the titles you use in your power exchange dynamic. Now, you may (like us) start by using the titles you were aware of. We started by using Dom/sub, and as we moved into more Leather circles we started using Master/slave. And after some time, we moved to using Belum/belet.

What a dance this is - on one hand, words are just illusions, constructs, and have no meaning beyond what we personally connect them to. Yet on the other hand, words can impact others, regardless of your intention. I used to argue that if my intent was good, then who cares about the impact? Well, the people being impacted certainly do. And if my intent was really so good, why not use different words?

If you are not digging this, you've probably already checked out, but for those still here, step deeper into this mess. When dawn calls me Belum, it reminds me that I have a role and a responsibility and an agreement with her and myself to maintain. When I call her belet, it is a title of honor, as well as a reminder for her that she is in my collar, in my service. So those words have power there as well.

So there you go. More words that could be of great impact, or convey honest intent, or be nothing more than illusions.

## Physical Body, Mental Body, Spiritual Body

As the Leader in a full time, unlimited power exchange relationship, I am as responsible for my follower's physical body as I want to be - or better said, I'm as responsible as we've negotiated me to be. In the case of dawn, that translates to avoiding injuring her - we do play in a BDSM space, so I can do this in a way that causes yummy pain, but not harm - and not doing anything or allowing anything that may lead to harm.

Now, I am not an expert in physical bodies, and dawn does a great job of paying attention to hers, so in general I choose not to drive much here. I have the right to tell her to diet, eat less, sleep more, get up at 6am, walk daily, or a variety of other things that I think might benefit her physically. But to be honest:

A. she focuses on her physical health as something she keeps in mind
B. I don't honestly know if that keto thing is really great or not great for her
C. I don't really want the job of being her physical trainer. If I see something clearly out of whack, I speak up, but I don't really want to micromanage her in this.

I am also responsible for her Mental Body. What this means to me is that she is taking care of the platform of her mental health. Now, to be clear, I am not responsible for dawn being happy, as much as I might like to believe I am, but instead that she has what she needs to be in a place where happiness can flourish. And at the same time, a place where her sadness can be processed. Actions around this could include telling her she can (or cannot) go back to college, because of the stress it would cause. I have been known to prevent her from taking on some new project because she had, in my view, enough on her plate already.

With the Physical Body, often if something is off, we know it immediately - my foot hurts, my arm aches. With the mental, it can be more challenging to see. And sometimes we as people either hide or simply can't see our own issues and challenges. As with physical, I am no expert in mental health. If you've already skipped ahead and read the chapter on being a survivor, then you know that dawn had some challenges coming into our relationship. The best command I gave her there was to call a counselor.

I did not command her to set up eight sessions with a therapist, or to 'just get over it' (Gods, no). And I did not try to work out her issues via a scene. No. Instead, I acted as the solid foundation to get her to launch the work she needed to do. And I was the person who can see her. Meaning, her own perception of herself was skewed by years of being told she was unworthy and unwanted. We talk about being the witness - just seeing what is, without attachment to it, and avoiding unskillful reactions. When dawn told me about some of the horrors she was put through, I heard her, loved her anyway, and I said 'Now go get me a cup of coffee, follower.' And that was just right.

And then we have the Spiritual Body. This one is tricky. If you have a clear religion you align with, then the spiritual life may already be well laid out for you. Do this on Sunday, don't do this on Friday, etc. And some power exchange couples I know work this into their power exchange directly.

But for me and dawn, I am responsible for providing a foundation for her spiritual life to be whatever it is. But do I have rights or responsibilities for her spiritual path? Well, barely. I have pushed dawn to pursue what she wanted to pursue; attending a clergy course. But the push was to give her the courage to do what she wanted to do, nothing more.

dawn has made slight modifications to her spiritual path a number of times, and none of that is my business. For us, that is where the line is drawn. If tomorrow she started to follow Jediism, and as part of that she was not allowed to have oral sex - note I don't know anything about Jediism, and this is just an example - then so be it. Even though this clearly has a direct impact on me, it is just part of our agreements that the spiritual path is one that you have to drive yourself.

I will make adjustments as needed for my own needs. In this case, I have other relationships so her lack of oral would hurt, but would not prevent me from enjoying it with other partners. But even if these choices impact the relationship, I adjust; I do not command it to not happen.

The same goes for dawn, in that if I decide to follow a certain path that directly impacts her, then she is expected to support me or get out of the way, but not influence me away from it. This most recently happened when I was studying Buddhism and decided that my path included becoming a monk. For some time, she had to make some adjustments for my path. These were small things, mainly with me wearing robes, but she never said 'but how will this impact our lives as authors or presenters?'

There is an exception to all this. There are some pretty unhealthy religions out there, so if for some reason dawn got caught up in one of those - and it would have to be clearly unhealthy, not just something I didn't dig - then I would intervene.

Now, we have to understand, the language here is a bit imprecise. Does a chemical imbalance causing depression count as a Physical Body or Mental Body? Let's not get too attached to those words, and instead get our followers (and our Leaders) what they need to be healthy in all aspects of their lives.

## Spiritual Objects

When I was a student of one spiritual path, we were told that the books related to this path should never be put on the ground, as it shows disrespect. I accepted this, not as a truth, but as a courtesy to that tradition. But in general, I think things are... well, just things.

Yet, I have a few things that I perceive as having an energetic charge, as a result of intent. For example, as noted elsewhere in this book, I recycle collars. Once a follower leaves my service, the collar is returned to me. That collar, full of sweat and tears and intention and hope and pride, moves on to the next person. And I make it sure they are aware of that - they are both adding to it, but they are also bound to uphold it.

## Spiritual Challenges

By the time I collared dawn, I was done with the 'does God exist' phase. I had decided there is probably some sort of higher power, and I'm not it. My spiritual challenge was more along the lines of, what is the point of me being alive. Not the meaning of life, mind you, but me specifically. This goes back to my days some thirty years ago of being a drug addict. If I died then, no one would really have cared - I was self absorbed, and generally not a great person. Beyond a few people who felt they had to, if I had died then, I'm not sure anyone would have shown up at the funeral. This led me to believing I had a second chance to do some good in the world, and that gets us here, to this question: "So I am alive. So what?"

This question led me to explore religion, and eventually led to a book on Buddhism which basically had a core view of 'if you are compassionate and nice to other people, they will be happier.' So I tried that, and it worked pretty well.

Now, if you are a student of Buddhism and want to argue there is much more to it than that, I will suggest that your attachment to your viewpoint is causing you suffering and that you should find a more skillful approach. (That is Buddhism for 'chill the f out.') By the end of this you might have decided 'this guy is no Buddhist' and I'm ok with that. But let's see where this is going.

So, I became both a Leader and a Buddhist. Like many other religions, there are many flavors of Buddhism; everything from a simple philosophy to a complex multi God religion. I started to look around to see where I fit. I tried a number of different schools of Buddhism, chanted in languages I don't speak, meditated on retreats, studied some sutras (buddhist texts) and books, spoke to a few monks and priests, and even committed to the path of being a monk not once, but twice.

Now, where in this story is the power exchange? Well, all of it. During these years I continued to be the Leader of dawn and multiple other followers; I ran for a Leather title, did a kink podcast, became a co-director of a BDSM club, and had lots of kinky sex. At the same time, I was running a sangha (Buddhist group) and for one period, I was wearing monk's robes.

The point that this became a spiritual challenge for me was that I was getting to the point of 'either/or.' Either commit to becoming a Buddhist monk, or stay in my current world - Leader of power exchange relationship, kinky as hell, etc. "Why not both?" was my view for a while, but… for me, it started to feel wrong. One of these people - either power exchange kinky Dan, or Buddhist monk Dan - was who I was, and I was running out of room for 'both.'

I sent my robes back, and spent a few years realigning myself. You do not need to identify as a Buddhist to be compassionate, or to have a desire to help people. I've found - and continue to find - the tools of Buddhism of great value to me. But the label itself got in the way.

## My Spiritual Foundation

### *dawn says*

Like power exchange, spirituality is a huge part of my life's foundation. It has changed slightly over the years, or better said, it's picked up hitchhikers through the years. Every time I study something new, I tend to add another label to my spiritual description of myself. At the moment I'm a Wiccan-trained, Buddhist-flavored, Goddess-oriented, shamanistic Qadishtu, energy-working witchy healer, as well as state licensed clergy.

I've thought of calling myself an Earth Spiritualist when someone asks, just to keep it short. I guess I could just say 'pagan,' but that means so many different things to different people. Regardless, I'm a lot of things, and I take it all very seriously.

Oddly enough, I found my spiritual path at about the same time as Power Exchange and my healing path. More than likely it's because that's the time that the internet became more accessible. I found me… or at least, a path to me.

For me, this is one of those items that would fall under a 'Need' in a contract. It's non-negotiable. I 'Need' to be able to explore my spiritual path. Whether it's healing rituals on the full moons, or sacred sexuality, I need to be able to find what speaks to my soul. Luckily, Dan is of the same mind, and watches my experimentations. Sometimes he tags along, but more often than not, he goes in his own direction.

So, let's pick this apart a little bit.

## *Wiccan trained*

While researching the web in the early days, I wondered what I was going to find. I started with researching my Native American past, just knowing that was going to be the path for me. I wanted it to be the path for me. It just made sense. But, only small pieces resonated with me. Not all of the paths or paradigms or pantheons spoke to me. I kept a couple of pieces that worked for me, and kept looking.

Next, I stumbled across a Wiccan tradition that really sang to me. I researched them, and then asked Dan if I could join their online school, knowing there would be chances to meet in person as well since they were a familial tradition. I was so excited, and he agreed. I took all the courses and worked really hard at making it through the degrees.

At one point, I had the opportunity to travel to their

physical temple to gather with elders, discuss becoming pagan clergy, and to receive some training. Oh how I wanted this... but I didn't want to leave Dan or travel that far on my own. Dan decided that this was when he was going to increase the size of my shark tank.

Have you heard of that saying? A shark only grows as big as its tank. Well, Dan has that feeling about followers. So, he wanted me to grow, and he knew I desired to grow. He pushed me out of the little tank and said I would be going and would do him proud in the process. I packed my bags and went. It was really weird, because I also wanted to be home taking care of him. But, he'd given an order.

I will always remember that trip. I was able to meet people that I'd only dreamed about meeting, and be part of the conversation on how to establish pagan clergy and create pagan churches. They also did a lot of clergy training while I was there. When I came home, I decided to start my own temple, and become licensed clergy through my own temple instead of the Tradition I had been a part of. You'll read several chapters in this book that mention my control issues. Well, I wanted to decide whose marriage I officiated. I was done with the Tradition telling me what I could and couldn't do. So, I did the thing. Created a Temple. Became licensed clergy. I've officiated hundreds of weddings since then.

The first wedding I did, Dan tagged along with me. There were 2 brides and the ceremony was in their home. Dan carried in my props and as I started setting them up in the living room, he asked me what I wanted to eat.

"Ummmm, Sir?..."

"Don't call me Sir here. What do you want to eat?"

"Umm, I can get it Si... umm, I can get it..."

"No you can't. You have a wedding to officiate and two nervous brides. I'm taking care of you tonight. I'll bring you a plate."

It blew my mind, and I had a really hard time with it. But, it finally clicked that he was proud of what I was doing, and it was up to him to decide to take care of me so I could do the thing. That was a nerve-wracking shift that took me a while to get used to.

I was challenged again with being asked to officiate a Leather wedding. Oh my. Me. A follower, officiating a Leather wedding. Not just any Leather wedding, but for the president of NLA-International. I had other followers, and Leaders for that matter, asking me how I was going to be able to do it. It shook my confidence a little bit. I was afraid of being judged as being cocky, or worse, as a bad slave. I was so confused at the time. But, the bride and groom really wanted me to officiate. And Dan wanted me to officiate. Luckily, when the time came for me to lead the practice the night before the ceremony, everyone listened to my direction. It felt so weird to be giving directions to covered Masters. Masters in leather, wearing their caps.

Dan sat me down before that rehearsal. He knew where my head was. He reminded me that I was a Priestess, that I'd done many weddings before this one, and that they must think I could do the job since they had asked me to do it. He also let me know that he was proud of me for doing all the work to get to that point, and that he knew I'd do a great job. And I must say, I did. It was beautiful, and I'd love the chance to do another one. This one had Leather and collars and leashes and whips and roses. It was so authentic and fantasy level at the same time.

But, it's not just about officiating weddings. I take being clergy very seriously. I even designed a clergy training program and have 5 people licensed with the state under my Temple's name. They have been trained in designing rituals, officiating weddings and funerals, and how to be clergy for a community. It's so much more than weddings. Even Dan took the training. I was his teacher, and that had me so confused until it clicked, and my confidence in what I was doing settled in.

I officiate weddings and handfastings and collarings. And even funerals. At this point, I've led more than a handful of funerals, with about 70% of them being funerals for members of the Leather community. It's hard, and an honor, and exactly what I'm supposed to be doing.

## *Reiki Master*

Around 2004 is when I started my temple, and that's also when I decided to learn Reiki healing. I mainly wanted to learn so that I could work on my own healing. Dan had been helping me so much, and though I appreciated it, I wanted to take some of the pressure off of him. As my Master, he was always there for me, but I also knew he'd be proud of me for learning new skills, especially if they helped with my healing path so that I could help myself.

This was back when Reiki was really popular and I was seeing it everywhere in magazines. So, I found a local teacher and took the first level. I loved it! A few months later I took the second level. Oh, this was for me! Dan was even excited for me. This blended in so well with my current spiritual path. Then, after some thought, I took that training to become a Reiki Master. This was when I started offering Reiki Shares in the kink community. I even went to outdoor events and offered 'Neiki'... which was my version of naked reiki. Plus, I helped others with healing circles during these events.

This could have been a real challenge if Dan wasn't so secure in himself as a person, and a Master. I was being asked by elders and High Priests and Priestesses for help, running my own temple and clergy training, holding rituals at events, and all the stuff that goes with being clergy in the kink community. There have been moments where he could have told me to stop. But instead, he takes pride in having a slave that is responsible for so much. I am a reflection of him and his training, as I've said before. It's with his support and help that I was able to accomplish this.

## My Master Lifts Me Up So That I Can Shine

### *Master vs Priest*

Dan and I are both spiritual beings on a spiritual journey. And though Dan is a Priest in some aspects, he is not my Priest. He is my Master - which can have the same energy as a Priest - but he is not my Priest.

Or is he?

What are the responsibilities of a Priest? Well, it depends on who you ask. But, the way I'm using it here is that a Priest is someone who guides a person on their spiritual journey. They are the teacher, the 'knower of things,' the Leader in ritual, the conduit between people and God/desses.

Is Dan my Priest? There are days that he is a Priest. There are days he helps me on my spiritual journey. There are days he is the 'knower of things.' There are days he is the Priest in my rituals along my journey of self-discovery and celebrations of accomplishments. There are days he is the conduit between me and the Gods, and he has great wisdom to pass on to me. So, yes, there are days he's a priest with me. But, he is not my Priest as my Master. He is a priest to me, as he is to many others. In our relationship, it's not a full-time job like being a Master is.

Dan is not my Priest or my spiritual guide, just as I am not His Priestess even though I am a Priestess.

This isn't to say that some couples don't interact this way. I do know a few power exchange couples where the Master or Mistress is also the Priest/ess in the relationship. And it works for them. It's just not how we currently interact.

Though, as I've said, it can take on a similar energy, Priest and Master. And at first, it can be difficult to separate the two.

## *Master vs. God*

At first, it would have been so easy to see Dan as God. As the supreme being in charge of my life. As the 'knower of all that is good and holy.' As the person, wait... the God, who never makes a mistake. As the brightest light in the universe, sitting upon the highest pillar. As the end-all, be-all of absolutely everything! Hail be to Dan!

Right? How easy it is to just surrender and hand over everything. This is a power exchange relationship, after all. But there is a concern with doing that. Even though I believe all of us have a spark of divinity in us, there is a danger in believing our Leaders are God, or treating them like God. Simply because they aren't. They are humans that are on a human journey, just as we followers are. Yes, we've put them in charge of our lives, I know I did, but that doesn't mean that they are going to be perfect with that Leadership role. They are still learning. They will make mistakes. And if you place them on that super high pedestal, damn, the higher you put them up, the further they have to fall when they make a mistake.

Don't tell Dan, but he does not know everything. And if I allow myself to think he does, I'm going to have a spiritual crisis the first time he makes a mistake, doubts himself, or I doubt him about something. If I put that kind of pressure on him, or if he puts it on himself, we are creating a landmine that will certainly be stepped on and blow up, leaving shattered pieces behind.

Thankfully, Dan doesn't have the type of ego that would allow him to try to fill the role of God. He knows his limitations and speaks them. He reminds me that he's just human and Leading a relationship that we've both agreed works in our best interest.

So, though I don't believe Dan is my God or even a God, I do believe that the Universe put him on my path at the right time. The time I needed him and this style of relationship the most.

## *Spiritual Surrender vs. Surrender in Power Exchange*

One of the things that confused me at the beginning was this whole idea of surrender. As I've said before, a lot was going on when Dan and I got together and decided to create this designer relationship. Not only had I had just gotten out of a long-term vanilla marriage and started my healing journey; I was creating a hierarchical relationship, and I had started my spiritual journey. I blame it all on the internet becoming more accessible.

So, through the beginning years, during my spiritual study, journey, and experience, I had come to this place of peace. A place of surrender. A place where I stopped trying to force solutions on situations that I couldn't control. I finally believed that the Universe wasn't out to get me. I stopped waiting for the other shoe to drop. I came to trust that the Universe was taking care of everything and showing me the way. I surrendered to the path that was laid out in front of me.

OK, that sounds like it was easy for me to just let go and let it be. It wasn't. But, the result of all the hard work and workshops and research was that I learned to trust what the Universe had in store for me, and that it knew me better than I knew me.

Sounds familiar, doesn't it?

This is also exactly what I was doing in my submission to Dan. I was learning to trust him. I was learning that sometimes he really did know me better than me. That's because he listened to me more than I listened to me. He knew what the relationship needed. He knew what we both needed.

And as with surrender in a spiritual sense, surrendering in the power exchange sense wasn't easy either. As I've said elsewhere, or at least meant to say elsewhere, I had gotten to a place in my life where I felt like I was the only one who could protect me from the world. I felt most people in my life were only in my life because they wanted something from me, and they weren't transparent or trustworthy about what that was. I had to fight against seeing Dan through these same lenses. I constantly questioned him and what he was doing and why I was submitting to him.

It took time to surrender to him. And funny enough, it's actually not something that either of us were aiming for. Dan wanted to lead. I wanted to follow. Dan needed to lead for his growth as a person. I needed to follow for my growth as a person. Each time Dan led and was trustworthy, it became easier for me to follow. Each time I followed without question, obeyed with pure trust, it became easier for him to lead.

My surrender to his Leadership ended up empowering him as a Dominant, a Leader, and a Master. And when he's empowered, I'm empowered. And once I realized I had surrendered, I was able to take that breath, and know that we were going to be ok. I had learned to trust.

Life is much simpler when I'm in a state of surrender to both Dan and the Universe. Experience tells me they both have my best interests at heart. Neither contradicts the other, so I haven't had to deal with any conflict. They both work hand in hand.

## Spiritual Teacher

Not only am I a co-presenter with Dan, I'm also a teacher of the spiritual/sacred arts and have been for many years at this point. This is my wheelhouse, so to speak. Sometimes we teach this stuff together, but Dan prefers that I teach most of the spiritual stuff and energy stuff. And I'm ok with that. Between being a Priestess, and a Reiki Master, a Qadishtu, and a Healer, this is what I do.

Again, people ask me how I can do this when I'm a slave. Well, over time it became easy. And it's easy simply because I do everything as his follower. He takes pride in what I've learned and accomplished. He realizes that my successes have involved a lot of hard work on my part, but also reflect all the hard work he's put into this relationship. My growth as a slave is something we've accomplished together.

# Relationship Building

### *dawn says*

Let's face it, this whole book is about building a viable, healthy relationship. Even though our focus is about a power exchange relationship, (or authority transfer or hierarchical connection or whatever terminology you want to call it,) it's still a relationship.

It will have some differences compared to a non-hierarchical relationship, and some stuff will be what an egalitarian relationship might incorporate. With our foundation being power exchange, our relationship building will be focused around that.

## Power Exchange Foundation

So let's start with that. What is the foundation of your relationship? Is it a power exchange? Is it love? Is it egalitarian/equality? If it's egalitarian, this book may not be for you unless you are thinking of giving power exchange a try.

For us, it's power exchange. Love is layered on top and I tell people that without love, this level of power exchange probably wouldn't be possible for me. But, in the end, the foundation for us is power exchange. Without the hierarchical dynamic, our relationship would not be the power house that it is. We have discovered that with power exchange, all good things arise. When we stumble, we go back to our foundation.

We've had people come to us for mentoring and more than once we've been told, "we are having issues, so we decided to put our power exchange aside to work on the relationship." I shake my head. Why would you put aside your foundation? Why not embrace it even tighter? It's like a couple that has a 'regular' relationship saying, "well, we are having problems so we've decided to put aside our egalitarian foundation." Why?

I speak from personal experience, because we made the same mistake. About ten years in, we started doing polyamory in a new way and it shook us up for a bit. I was having issues with it that were complicated enough that we decided to put power exchange aside. The idea was that Dan would know I was making the decision to move forward as his partner, not because I was a slave and just submitting to the situation. Because of our experience with this decision, we recommend others don't take the same path.

Why? Well, when we decided to remove the power exchange after ten years of having it as our foundation, we no longer knew how to interact with each other. Everything we had built that worked for us we were now stumbling over. I was stumbling over calling him Sir. He was stumbling over telling me to do things. We no longer knew how to respond to each other. We weren't sure how to communicate.

Imagine being vanilla and you are having issues so you decide 'we are now power exchange and this is how we are going to be until we figure out how to resolve the issue we are having.' It's a whole different skill set. It's a whole different way of relating. For us, dropping our power exchange foundation was absolutely confusing.

We realized after a week or so that we'd made a mistake and made the decision to bring back the collar and to interact as Leader/follower, which is what we were good at. It didn't totally resolve the original issue we were having, but it gave us back our tools that we were used to. We now had our chainsaws back instead of plastic butter knives to deal with the situation.

Power Exchange is our foundation. It is our seat of power as individuals and as a couple.

## What Does a 'Real' Power Exchange Relationship Look Like?

Well, it depends on the relationship. We were just at a friend's house where the follower was always naked, she did all the domestic stuff, and she sat on the floor beside her owner as the owner sat at the dinner table. The follower never sat on furniture and always spoke in third person. There were smiles on both of their faces. This is exactly what they wanted, so it's what they designed.

Another couple we know are far more subtle. If

you go to their house, the follower is always taking care of the Leader, but it's hard to notice. They don't use any particular language, but the Leader will nod their head and the follower will know what's needed. Sometimes you'll see them lean into each other to ask or say something. If you weren't aware, you wouldn't pick up on it.

For us, it's changed over the years. We've had our high protocol days and now we are more relaxed except when we have the opportunity to be high protocol in certain situations, like visiting the first couple I mentioned. I don't sit on the floor during dinner. But, I did that night of the visit. I used to sit at his feet all the time. If we had company, I'd still sit at his feet, but it just looked loving, not like it was a 'thing.'

But then he decided he liked me sitting with him on the couch. It did take me a while to adjust to sitting next to him, though. We can pass as any other couple, except it will become noticeable if you are around us enough. You'll see that we don't argue and we seem to have a secret code for knowing what is needed in the moment. Dan's cup of coffee is never empty. If he says my name a certain way, I know it's 'Master Dan' talking, not husband Dan. Others don't know the difference. When around us, you'll also see that there is never a power struggle. If Dan says, 'sit here,' I hear Master Dan when others may not. I sit there with a smile. I may even say, 'perfect spot, thank you.' He hears, 'yes, Sir.'

## Interdependency

You'll see Dan taking care of us, and me taking care of him. That's our interdependent relationship. It's two people that work together as a team, not two individuals trying to be independent. Nor are we so enmeshed that we can't do something without the other, though I'm sure it can look that way from the outside. Actually, it would depend on the day. It could look enmeshed, or it could look independent. The trick is, that's just the cover layer of what's going on. It's the layer underneath, the roots underground, that wrap together in power exchange interdependence.

It's taken us a while to figure out this balance. We both came into this relationship pretty self focused. Our past relationships had required that. They had involved so much power struggle that we had some resistance to the whole 'teamwork' idea. I don't know if it was because we were resisting what we had seen with our parents or media or maybe our notion of what women's lib was.... I'm not really sure. But we as two individuals came together and added the power exchange dynamic, and it felt so good that we had to make sure not to lean too far into it - to not become codependent. It would have been easy. I can remember driving around in the car having conversations with Dan talking about my fear of becoming codependent.

What is codependency? According to an article in 'Psychology Today' it's a term used to describe a lopsided relationship where one person does all the giving and one person does all the taking. One person is in the role of a constant caregiver. From the outside, this could be what a power exchange relationship looks like, right? The Leader is always asking for something and the follower is always serving. Or vice versa. The follower is always needing something, and the Leader is always providing.

But, if you look closer, is that so? In our relationship, I take care of Dan. But he takes care of the relationship. He provides service, it just looks different than what I do. It may not be as visible to the outside world. We work together to support each other and to make sure our relationship is mutually beneficial. And not only do we support each other, we push each other to be the best people we can be. The best Leader and individual that he can be, the best follower and individual that I can be. Mutual growth. All of that benefits us and our relationship. We are interdependent.

## Relationship Hacking

I would argue that designing a power exchange relationship is the ultimate in relationship hacking. We are constantly looking at how to strengthen the relationship and constantly trying new techniques. Even the week that we took off from our dynamic was a strategy in relationship hacking. Thank goodness we found out early that that wasn't beneficial to our relationship.

Over the years we've tried incorporating different 'hacks' into our relationship. Some have worked to make it stronger. With others, we wondered what the hell were we thinking to try such a thing. Yet we are constantly trying new things without even realizing it. You could call us relationship hacking junkies.

Personally, I think all relationships could use a little of this. Don't rely on what your parents did, or what you may have done in another relationship, or what you see others do, or even what you read that we do. Every person is different. Every relationship is different. Try things, and see if they work for you.

Something Dan and I are always open to and still

learning even after this many years, is figuring out what our strengths and weaknesses are. And we've discovered that some remain our core strengths while some have changed over the years. For example, I used to be a book learner. Give me a book full of details and my photographic memory would tell you what page and where to find an answer. As I've gotten older, this isn't the case anymore. I remember just enough to be dangerous, so we can't always believe what I recall anymore. Just last night I remembered reading something about why the interstate highway was built. Dan looked at me like I'd lost my mind because he had never heard of that before. The problem was I could only remember a few of the details. Thank goodness for Google! So, my strength used to be my memory recall, now it's knowing how to research for information.

## Hawk and Mouse

### *dawn says*

Elsewhere in the book I mention that Dan's default is to look at the big picture while my default is to see the details and logistics of a situation. If we didn't look at that as our personal strengths, it would drive each other crazy. Instead, after realizing each was indeed a strength, we were able to see that they complemented each other. A lot of what we do is complementary. He likes to lead, I like to follow. He likes to create, I like to bring his creations to life. He likes to solve puzzles, I like routines. He likes spontaneity, I like structure and plans. Because of these complementary personalities, we've been able to create an amazing relationship. It works out well for us.

Mix that with my spiritual path, which involves lots of pagany stuff like spirit guides and animal totem medicine, and I've come up with another explanation of why we work together so well. One of my spirit animals is the mouse. I haven't wanted to admit to that for years, because I have some amazing spirit animal guides in my life like: Black Panther, Blue Heron, Red-tailed Hawk, Whale… and mouse always seemed, well... small. I feel larger than a mouse. But, am I? Really?

The more I look at it, the more I understand my personality. And Dan's. You see, Dan has some spirit animal guides in his life as well. Hell, we built House Metta around Skunk medicine. And what I've figured out lately is that one of his main medicines when working with me is Hawk. He sees the larger picture. He has vision. And because he's working with the big picture, sometimes he misses details. That's my responsibility.

### *Dan says*

You can read more about spiritual aspects - be it how I incorporate Buddhism or dawn's, as she said, 'pagany stuff,' elsewhere in the book. Whether you dig totem guides, see them more as archetypes, or think it is all crapola, it doesn't matter. Or it does matter, but only if you let it get in the way of finding something useful.

I read a story about a fellow who went to university and before a big test he would pray to Spock. You know, the Vulcan from Star Trek. It was pointed out to him that not only was Spock not a deity, but he wasn't even, well,

Spock. Instead he was Leonard Nimoy (or Zachary Quinto, depending on your era). The student said it didn't matter - the prayer reminded him to take his time, be cool, be logical, and to do his best.

With that in mind, when dawn and I come into conflict in planning - I suggest it might be fun to go see a friend in Texas on the spur of the moment; she reminds me that I have work, it will cost money, and lots of people don't like those that suddenly drop in on them. I feel like she is being a killjoy but she will say 'Hawk and mouse,' and it will remind me that we both have our own views and roles and together we accomplish things. So I will say 'make it happen' and she will say 'Yes Sir. Now you'll have to put in your time off at work and we'll get someone to watch the dog and do you think we should mention we are coming...?'

### *dawn says*

As for me, the mouse, I see all the details. Sometimes he says I burst his bubbles when he's dreaming. I don't see it that way. When he starts dreaming up a new plan, I automatically go into logistical mode. "What about this?" "Have you thought of that?" "What about when this happens?" I've had to learn to just let him get his dream spoken into the air. Let him dream big. Then, I can go into logistics. He thinks I'm a bubble popper, but what I'm really doing is going into a space of trying to figure out how to make his dream real. And that involves asking (and answering) lots of questions.

Dan sees the big picture. The future vision. I see the details that are needed to make it happen. As Belum and belet, he tells me what he wants, and I use all those details I've organized to help create his vision. Picture it like designing a story or paper the way we used to in school - he creates the outline, I fill in all the items with the roman numerals.

Another way Hawk and mouse works for us is the realization that he has the power to devour me, and doesn't use it. This is one way he's earned my trust over the years. Mouse is not very trusting. She sees danger everywhere. Dan as Hawk is actually my protector. Not because he has to be, but because he's chosen to be, and because of that, I can relax a little and not be scared of all the shadows around me.

## Finances

Now, on to more logistical things. Finances. Did you know that at least 25% of breakups are over finances? At least according to some of the research I did. That's no small number! And honestly, it's not surprising. Dan and I both went through relationships that had finances involved and weren't happy with how they were dealt with. I could even say that my 14 year marriage broke up partly due to finances.

So, Dan and I went into our relationship knowing that we wanted to deal with the money differently than we had in any other relationship. It took a while to figure out what we wanted as we struggled with what we 'should' do as a power exchange couple. What we discovered was there is no right way or wrong way to do things, including finances. This is a designer relationship. We built it how it was most comfortable for us.

We each needed to know what was going on with the money we were both bringing into the household. Now, this doesn't mean that we both had the same responsibilities. Remember, Dan is Hawk and I am mouse. We have different strengths, different goals. How we've done this has changed over the years. Currently, we sit together as partners each week and at the beginning of each month. Dan is on his computer with the bank website pulled up. I'm on my computer with the budget app pulled up. We reconcile the bank accounts and credit card together. We each know exactly how much money the household has and what's being done with it. This makes us both feel on top of our finances and in control (read more about my control issues elsewhere in the book). Dan could change this at any time, but why would he? It's working for us.

Now, we also each get an allowance to do with as we please. We had spouses that would spend household money on personal things and then there was scrambling to pay bills. We didn't want that in our relationship, but we also didn't want to have to ask permission every time we wanted to buy a little something for ourselves, or a gift for each other. So, we each have our own personal accounts that the other doesn't look at. We could, as we have each other's passwords to all bank accounts. But, these personal ones are ours to do with as we please.

This helps Dan and me both feel secure in our financial situation. Keep in mind that we also run a business, so our finances can be a little more complicated than others.

This is what we designed because it works for us. And in the end, Dan gets final say with what happens to the money. Recently, he wanted to invest some money from a sale. I wanted it to be a safer option, as is my nature. He was willing to do something a little more risky since we are closer to retirement and need the possibility of earning more than my safe option. I spoke about my concerns. He still wanted to do the riskier option, so we did. We'll see how it turns out a few years from now. I'm betting his was the right move. And if not, we shrug it off. It was his decision to make.

Other relationships do it differently. One couple we know decided to invest some of their money from a sale. The Leader told the follower to do the research and make a decision. How scary, right? But, he knew that that was her skill and she would invest the money wisely.

Yet another, the follower does all the finances because it's their skill. But then another couple we know, the Leader does all the finances because it's their skill. Figure out your strengths and desires. Even if finances isn't my strength, it helps my sanity to know what's going on with the money, and Dan likes it when I feel secure.

You do you. There is no right or wrong way. There isn't a power exchange police. Well, unless you run for a Leather title, and even that is limited (but you are inviting some judgement into your life).

## Transparency

After reading the financial part, you might have guessed that part of what works for us in our relationship is transparency. I'll even go so far as to say that it is a huge piece of why our relationship works so well. For some, they would say that it's not needed, especially by the Leader. I disagree. And the reason I disagree is because one of the pieces that cements our foundation is trust, and transparency can lead to trust.

For me, as a survivor (more on this in a later chapter), if I feel that anything is being hidden, it's a major issue for me. It feels like a secret, and I can't trust someone that is holding on to secrets. We learned about that in the beginning years, before creating our contract. So, transparency is in our contract, or at least words to that effect are in there.

As for me, I like having transparency be a requirement. I don't like having secrets. I can't fully surrender when I'm also holding onto secrets. Personally, I think one of the reasons we ended up together is because we shared so many of our personal secrets at the beginning. I told Dan all my memories of my trauma - not on purpose, mind you. I had gone to a workshop, Dan had tagged along, and we ended up being the only attendees. The workshop facilitator broke down my walls during the workshop, quite by accident. (I believe the Universe had a hand in this.) I ran out into the parking lot, Dan followed me, and I poured it all out to him. When I realized he wasn't going to judge me and instead saw my sharing as a vulnerable gift, well... that's when our friendship started to change into something else.

I share everything with him. He shares everything with me. Well, maybe not his tricks on how he Leads me and our relationship, but the important stuff. We live in glass houses. I know all of Dan's triggers and things that could hurt him. He knows all of mine. And we choose not to use that information against each other. How powerful is that?

## Business Meetings

So, when you are extremely busy like we are - or even if you aren't - how do you keep on track with your relationship and all the things involved with it? Dan and I find it very important to keep on top of things and to be proactive with being transparent and informative, so we can nip issues in the bud that could be growing without our awareness. We do this with business meetings.

Just the other night, during our bi-monthly call with some other power exchange friends, one of the Leaders brought up the topic of the importance of meetings. They didn't currently have them, wanted to hear if others thought they were important, and their frequency if we did think they were important. Some said yes, some said no. For some it was an annual review at their contract anniversary date, some were weekly, some formal, some informal. Get the gist? Do what works for you.

Dan and I have always had some sort of meeting schedule. Maybe it's because we both come from the corporate world? I don't know, but it works for us. At the beginning, it would be every Sunday. Before we had a contract, the Sunday meeting would cover household and parenting. After the contract we added a little time to review a piece of the contract to keep it fresh.

Currently, we have a daily check in, like an office "Stand Up" meeting, though we don't really stand up for it. We go over our calendar for the day/week/month and go over what we'll be working on that day for the business - books, podcast, zooms, presenting, and so on. It keeps us both in the loop with what is going on. We may also bring up some bigger ideas that we are thinking about, with the idea that we will schedule a time to talk about these in more depth later.

This meeting replaces the email I used to send him

every morning outlining my day. When he drove in to work, the email worked better. Now that he works from home, the 5 - 10 minute check-in works better.

Then, for the bigger topics or emotional issues, we try to schedule a time when we can go for a walk or a car ride to talk. It gets us out of the house and away from distractions. We used to save these talks for trips to wherever we were presenting, and had hours in the car or on a plane. Once in-person events start happening again - we are writing this during the covid pandemic - I'm sure that will become our practice again.

We also keep a list of things to talk about, if they can wait long enough for the car ride. This is one of the ways of keeping things from escalating to a 'porch time' moment.

## Raising Kids

Of all the things we had to deal with in the building of our relationship, probably the most cumbersome was raising the kids. Our sons were from my previous marriage, though they had known Dan their whole lives. So, our situation was probably a little different than most.

Dan and the boys were shifting from a 'Friend Dan' to a 'Stepdad Dan' relationship. They used to be able to get away with quite a bit when Dan was 'Friend Dan.' And Dan was willing to get them in trouble when he didn't have to deal with the outcome. 'Here they are, we went walking in the creek,' even though they were wearing their new shoes. So, not only were they upset that that relationship dynamic had changed, they were upset that I'd left their dad. We all had a hard time adjusting to the changes.

As for having power exchange as a basis for my and Dan's relationship, the kids were never aware of that, or that it had a name. What they did see was that Dan was in charge and I was happy. This provided a stable environment for them. And it's not that Dan was in charge of them. He left most of that to me. But he was in charge of the family. That meant that as their mom, I made most of the decisions regarding them. Dan definitely had input though, and his input trumped mine. He just chose not to use that option that often. And the kids knew that they couldn't play off of us. They went to me. If I went to Dan, his word was the law.

This relationship also benefited from meetings. Once a week we would have a family meeting. We kept a notebook of what was brought up and decisions that were made. The boys felt like they had a voice, which I found so important. They could pretty much bring up anything, and they did. For bigger topics, we'd employ the talking stick method. We talk more about this in the communication section.

From the outside, we look like a normal family. Our kink stuff was locked away. The kids were not aware of what we did when we went to parties. For us, there is a line that we don't cross with children. It's not everyone's line, but it was ours, and still is ours as we now have grandchildren.

The boys knew that we taught on spiritual subjects and went to events to teach sacred sexuality topics. At home, I ran a spiritual group that had all kinds of 'alternative' people in it, even a polyamorous family or two. So, they knew we were very open-minded when it came to people and life and alternative ways of building relationships.

They knew that they could ask us anything and tested that line a few times. I would usually start my answer with 'Give me a second while I try to put together an age appropriate response' or 'Are you sure you want to know? I can't take it back once I speak it.' That would usually make them pause, but not stop the question if they felt they really needed an answer. They also knew that if we didn't know the answer, we'd find someone who might.

So, for us, we did not use the lingo involved with our power exchange. Dan never called me slave in front of them. That would have the potential of creating friction in the relationship between me and the kids. He didn't want any misconceptions. And at the beginning, he didn't want them going back to their dad with tales that could have caused issues for all of us.

At the beginning, I had one friend ask me what the kids thought to see me chained to the furniture! I have no clue where she got that concept. Too much fantasy erotica? I don't know. My response to her was that I didn't have time to be chained anywhere. I had too much work to do with taking care of Dan and the household. Chained to a chair? I wish! That would be a vacation for me!

Well, the kids are older now, with kids of their own. We feel like we've done a good job. They have great families. One is into power exchange and polyamory, the other is not. We raised them in such a way that they could make choices about who they wanted to be, and find what makes their hearts sing.

Yet, I can tell you stories of how others have raised their kids, different from us, and their kids turned out ok as well… or didn't. Who knows if it had anything to do with being aware of their parents' power exchange relationship or not? Ours could have turned out differently as well. Kids turn out ok and not ok coming from any relationship style.

# Victim, Survivor, Thriver

*Though there aren't any details of my trauma here, the things I talk about can still be triggering. If needed, take your time with this chapter and take care of yourself.*

## *dawn says*

### Part 1 - A Piece of My Story

I am a slave. I am a survivor of childhood trauma/ abuse. I'm diagnosed with PTSD. And yet, I am a thriver.

Once people find out that I'm a survivor of childhood trauma/abuse, I get a lot of questions about how we make our power exchange relationship work. I'm not going to lie, it's been challenging. I came into this relationship with so much trauma baggage that it definitely caused issues at first.

I was aware of some of my issues, but I also had a shadow self that I wasn't aware of. It was locked deep down and she was running the show without me even knowing it. I was living as a victim without realizing it. The anger, the control issues… for me, at least… are signs that the 'victim' me is in control.

I tell people all the time that I was lucky in finding a Master who had recovery experience. He knew the power of shining a light on the shadow self, so that it can't hide. Like he told me, he wanted to be in charge of me instead of allowing the shadow to be in charge of my actions.

What we didn't know at the time, but quickly came to recognize, was this. For me to embrace being a slave, I need to:

- Be vulnerable/Being vulnerable is triggering
- Be honest/Honesty can be triggering
- Share all my thoughts/Being this open can be triggering
- Trust another human being /Trust can be triggering

- Be focused on someone else/Focus on another can be triggering
- Trust someone else with my safety/Not feeling safe or in control of our safety can be triggering

Fear of triggers by the submissive and fear of triggering the submissive by the dominant, can make us walk on eggshells to keep from stepping on potential landmines. Yet, walking on eggshells can make a survivor feel broken (at least it makes me feel broken), which is triggering.

Triggers are a huge deal in my world. I don't use the word 'trigger' lightly. It can mean different things for different people. But, it's not just a feeling of being uncomfortable, which is how it seems to be used in today's world. For me, triggers are totally out of control feelings. My triggers involve flashbacks, physical memories, emotional memories, a feeling of being completely out of control. They can be hard to deal with for both Dan and me, and that is the reason why I talk about them and how to handle them. For some of us, the triggers can be so painful that we'll do anything to not experience them. As much as we want to be a follower, the fear of the triggers can be more powerful and really get in the way of full submission or surrender. It's scary.

Neither Dan nor I wanted the reactions to control our destiny. So, we spent a lot of time working through these responses. I would like to point out that it's not something you can just command someone to stop doing. You can't stop them by commanding, 'You will have no more triggers' or 'You will not respond to ____ with flashbacks." It's not like in the movie "Secretary" where the guy told her to stop cutting and she threw her cutting supplies away and just... stopped. It's just not that easy, even if we truly want to obey. It takes time and patience and positive experiences, over and over again, until the positive experiences and new memories of good stuff outweigh the memories of the past. Layers and layers of good memories. The old memories will never go away, but we can calm them down.

Thankfully, Dan did not take on the responsibility of trying to 'fix' me. For one, he didn't see me as broken. I was stuck in a cycle of reaction, but not broken. His goal was to help me be my best self. He saw my light, and he wanted me to see it as well.

He knew the importance of therapy and guided me in that direction so that I could get the help I needed with that past baggage. The Universe was looking out for me when they put Susan, my therapist on and off for 10 years, on my path. With her help and Dan's fortitude and my determination, I not only became a survivor, but a thriver.

That's how I describe myself now, after so many years. I'm a thriver. I don't let the shadow of the past rule me or my reactions to the world. When my actions aren't what Dan expects of me, or what I expect of me for that matter, I start using my tools I've learned over the years. And if they don't work, I ask myself "What is going on? What work still needs to be done? What story is going through my head/ heart? Am I feeling rejected by someone or something? Am I feeling judged?" The judged part doesn't bother me as much as it used to, but even with all the work I've done, the fear of rejection can sometimes raise its ugly head.

What is rejection to me? Well, it's not the same as abandonment. Abandonment is about someone who decides to leave. Abandonment, for me, feels like it's their decision and has to do with something about them. But, rejection... that's more personal. Rejection is about the person judging me as unworthy and then deciding to leave. Or my work being judged as unworthy. Or my contribution to the community, or my service to someone, being judged as unworthy or not-good-enough. That digs under the skin, and sometimes I'll react before knowing what I'm reacting to.

Sometimes the feeling of being rejected interferes with our power exchange without me even realizing it. Currently, after a lot of work, I am more aware of my reactions and body feelings so it's hard for feelings of rejection to sneak up on me. But, I will admit, even after twenty years of doing this self work, it can still smack me out of the blue.

So, I have fears like 'rejection' to work with, and I also have other reactions to work with. A big reaction we worked on was my passive-aggressiveness. It was an automatic response when I was younger. I couldn't show anger or tell someone no, so this tool showed up instead. Nowadays, it's considered snarky. Dan doesn't do snarky. Snarky is meanness hidden as something pretending to be funny.

Now, I can see and feel when that response sneaks up on me. It feels dark and manipulative. It's meant to make someone feel a certain way. That's certainly not how Dan wants me to respond to the world and the people in it. And it's not how I want to respond. So, I catch myself, apologize if it's needed, and find other ways of communicating. Dan will point it out to me as well, and remind me that passive-aggressiveness is manipulative and manipulation won't be tolerated. If I want something, ask for it. If I need to express something, find a way to express it that is more in line with what he expects of his slave - courtesy and graciousness.

A couple of other reactions that were created because of my situation as a child were learning to be hyper aware of my surroundings, never feeling safe, and not trusting anyone. You can imagine, I'm sure, how this would not only affect my interaction with the world on a negative level, but my acceptance of my desire for a power exchange relationship.

What is needed in a power exchange? Trust, feelings of safety, allowing someone else to be in charge, among other qualities. So, even though I knew I wanted to be in this style of relationship, and craved it, it was hard for us at the beginning.

I trust Dan completely, with all of my being. He has proven time and time again that he is trustworthy. I had known him for a long time before we started this relationship, and I knew he had grown into a trustworthy man. Yet, I made him prove he was trustworthy over and over and over again because of my core lack of trust in people. I figured at some point he'd be hiding something, or have an ulterior motive involved. This never happened. He helped me learn that people can be trusted after all.

As a child, I never felt safe. Because of not feeling safe for so many years, and that being part of my developmental years, I still have moments where I don't feel safe. A lot of my actions are based on my concern for my safety. Some of that is valid in this day and age and as a woman, but not to the level I take it in some areas.

One of the hardest things I did when I became Dan's property was to trust him to be responsible for my safety, to trust his wisdom in certain areas. I'm sure some of you understand how hard that can be. I wanted him to be responsible, but having a core distrust of everyone and everything, means I'm always double checking what he's doing. And knowing that he trusts people and situations so easily, makes me second guess his choices. I'm lucky that he allows me to speak up when these moments happen.

Over time, I've learned how to vocalize my concerns. "Sir, may I share with you how I'm feeling about this situation?" or "may I share the story that is stuck in my head?" is something that I can now say with ease. I know he'll listen to what I have to say, realize that I'm right in some situations and wrong in others. He relies on his confidence and experience to make the choices he thinks are right. And if he ends up being wrong, he chalks it up to gaining more experience, apologizing if needed, and fixing the situation. Because he's able to do this, I trust his decisions more.

My hyper-awareness on the other hand can drive him a little nuts. I notice all the little things. If someone has been in my house, I'll know. I can spot every little thing that is out of place. I'm constantly checking our surroundings. I can spot the thing that looks abnormal in a situation. I have stories in my head as to why things are out of place. As a kid, this was a way of protecting myself. A way of staying safer than if I wasn't paying attention. I hear sounds that others don't hear. I can hear or feel someone coming up behind me. And if you are one of the few that can sneak up behind me, prepare to be punched or head-butted from my terrified reaction. And once that adrenaline is pumping, it's hard for me to calm down. Hell, just seeing stuff out of place in or around my house will start the fight/flight/freeze reaction.

That reaction always seems to be just under the surface of everything I do. It seems to be hard-wired in. I worked on this a lot with my therapist and she helped me work through some of it and to recognize when it happens. Self-talk is my friend in these situations.

I will admit that hyper-awareness, used correctly, can be an amazing tool. Not only does it help me in service to him on a personal level, as I'm always aware when he needs something, sometimes before he knows it... it also helps me when producing events, or teaching or with many of the other projects we are involved in. I'm the keeper of lists and details. Many times you will see me at events with a clipboard, making sure everything is on track.

Another thing that helps me a lot when situations like this happen and keeps me from reacting as 'old Dawn' would react, is to remember that Dan considers me to be a reflection of him and his training. I always think about what he expects of me. I literally ask myself, ``What would Master do?" in such a situation. It helps calm me down, so that I can think and make a better choice than 'old Dawn' would make.

I remember the first time I shared this 'What would Master do?' idea with kame bat. I was taking her to an event in Cleveland, her first event. We were on the way up and I realized that I had forgotten to ask Dan about something and get a decision from him before heading to the event. I started to panic. I didn't mean to, but the adrenaline started pumping. I pulled over to the side of the road and texted him. No response. I took some breaths and bat asked what I was going to do. She was really new to this whole power exchange thing and hadn't really spent any time around those that live it as a relationship style. I took a couple more breaths, calmed myself down, closed my eyes and told her that since I could not talk with him, and a decision needed to be made right then, that all I could do was to make the decision that I knew he would make. I had known him long enough that I could make a good guess, and as long as my intention was to guess as to what he would do, I wouldn't get in trouble even if it was the wrong answer. Knowing this would be the result from Dan, made it easier to make a decision. So, I did so. I made a choice, and we went back onto the road to finish the trip.

This was one of those moments when I realized I wasn't behaving as a victim. I was a survivor. And I continue to use that tool today. "What would Master do?"

## Part 2 - Tools We've Developed and Used Through the Years

Our power exchange relationship has been the most powerful tool for my healing from the past. It may not be for everyone, and I'm not trying to say it is. But for me, I tell people it was the best decision I ever made even though I didn't realize at the time how healing it would be. I'm so glad we stuck it out through the hard times.

We've gathered and created a lot of tools for our toolbox over the years that contributed to the goal of thriver. We'd like to share some of them here. You'll hear us talk about these in our polyamory classes, but many of them were specifically needed because of the years I was wired as a victim. It's because I needed to be a survivor for our power exchange relationship to work, that we developed these tools.

These are not in any particular order... except the extra safeword was the first tool we created.

## Extra Safeword

One of the first things we discovered we needed was an extra safeword when we played, or when we spent the weekend in D/s 'Lite' mode. (That's what we called it when we first started experimenting with power exchange while the kids were gone for the weekend.)

We found that if we stepped on a landmine while playing, I needed to be able to share in a simple way that we had done so. Since it's impossible to know all the landmines with a survivor, we wanted a code word so that we could stop and look at what happened and come up with a plan of action.

The word he gave me was 'abort.' It's very different than 'yellow' or 'red.' For us, 'yellow' means slow down and check in. 'Red' means to stop, but for a regular reason. I don't like it… something hurts too much… not in the mood, etc. But, 'abort' means a landmine was stepped on. I'm falling (crashing) into fight/flight or freeze mode, a dark place, not the endorphin driven happy place. I've only had to use it a couple of times over the years. It's an instant reaction from Dan. Everything stops, he knows it's not physical and he wraps me in his arms to calm me down. More emotional care… a different emotional care… is needed if I use that extra word.

Honestly, I hate having to have it, let alone use it. I don't want to be different. But, it was absolutely needed when I used it. Neither of us had a clue a landmine was even possible with what we were doing. Using the word was exactly what was needed though. We were able to work through the situation. With him knowing what I meant with the word, and instantly stopping what we were doing…

that helped build the trust that is needed in this type of relationship.

## The Contract

This is discussed in more depth elsewhere, but I wanted to mention here how important this tool was for me. I was able to help build a consensual designer relationship. I talked about what I wanted and needed. I was able to look at what would help create our relationship and build me as a person and as a follower.

## Commands

There are two commands Dan can use when he sees me spiraling emotionally; *Breathe*, and *Kneel*. These words are anchors that short-circuit my emotional response. Because I want to please him, my brain will latch onto the word.

If he says *'Kneel,'* I instantly kneel. My knees feel the solid floor/ground beneath me. At this point, I know nothing else is expected of me. I kneel and breathe. He may put a hand on my head to help ground me and remind me to stay in the present. He may not. I have to learn to help myself. I have to remember to breathe, and bring my thoughts back to the now.

Use what works for you. These came to Dan intuitively. He was frustrated that I just couldn't stop the spiral. He took control and the word that popped out of his mouth was a firm, don't question me, *'Kneel.'* I dropped to my knees. Bam. We had a new tool. Go with your intuition.

## Grounding

This one is huge for me. Oddly enough, when we started our Power Exchange relationship, I also started my current spiritual path. One of the first things I was taught, and one of the first things I teach others, is how to ground. This can be the commands above that Dan uses with me, or literally standing on the ground or against a tree, feeling their solidness. Breathing is grounding. Placing my hand on my stomach and feeling my breath is grounding. Anything that makes me feel my body in the present, is grounding to me. Sometimes Dan will wrap his hands around my wrists to remind me where I'm at, and that I'm his. That will usually snap my head/emotions into place.

## Anchors

Did you know that a collar can be an anchor? Ask a slave/sub/follower what their collar means to them. Ask them to take it off and see their reaction, beyond just being offended at the question.

My collar is my anchor. When I'm feeling emotional, I can reach up and hold onto that chain around my neck, reminding myself who I am and where I'm at. It gives me comfort. It reminds me that I'm worthy.

And it doesn't need to be a collar. I'm betting that has something to do with the feeling of wearing chastity devices, or slave bracelets, or chains. It's a physical thing that we can touch and feel. It's an anchor to the present moment and to who we are.

For some, I've even suggested stones in their pockets,

coins, anything solid that can be reached easily in case of an emotional spiral. Use what works for you.

## Change the Story

The biggest story that we need to change is the one of being the victim. If we label ourselves or think of ourselves as victims, we will base all our decisions with this in mind. A victim feels powerless and at the mercy of others.

We need to change the story. I am no longer a victim, I am a survivor. And survivors handle life differently than victims. Survivors have reclaimed their power.

Then, once we are able to handle life as a survivor, we can move on to thriver. Flourish in our life.

For example, a survivor can have low self-esteem, feel unworthy and full of shame. As a survivor, this can move to seeing yourself as wounded and healing. Then, as a thriver, this shifts to seeing self as an overflowing miracle. That's what happened to me. It wasn't a quick process. It took a long time to change the story. But, it's possible. I did it with self work and a patient Master throughout the process.

Another story some of us may need to change is the one where we believe that we were the reason the abuse and/or trauma happened to us. This is unfortunate but how it works, especially if our perp wanted us to believe that.

Because of this, we may be left with the feeling of being responsible, or being weak, or unworthy, or even unlovable. These feelings and beliefs can be very hard to work through.

After a lot of work with my therapist and somatic

therapist, they helped me to change the story that had been in my head for so long.

## Reframing

Reframing works hand in hand with 'Changing the Story.' This was a big one for me. Sometimes it's as simple as stating, "Dan is not my perpetrator from the past." Though the statement is simple, it doesn't mean it's an instant change. For me, it was years of repeating the same line and reminding myself.

To this day there are things that will catch me by surprise. The memories will pop up unbidden. I have to breathe, slow down my thinking before my body runs away with the emotion. I have to change the story, reminding myself that I'm in the present.

Trauma distorts our thinking. For me, I automatically don't trust people and think they are wanting something from me. It's easy for me to get into the mindset that my outlook is the only way to look at a problem. Reframing taught me to ask myself questions like, "Is there another way to look at this situation?" or, "What are some other possible reasons this could have happened?" Pointing out alternatives can help me see things from another view.

This is where having a Master that can see when reframing a situation is needed, comes in handy. If Dan sees me upset and stuck on a particular thought about why something is happening, he will point it out, and show me another point of view. Knowing that my thoughts are not necessarily the truth of the situation is big in helping me see the situation differently so that I don't spiral.

## Mantra

Developing a mantra isn't a new or original idea. But this tool was very important to me at the beginning of our relationship, when I was working on my healing path and it was getting in the way of me being in the 'now.' As I stated at the beginning of this chapter, some of the core structure of our power exchange relationship was difficult and triggering. Plus, I was new on my healing path and working on some deep, dark memories.

I can remember having a hard time one night and thinking that I was going to have to give up on the power exchange dynamic because I just couldn't handle the feelings it caused. I certainly didn't want a non-power exchange relationship, but not being in control of what was going on around me was terrifying.

And being terrified was not good for my emotions. The spiral had begun.

I was driving around the outer belt of Columbus, OH. It's about a 45 minute ride and I used to do it when I needed to think out loud. I'm an external processor and need to vocally get thoughts out of my head. Well, this evening all I could think of was how I must be driving Dan crazy. I was depressed and anxious, feeling like a failure when I questioned commands, and just feeling high-maintenance overall.

On that drive, I yelled at myself. I had to get the thoughts out of my head to process them, and that involved yelling. I was able to work through the shame and guilt by throwing the words into the air and looking for truth in them. Then, I asked myself what the truth of the situation really was.

The truth that I knew deep in my heart, regardless of all the other crap that was in my head, was that Dan loved me. He might have been stressed with everything we were working through, but he loved me.

Not only that, but I knew I could trust him. He had worked very hard at the beginning and through the time I was in therapy, to make sure I knew that I could trust him. For a survivor, at least with me, trust isn't automatic. It comes through experience.

The next word that popped up as truth was faith. I had faith in us. I felt the Universe had faith in us. Things felt like they were the way they were supposed to be, regardless of the tough times we were going through.

So, I had three words that felt like I could see them written in neon: Love, Trust, Faith. I chanted these words to myself until I calmed down. Many times later, these words would become my anchor to calm me down when I was full of doubts.

## **WAM** (What about me?)

This tool was a HUGE discovery for us. WAM is short for 'What About Me?" To a lesser extent, we also use the words "blip" or "hiccup." This tool is pretty much about recognition. Recognition of what is going on during a spiral.

I was having a moment one day and was processing out loud one day with Dan, loudly. I was trying to explain my brain and thoughts and feelings. I was in a rough moment and I just couldn't get to the nugget of how I was feeling, except that it was heavy and dark and confusing and not how I wanted to feel or think, and I just couldn't find the correct words to explain what was going on with my reaction to the situation... I don't even remember what the situation was that had me in such a spiral. The words that kept coming out of my mouth were 'what about me?'

Of course, he wasn't hearing everything else I was trying to express, because the question 'What about me?' was what he was trying to answer. But, that wasn't the real issue at hand, and neither of us knew that. I realized that every time I said that, or thought that phrase, I would have a crappy feeling in the pit of my belly. Heavy. Dark. Something was wrong. I mentioned this to Dan. And I started putting things together.

After working with my somatic therapist, I remembered that triggers can show up as body feelings. Wait a minute, was this a clue that I was in a triggered moment? We weren't just having an argument, I was responding to a trigger - and not only was my body giving me a clue, but so was my brain with the 'what about me?' response.

I started looking at my past responses to uncomfortable moments. Shit. I didn't even know my anger and frustration was coming from victim responses. I thought I was angry at current stuff, but instead it was stuff that was reminding me of the past and I was reacting to the past. My body had been talking to me this whole time. I just didn't know the language.

Now, when I hear the voice in my head asking 'what about me?' or I feel that heavy feeling in the pit of my stomach, I can recognize what is going on. Usually I'll tell Dan that I'm having a WAM moment. This is a code to him that my responses aren't based in the present moment. I breathe, and he asks if I know how he can help. Sometimes I have an answer for him of how he can help, sometimes just the recognition of what is going on is all it takes for me to reframe things, or change the story.

WAM is usually a large response, whereas blip or hiccup are the words I use to describe a smaller trigger response. Such as, when Dan tells me he's going out with his girlfriend. Oops, there's that feeling in the pit of my stomach, a tightening. Dan sees my reaction. "Is something wrong?" he asks. "Just a blip moment," I respond. Again, that tells him that he is correct with what he saw or felt with my reaction, and I can admit to it as a moment of reaction that isn't based on the current moment. (More on this in the shorthand section.)

Dan has learned to recognize these moments within his own reactions as well.

## Journal

The kind of journal I'm talking about here is one that is *not* private. This is where you can document your feelings and thoughts, but it is open for your Dominant to read. This was very valuable in our early years. I bought a red velvet book and wrote a lot. Dan would reply to each entry that he felt the desire to respond to. His responding wasn't an expectation with each entry. It was a way of him getting to know how the thoughts in my head worked. I pretty much did free-form writing as any thoughts came to me.

This can be difficult. When spiraling, the thoughts you put on paper and then look at in ink… yeah, those were hard to share. I found out that I had hidden my true thoughts from the world for a long time. But, it was good to get it all out and have someone read it, and see how powerful writing it all down and sharing it was.

Dan was able to see why I would have issues with following him and understand that it wasn't about him, or us. Sometimes you can 'hear' things easier in writing than verbally.

In later years, we did this through a document online. Personally, I liked the physical journal better, but doing it online meant we could access it anywhere at any time instead of keeping track of the velvet book, which was usually locked away because of having kids at home.

## Working Journal

I love this tool because it's something physical that I can do. Something other than changing how I think about something, which a lot of our tools are about. With a working journal, I write things down that I try and then keep track of whether they work or not.

For example, say I'm feeling triggered, so I walk outside and put my feet in the grass to ground myself and my emotions. I breathe and concentrate on my breath. Did this work? Document it in the working journal. Did it not work now, but has in the past? What was different? What did I try instead? Did I try the other tools?

I may talk about these things with Dan. He likes to keep track of what I've tried and what works and doesn't, but this isn't a journal that I share with him like the one above. It includes elements of:

- What happened?
- How did I feel?
- What did I do to try to resolve the reaction?
- Did it work?

## Meditation

Along with being in a power exchange relationship, meditation is the second most powerful tool we've come across. It is a way of training your brain to slow down. It helps you recognize stories are happening, and gives you a chance to stop them. It helps to create a sense of mindfulness.

Mindfulness is all about being in the moment. And when you are in the moment, you aren't living in the past or afraid of the future. It's all about being in the present. Mindfulness is so big and important that we will give it it's own chapter in the book.

Obviously, not all these tools are going to work for everyone. Take what you like and leave the rest. Modify them to work for you. Keep a look out for others that present themselves to you personally, in your readings, in your therapy, in your dynamic.

# Part 3 - What Does Being a Thriver Look Like?

## I am a Thriver

I'm sure some of you have heard of that term "thriver" and I'm going to give you a definition, but what does it look like?

One definition of a thriver is someone that flourishes, living life to the best degree possible. For me, as a thriver, I have embraced new skills that help me live a more balanced life. I've done the work as a survivor, learned new skills, have put a lot of the past behind me, and can embrace future possibilities with excitement. I've blossomed.

Visually, as a victim, I was cocooned in a hard shell, numb to the world, in my own bubble of protection. As a survivor, the shell had started to crack, showing some light from within, allowing me to feel some of the world and let people in. As a thriver, I've thrown off the shell, light shining bright!

As a thriver, one of the attitudes I've learned to embrace is equanimity. I've actually embraced this as a calling. I strive for equanimity in all my actions and reactions. What is equanimity? As a victim and survivor, I couldn't tell you with any confidence what it meant, because I hadn't had much experience with it.

Equanimity is a mental calmness, composure, and evenness of temper, especially in a difficult situation. Me, calm? That is not a description that was ever used to describe me. Angry? Sure. Abrasive? Absolutely. Ready to bite the head off anyone that crossed my path or I felt was treating me wrong? Hear me roar! Dan knew me back then. He can tell you some stories. My kids can tell you stories of us going through drive-thru at fast food places. They hated it.

One of the reasons I was drawn to a power exchange relationship with Dan is that I knew he wouldn't stand for that type of behavior. And I didn't want to be that victim person anymore. So, after time developing this power exchange relationship, working with my counselors, studying my spiritual path, and perseverance, here I am. For the most part, it's a natural state of being for me. I do a lot of 'changing the story' and 'reframing.' And on great days, it's just my way of being without needing the tools.

I've become ambitious, courageous, fearless, grounded, joyous, playful, resilient, gracious, and grateful, just to name a few. I have expanded beyond the confines of being a victim or even a survivor.

If you can visualize… I was a victim, curled in a ball at the bottom of a hill wondering what was the use of even trying to climb the hill. As a survivor I decided it was worth the climb. There had to be something better at the top. After years of doing the work, and climbing that hill, I've reached the top. As a thriver, I get to dance at the top of the mountain, feeling the warmth of the sun, being kissed by the breeze, dancing in joy, feeling love and loving, open to what life has to offer.

As a victim, I took it personally each time Dan corrected me. I had to drag myself through the days, wondering why he would want to be with me when I was so much work. I cried a lot. I resisted commands a lot, wondering if he had my best interest at heart. As a survivor, I had started the healing path, but still stumbled a lot, still didn't understand some attitudes, still would hide from the world on occasion, wondering if all the work was worth it. As a thriver, I'm confident in who I am as a person and as a follower. I've chosen the right Leader, the right lifestyle, the right path.

## Part 4 - How Leaders/Doms/Masters Can Help

There are various things that a Leader can do to help out a follower that has baggage from past trauma. As I stated before, not everything will work for everyone, but there are some basics that should be kept in mind.

### Don't treat a survivor like they are broken

The most important thing that Dan did for me was to not treat me like I was broken, or even let me talk about being a victim or being broken. Well, he'd let me talk about it, but he wouldn't agree with me. As someone that lived as a victim for a long time, if he had agreed that I was broken or would be nothing but a victim, that would have destroyed me. I needed someone that could see my light, see my struggles, but know that I was trying to pull myself out of the dark, see that I was someone special that was good enough to be his.

That's literally what he would tell me, that I couldn't be as bad as I thought I was, because he had chosen me, and he trusted his judgment and intuition. And because I trusted him so much, how could he be wrong? That was the beginning of me re-writing my story of who I was. It wasn't an instant change, but each time I had doubt about myself, he would tell me again that he chose me because he believed in my strength and my courage, even when I didn't believe in myself. Over time, these layers of belief helped create who I am today.

## You are not a therapist

Another thing that Dan took very seriously was the fact that he was not a therapist. He would offer advice, but knew his limitations. And he was confident enough in himself, that he was able to say 'I don't know what's best for you right now, make an appointment with a therapist.' He didn't require me to go see a therapist, but did command that I make an appointment. Smart Master that he is, he knew that making the appointment was the hardest thing for me to do, so I needed a shove. And he knew that as a follower, I really wanted to obey him and make him proud of me.

So, I followed through with making the appointment. I got lucky and found someone through my women's drumming circle. I made the appointment and followed through with the first visit. I ended up seeing Susan on and off for 10 years.

## Be confident

After a few years with my therapist she suggested Paul, a somatic counselor. I was terrified of working with a man and working with body issues. I was scared that I would be 'fixed' enough that I wouldn't enjoy BDSM anymore. Why I thought that, I have no idea. My enjoyment of BDSM is totally separate from what happened to me in the past.

But, I had no idea of what to expect with the therapy. I actually thought that since Paul was an Aikido (form of martial arts) instructor as well, that I would fight back in the scene. Dan and I talked about it. My journey towards becoming a survivor was more important to him than our play time. Like he said, we'd figure out how to deal with it if it became an issue. He was totally supportive of my journey, and totally confident of our power exchange dynamic.

Survivors can't just 'get over it.' There are reasons that victims of abuse can't just 'get over it.' If it's something that happened in childhood, mis-wiring happens during the trauma. The trauma literally changes how the brain responds to stress hormones. Many of us get stuck in a fight or flight mode and our bodies constantly pump cortisol as a result, The body goes into survival mode, which compromises normal emotional, cognitive, and mental development. This is why therapy and other tools are so important. It can help us survivors get over these challenges.

I'm proof of that. It may take time, but with patience, it is possible. No matter how good of a Master you are though, you can't just tell a survivor to get over it and they obey. This isn't 'Secretary.' As a matter of fact, if you tell them to get over it, knowing they can't, you've just set them up for failure. Bad form.

## Be willing to deal with landmines

Know this - triggers are going to happen. After all this time on my healing path, I still have triggers. At least today I know what they are, what they feel like, and I can deal with them easier. They happen and we don't always know what will cause them, which is why some can be landmines. You are walking along, no clue what lies in wait and then bam… everything spins out of control. Keep your cool.

I can remember when Dan and I were in the middle of a scene, no clue that things were getting ready to get knocked sideways. I hear a noise and totally freeze. It takes a moment for Dan to realize something is wrong. I'm not responding. He's not even sure if I'm breathing. Instantly I'm in flight mode and my way of flight is by freezing, hide, don't draw attention to myself.

This was totally unexpected and he'd never seen me respond like this before. The scene is over. He lays next to me and just talks to me softly. He tells me I'm safe and is able to bring me out of it. We are able to talk about it later, to see if it's something we want to try again. This is where he gave me the extra safe word. Knowing that I can say 'abort' to signal a triggered response is happening, might have made me vocal enough to be able to speak up and give him a clue as to what is going on.

Even after moments like this, he doesn't treat me like I'm broken. He doesn't run away. He stays with me until we get through the challenge. Because of this, I've learned to trust him deeply. He is there for me. I can surrender to him in so many ways because of this knowledge and experience.

It doesn't have to be a scene that can cause landmines. Remember all the things I listed at the beginning of the chapter that a power exchange relationship is about? Even obeying a command or anything else on that list can cause an unknown landmine reaction. Be confident enough to deal with it, even if you have to fake it til you make it. They need to know you have their back.

## Don't walk on eggshells

Knowing that landmines can happen, it's still important not to walk on eggshells. At least, that's the way it is with me. As a compassionate person, that was Dan's first response. But, our power exchange dynamic is the foundation of our relationship. So, if he becomes too… soft… it pokes holes in our foundation. If he lets me get away with things, I don't feel like I'm a follower any more, or worthy of being a follower. I need him to hold me accountable for my actions. Even if I can't control my emotions, he expects me to control my behavior. He will remind me that I am a reflection of him and his training. My actions matter.

If Dan walks on eggshells, I feel broken. If it comes across that he doesn't trust me to do better, then I'm going to feel like a failure, and my brain will spiral with the beginning thought of, 'who wants a failure for a slave?' I need him to believe that I can do better.

And this doesn't take much. It can be a simple command of *'Kneel'* when I'm having a difficult time. This gives me a simple command to obey. And obeying him is my highest priority, even in challenging moments. My agreements with him are very important, and I know they are the lifeblood of our relationship. Once I'm on my knees, he will usually tell me to breathe. I'm sure he's taking a breath as well, as he settles in to deal with the situation.

## You may need your own support network

Masters are not all-powerful, having all the answers to every situation, and full of unlimited energy so they can deal with every situation. There will be times of uncertainty and confusion of how to deal with a situation as a Leader. You'll be able to research some ideas of how to be a partner. Ideas are everywhere from online to the grocery store checkout line magazines, but these are written for the egalitarian partner, not the Leader in a power exchange relationship with certain responsibilities. Hell, most self-help books for couples and relationships are not designed for a hierarchical relationship.

You'll need to find another Leader in a similar situation to bounce ideas off of, or just to chat with and maybe even vent to if that's your thing. This situation can be taxing, and you may need the support to deal with the heavy times, if this relationship is important to you.

You may also need your own therapist, as dealing with your follower's triggers can trigger your own stuff. I could make the same list for Masters that I made for slaves at the beginning of this chapter, and it could also cause triggers for the Master. Don't let it rule how you Lead.

## Be careful of cathartic scenes

I'm not saying not to do them. But, I am saying to be careful. Regardless of how good of a top or dom you are, things can go wrong, and you'll end up dealing with someone's emotional and mental state. If landmines happen, you have to be willing to put the energy into putting the sub back together again.

Even if a noticeable landmine doesn't happen, there is the possibility that the survivor will transfer their feelings of the event or perpetrator onto you, the facilitator of the scene. We learned this from my somatic counselor. Dan came to one of my appointments to see what Paul was doing with me. It was some simple but powerful exercises. Dan offered to continue the practices at home. Paul was adamant that this not happen. In his experience, if Dan triggered me on purpose like Paul did, and wasn't able to pull me out of it, I could forever associate him with my past trauma. Paul the therapist was willing to take this chance because I could walk away from him at any time, if I felt unsafe. With Dan, it could cause me to never feel safe around him again. It could destroy our relationship.

## Part 5 - Advice for Survivors

So, I have some advice for the survivors. Even with the tools I've given you, and the tools your therapist will give you, and with the support of your Leader, this is not going to be easy. Yet, it's totally worth all the work. Your power exchange relationship can help you through this.

## Obey

This is the simplest thing you can do. They tell you to kneel, kneel. You might have a temptation to resist. Don't. If you resist, it will affect the foundation of your power exchange. Your power exchange relationship should be giving you strength during this time. Obeying will help fortify your foundation.

## Be Understanding

Be understanding of yourself and your Leader. They are not a professional. And as much as you may want them to be, they are not God. They are fallible, do not have magical answers, and have their own issues to deal with. Sometimes your triggers may trigger them. You have to work together and you as a victim/survivor have to put in the work.

## Recognize Triggers

Learn to recognize your triggers and remember that those emotions you are feeling now, belong in the past. Even though they feel real, they are not based in the present moment, and therefore do not serve you in the present moment. Most triggers can be felt in your body when they happen. I feel mine in the pit of my stomach and some of the words in my head are 'what about me?'

Where do you feel yours? What trigger phrase do you have? When I feel the feeling and hear the words, I can tell Dan that I'm having a WAM moment and he knows what that means and will usually ask if there is any way he can help, or will tell me to kneel so that I can breathe through it. Find what works for you.

## Don't Think of Yourself as a Victim

If you think of yourself as a victim, whether you use the actual word or not, your 'self' will hold onto that label, resisting change. It will white-knuckle onto all the fears of the past and fears of the future. It will make up stories to fit the victim persona. It will be a self-fulfilling prophecy, and fight against any progress you might make towards being a survivor.

You may have been a victim in the past, and developed methods of surviving being a victim. But you are no longer in that situation. You are a survivor. You survived something and came out on the other side. So, don't let your 'victim self' control your life. Create a new label for yourself that your psyche can work with. Survivor. And after putting in the work to recognize all the ways the 'victim' has controlled your life, and you feel comfortable with knowing you are a survivor, take that next step to become a thriver.

Turn, "but I can't do that because it scares me, or reminds me of something" to "Yes Sir/Ma'am, I can do that" and embrace all the joy and pride that comes with being able to do the things you couldn't do in 'victim' mode.

## Seek Professional Help

Interview therapists. They work for you and you don't need to stay with one that doesn't understand your trauma, or the results of your trauma. Therapists go to different schools with different focuses. Some are religious, some not. All of them are biased about something. Keep this in mind.

If you can find a therapist that is not only aware of power exchange dynamics but has a positive outlook on non-normative relationships, so much the better. Otherwise you may be spending all your time defending the validity of your consensual relationship choice. After my therapist of 10 years retired, I interviewed 5 more therapists before finding a match. For me, I feel my recovery is an obligation towards my personal health and the health of our relationship.

So, I hope you didn't read this as all doom and gloom. Yes, coming into a new relationship can be daunting when you have past baggage. Yes, being the Leader of someone with trauma baggage can be a bit of a challenge. It will involve work and understanding from both of you. But, a power exchange relationship is the perfect foundation for this. There are consensual agreements, transparency, honesty, trust, and expectations.

This is why I say that our power exchange relationship was my savior. It certainly wasn't meant to be. We got into it because of the kinky aspect and the erotica we'd been reading. My healing was a side effect of what we'd built.

## Dan's Comment

### *Dan Says*

I am at a loss for words, which isn't what anyone wants to hear when they are co-writing a book. But the above is a skillful reflection of the journey that dawn has been on that started with her teaching a class on being a survivor. That first class, over fifteen years ago, was the first time dawn spoke up in a bunch of peers - these happened to be Leather folk - and admitted to having been a victim of some pretty serious shit.

Although afterwards dawn suffered through some triggers - dredging up the past is not easy - she stuck with it, revising this class and continuing on her own healing journey. Now she is able to say, without doubt, that she is not only a survivor, but a thriver as well. And she did that so she can say "and you can be too." She continues to do so in classes around the nation. Her experience with trauma has become something she uses to teach others how to get through - and beyond - their own trauma.

My role in all this has never been complex. She outlined it above, but beyond that, it is to simply see her as who she is, never who she was. She is my follower, slave, wife, lover, friend, belet. I don't allow her to slip into who she was. I continue to emphasize who she wants to be, who I want her to be, and the path to become that.

# Submissive Vs Wife

## *dawn says*

Though someone can be both a follower and a spouse, as I am, I must say I had some really hard times with wearing both labels at the beginning of our relationship.

At the beginning, Dan and I decided that our relationship dynamic was going to have a foundation of power exchange. I was nervous and excited at the same time. I'd already tried a 'normal' white picket fence, pretend-egalitarian style of relationship with my past husband. That didn't work, and it certainly wasn't what I wanted this time around.

Though they say mainstream, 'normal' relationships are 50/50 or egalitarian... they really aren't. At least that's my experience. Most 'normal' relationships I've been part of or witnessed seem to be full of power struggle over what really counts as equal. For me, this always led to resentment. Who was supposed to take care of the kids, the house? He thought I should, and I thought he should help... there was daily struggle, based on how our parents lived, or how the media showed us we were supposed to relate.

Not only was it about power struggle based on expectations of what spouses are supposed to do in a relationship according to our parents or TV and movies, but marriages also seem to be about hiding mistakes or not sharing fantasies. That's because all this knowledge can be used against you. Why in the world would I want to be in that type of relationship again? Of course, not all marriages are like that, but my experience tells me for every one that isn't, I can list many many more that are.

So, I wanted something different in this relationship. Power exchange excited me for many reasons. Not only do I find dominance and submission super hot, but I was also enjoying the whole process of consciously designing our relationship. We were looking deep within ourselves to build something that would work for both of us. Time was being spent on looking at our needs, wants, and desires, and making sure they were shared with each other and added to our contract that we were writing.

We were discussing rules and expectations and duties and all that stuff that we wanted in place, and agreed to before the collaring. We were designing our fantasy relationship with intent… tweaking the design so that it would work in the real world. Power struggle would no longer be a thing, well, for the most part. And since we didn't really know anyone that was living a dynamic like this, we could create what we wanted. We certainly didn't have tabloids or supermarket magazines or TV shows telling us how to relate as a power exchange couple, right or wrong. We would create what we wanted, defining our own expectations, our own communication tools, and more.

After a year and a half of trying out this relationship style in our D/s 'Lite' moments, and creating a contract that worked for us, Dan officially collared me. This was an ordeal ritual that I had to make it through the other side of. After making it through the ordeal ritual, I was now his, wearing his collar, which I still wear to this day. What a feeling! Dom and sub was the language we used then, and it felt so right. I can still feel the tingle of that moment.

At that point we were no longer D/s 'Lite.' Full-time power exchange became our focus. Continuing to build that foundation became our focus. My brain tried to stay on track with my feelings and would be in logistical mode a lot as we created this new dynamic.

How did we interact? The way we had agreed to in the contract. Why was I obeying? Because it was fulfilling to me and what I had agreed to. How did it feel to clean out his car or make his bed or pick up his socks? I loved it. It's a very different feeling to take care of someone as an act of loving service, compared to picking up after someone who expects you to because you are their wife. My service was an expression of my love for him.

Then, our world turned upside down. Nothing super drastic… well, yes it was. Dan was laid off from work, and I became the breadwinner. He lost his health insurance. My company didn't have insurance available for domestic partners, which is legally what we were. No one recognizes a collaring as having any significance. It's a commitment ceremony, but not a joining in the eyes of the law or my company. What to do?

We had agreed at the beginning of our relationship that neither of us wanted to get married again. That wasn't in the plans. It didn't fit with our designer relationship. But, we were in a situation we hadn't thought we'd be in. Yes, layoffs happen, but this was our first experience with them, and he needed health insurance.

After discussing it, we decided that marriage was the least complicated option. And marriage wouldn't be all that bad, would it? We had been living together for almost two years, owned a house together, were raising kids… it's like we were already married, wasn't it? But, it wasn't.

Dan asked me to marry him, not knowing how I'd answer. We were in the dungeon where we'd had our collaring ceremony, so of course I said 'yes.' But, later it hit me. Getting married meant I was going to be a wife. His wife, yes. But still a wife. I didn't like that feeling. Didn't like that feeling at all. My whole belly twisted up in a knot. I was his sub. We had a great foundation built. I didn't want to be a wife, but it was the right thing to do in our situation.

I was so stressed out and it bothered me so much that I ended up talking to my therapist about it. Being aware of power exchange but not totally understanding it, she tried to get me to see that nothing would change. But, it would. I could already feel the change within me. The expectations the world has on the label 'wife' are different than what our community had on a sub, slave, or follower. As a wife, if I followed Dan without question, there would be so much judgment from the outer world. Or at least, I thought there would be. And if not from the outside world, then from my inner self. Labels have a way of changing us just in their very nature, regardless of what we think about them.

I wanted what we had created. My therapist convinced me that it would be ok. She had met Dan, knew of our dynamic, and knew that he had a lot of faith in our foundation. I still couldn't get over the idea that it was all going to blow up.

Dan and I talked a lot about this fear. And we made the decision to be courageous and walk through the fear. That was our motto a lot back then, "walk through the fear." We had to have trust that it was going to be ok on the other side. So, that's what we did. We went to Las Vegas and eloped. As a side note, oddly enough, we got married in the same chapel as his parents did. We didn't know that until we sent a picture of our wedding to his Dad. Of all the chapels in Vegas, what are the odds? The Universe is so funny sometimes.

The morning of our scheduled ceremony, we still hadn't written our vows. We didn't want to go with the standard vows that would be provided. We'd both already done that in the past and they are so generic that I don't know that they have any meaning at all. We wanted our vows to be personal, but weren't sure of what to say. We were eating at a Vegas buffet with the kids, and realized we had to write them there while the kids ate. We were out of time before the ceremony. Have you ever been to a Vegas breakfast buffet? If so, you'll be able to picture all the noise and motion. Finally, vows are written on scraps of paper, or maybe it was a napkin, I don't remember. Breakfast done, we headed to the chapel, neither of us sharing what we had written.

We've been waiting outside the chapel with the kids and it's finally our turn. We are standing in front of the preacher and we get to the part where we say our vows. Surprise, surprise… in Dan's vows to me, he talked about how he would always take care of me. In my vows I stated that I would follow him anywhere and I was completely his. The preacher looked at us kind of funny. In this day and age, I doubt he hears stuff like that anymore. But, at that moment, hearing what we were promising each other, I knew we were going to be ok.

We had a couple of slip-ups after that… "But I'm your wife!"... "No, you are my sub and you will do as I say, like you agreed to"... boom… back on track.

Our power exchange is our foundation. Our collaring is the anniversary we celebrate each year. Our marriage is legal paperwork for the benefits that a married couple receive, and will help protect us in the future if something happens to one of us.

# The Punishment Dynamic in Power Exchange

## Why Bother With Punishment?

### *Dan says*

In our relationship, not only do we have punishment, but we also clarify the differences between correction, discipline, and punishment. But why bother? In the past ten years, we've seen the no-punishment dynamic version of power exchange gain a lot of momentum, including people whose approach to power exchange and relationships we greatly respect.

As we explored this with those peers, we've come to see that this is often a matter of terminology. For example, one couple we chatted with is very clear they don't have a punishment dynamic. But the Leader has clear expectations and, if the follower does not meet them, there are consequences.

The thing most people get tripped up on is thinking that punishment is physical (spanking or pinching or kneeling on legos). Those are simply options. But so are letters of apology, clearly repeating back why a situation was not acceptable, or denial of being allowed to serve (another part of this book includes a list of both physical and non-physical punishment ideas).

The other thing is that punishment is used for is... well, to punish. If you scold your child for running into the street without looking, your desire isn't to make them feel bad, but to stress the gravity of the situation. When I punish dawn, it isn't to make her suffer; instead it is to clearly align her with my expectations and to emphasize that she has strayed from them.

In my opinion, whether you have a punishment or non-punishment power exchange dynamic isn't really important, nor does it suggest that your relationship is solid or not. What does matter is that the Leader has standards, communicates them, and holds the follower accountable to following them. And if they don't, the Leader responds in an appropriate way that drives greater accountability from that follower. For some, a quick pinch on the thigh. For others, the look of disappointment and a simple 'do better' is the best tool.

### *dawn says*

There are a couple of reasons I like punishment being part of our dynamic and why I'm ok with defining it as having a punishment dynamic. It doesn't mean that I want to be punished. Or do I? Let me explain.

There was a time that I was punished at a small Leather gathering. I had done something wrong. It wasn't with intent of malice but it was something wrong that needed to be corrected. Even though I didn't like being corrected in front of everyone, for me, it was much better than seeing the wrong thing, knowing that he saw the wrong thing, and then him doing nothing about it. I would have beaten myself up all evening. I would have not only beaten myself up, but knowing that he'd seen it, I would have felt the energy of his disappointment. That would have messed up the whole evening.

Dan's decision to take care of it right then and there, making me kneel and calling me out on it, fixed the moment. Yes, I was disappointed in myself for allowing that thing to happen. Yes, I knew he was disappointed when I saw the emotion cross his face. But, it was taken care of then and there. Done.

And I've learned with Dan, that when punishment is done, it's done. We may talk about it later, but it's done. I can let it go. Atonement made. Done. For me, that's one of the benefits of punishment.

That doesn't mean that I'm into being punished for the sake of being punished. It doesn't thrill me or excite me in the least. I'd be ok with serving him in such a way that I never have to be punished again. I strive for perfection.

But, I also don't necessarily want him ignoring something that he doesn't think is right. Correct me, absolutely. Discipline me, if you have to. Punish me. I strive not to have that happen but I accept it when it does. It's what I asked for, and what we agreed upon.

It's been years since I've had to be punished. And I'm

ok with that. It means when it does happen, it's for a serious matter. I will never do something just for the attention of punishment. It's not play to us.

A few years ago, we had someone tell us that they didn't believe we were in a power exchange relationship because they had never seen Dan punish me. Good! That means I've learned what he wants and needs and am following through with my part of the agreement.

## Correction, Discipline, Punishment

***Dan says***

As the Leader in a power exchange relationship, I am responsible for making sure the relationship not only runs well, but runs the way I deem it should run. This means I have the responsibility to correct things when they are not running well - either my own actions, or the actions of my follower. And whether it is a loving relationship style of power exchange, service based, or more of a military mindset, the tools of accountability I use for my follower are the same - correction, discipline, and punishment.

## Correction

Nothing kills a power exchange relationship quicker than complacency. Ignoring those little things is, well, easy. It doesn't take power, you don't have to do anything, and after all, it is just a little thing. So what if you wanted your follower to remind you at 9:30 to take your meds, when they did a great job the last five or ten nights in a row? Or if the bed isn't made? Or if the dog wasn't taken for a walk when you got home and you ended up doing it?

Correction is what I use to address times like this. Correction is about 'the thing.' Not about the follower who didn't remember the thing - we are, no matter how long we've been doing power exchange, (or relationships at all,) merely human. And thus, we will forget things. Leaders and followers alike. Elsewhere in the book we will address how to correct those Leaders! But for our followers, we realize that sometimes intent is good, but they just plain forgot. Correction is not intended to make them feel bad or chastised, but to acknowledge you (and in truth, you both) have high standards for yourselves.

And that you are paying attention. Part of the power exchange is your follower makes the bed. And you, Leader, notice that it is made. Or not. So instead of just thinking to yourself 'ah, one night of the bed not being made isn't worth mentioning,' you speak up and say 'By the way, you forgot to make the bed,' which tells your follower you are engaged and paying attention. I would likely continue that sentence with 'and you've been doing very well with that task I gave you, but tonight you must have forgotten. Let's not make a habit of that.' And they acknowledge, and it is done. No big deal.

## Discipline

In the scenario where not only was the bed not made tonight but it wasn't made last night as well, or the daily cup of coffee I am expecting isn't happening every other day, or when I give my follower a new task or command they do not implement it, then we move to discipline. Where correction is about 'the thing,' discipline is about the person and a lack of attention.

Often in these situations, when it is pointed out, I'll hear excuses that sound like 'I forgot' but are really 'Something else had my attention and I did not manage my priorities appropriately.' For discipline, the conversation isn't that dissimilar to what I might say in a correction, but the setting changes. I have my follower totally stop whatever they are doing, to sit (or kneel) with me, and give me their full attention. I then clearly state what it was I expected, and what they will provide moving forward, and get clear acknowledgment of their understanding.

I will not listen to any excuses, but will ask if there are any 'blockers' - items that may prevent or impede the implementation of my command. And if the answer is yes, I ask them if they want my input on how to fix it, or I just fix it. If the problem is they are too involved in a PC game or TV show, I might command them to engage after all the tasks are complete. You might have been expecting the discipline to be taking the thing (PC game, TV show) away. That is on the table. But not my first response. This isn't some horrible thing they've done after all, just an area where we need to move focus. The key to both correction and discipline is that they are not done with poor intent.

## Punishment

Where correction and discipline are about the thing in question or the attention to the action, punishment is about the dynamic. It is rare in a healthy power exchange relationship. Often I've had years go by without punishment. I have punished dawn, who I've been with for 20+ years as of the writing of this chapter, no more than five times. And I can only remember two.

Punishment is when you need to fully step up and make it absolutely fucking clear without any doubt who is in charge. Or, put another way, that this is a power exchange relationship. Any flexibility or cooperative aspects are, when it comes down to it, at your whim. That it is, after all is said and done, my way or the highway; that when push comes to shove, you'll shove.

Now, if you know me and my relationship with dawn, you know we are a team and we work together on many projects. We co-host a podcast and co-present classes and workshops. She is a capable and wise and wonderful human being. I rely on her intelligence and insight for many of the day-to-day operations of our relationship and our family. But that does not preclude our power exchange relationship and my responsibility in the Leadership of it.

Punishment only comes up as a result of a power struggle. It often starts with my command to kneel and then my clear demonstration of who is in charge. It is done in a way to shatter any illusion of who we are, what our roles are, and who gets the last word. It always feels harsh and to be honest, it is harsh. It is determined. It is a statement of fact - I am in charge, you are a follower, so either follow or get out of the way.

You may have noticed that unlike what people normally think, punishment is not only physical. As noted before, examples of punishment are included in this book, but knowing when the appropriate punishment is four cold whacks with a paddle or when it is staring your follower dead in the eye and saying 'I am disappointed in you' is the right way to go - that is the key. Nearly every follower I've ever had in my collar has said they would rather be caned than be shown they have disappointed their Leader.

## Examples of Correction, Discipline, and Punishment

### *Dan says*

As expressed above - correction is about the thing, discipline is about attention, and punishment is about the relationship dynamic.

Punishment should be approached like edge play. You as the Leader must be in control of yourself, not reacting in anger or because of a bruised ego, and choosing the right tool for the situation. And don't get confused with punishment (what we've been talking about) and "funishment," which is 'you've been a bad little subbie, you are going to have to get a spanking' role play. Some of the below examples are physical, but you may find you need to be most careful on non-physical (emotional) ones.

If you and your follower have a negotiated list of soft and hard limits… those are off the table for punishment completely. You might think that if someone has a hard limit of no public nudity then that would make for easy punishment, but the harm caused - including a lack of trust and faith in you as a Leader that respects boundaries - makes this a very poor idea.

My initial thought was to break these out in three sections (this is used for correction, but that is used for discipline), but there is an issue with that. One follower might see a pinch on the thigh as a minor correction, but another as a punishment. One slave might take a disapproving word as a reminder to do better, another as a sign they are a failure.

So instead of breaking them out into the three types of punishment, I've left that to you. Perhaps you and your follower sit down together and go through the list (prior to it being needed, one hopes!) and have the conversation. Does that pinch on the thigh strike you as a small reminder to attend to something? If so, I'll note it as something to be considered for correction. Does holding a penny to the wall with your nose for five minutes feel like something you'd like to avoid but would surely remind you to be more attentive to your tasks? Then that could be noted as a discipline.

Finally, the below is a list of examples that we have used, that friends have shared, or other sources such as advice in a class or workshop. They are, as the title says, simply examples. Take what you want, add new ones, or use this as a guide to creating your own list.

## Examples

- pinching is a simple way to express "hello, pay attention"
- have your follower stop, breathe, and then wait. Count

to three in your head. Just stand there looking at them. Then say whatever you need to attend to.

- A popular one we used to hear a lot was to have your property kneel on a green lego mat. An alternative is a tray of rice.
- Have them hold a penny to the wall with their nose. For a minute… or five.
- One of the ones that dawn dislikes the most is me looking her in the eye and saying 'you are disappointing me.' Not as bad but not by much is 'you are disrespecting me.'
- In an appropriate setting, a significant and powerful one is a public dressing down among our peers, possibly including explaining a follower's failure. Doing so in private is a serious gesture. Doing so in front of others is huge. (One should get consent prior to taking this action of the other people in attendance.)
- Relative writing (I will remember Master's coffee) 100 times
- Another writing exercise that leads to a different result is to have them write why whatever it is you are addressing happened. And that they must keep writing until the page is full. This exercise is useful when the reason for the behavior is 'I don't know.'
- Having to surrender something like time on phone games, social media, ice cream for a period of time, or until an objective is met.
- Orgasm denial if used correctly (instead of just a sexy thing... which it can be) and/or enforced chastity.
- Denial of being allowed to serve. Yes, that is a real one.

- Denial of contact is one you need to deeply consider before using. It can be devastating because it feels a lot like rejection. Even the harshest of punishment should, when it is all said and done, be constructive and bonding. Denial of contact can end up being destructive if not handled correctly.
- Physical BDSM. There is a significant difference between physical BDSM with the intent of discomfort instead of pleasure. Some would suggest that if your pet enjoys spanking, that spanking can't be used as punishment. Or that anything you do to a masochist they will just enjoy, leading to bad behavior. This has not been the case with us. dawn likes a good caning. If she is warmed up, relaxed, maybe a spanking first to wake things up. The caning without that warm up and with intent to demonstrate displeasure feels and is received very differently. The list of BDSM punishments is complex and long and totally subjective. I had one collared submissive who would have felt clothespins on the nipples as significant punishment. dawn thinks of that as foreplay.
- Chores or modification of chores. Classic bathroom with a toothbrush and such.
- Enforced bedtime or enforced get out of bed time.
- Hand in the hair and force them to look at you and say what needs to change.
- Have them fully stop whatever they are doing and focus on you fully, while you convey what you want to convey.

And on and on. Hopefully this will give you a good feel for guidance on what will work for you or your situation.

### *dawn says*

Assuming you have a punishment dynamic, Dan has given a great list of ideas. The trick is to learn what will work in your dynamic. It may be something that isn't on this list. There are things on here that only work if I can feel his disappointment behind the action.

And though I feel correction is normal in a growing relationship as things change, I have no interest in being disciplined or punished. The idea that he has to stop what he is doing to address what I'm doing... I just don't like that feeling at all. Further, when it comes to being disciplined or corrected in front of others, this type of humiliation is not the kind that turns me on.

I realize how much work this is for Dan. He has to follow his instincts and I know that he is making sure not to harm me, but make sure I understand the importance of why what I did was wrong. That's a bit of work on his part that I caused. He also doesn't want it to come across like I'm being a chastised child. He knows that will cause me to resent and/or resist what's going on. What a position to put a Leader in.

# Relationship Shorthand

## *Dan says*

A few years ago, we were driving to find someplace to eat. I had a vague sense of where we were going but also had the GPS going. Said GPS suggested I turn left and dawn spoke up and said 'What?! Why would she want to turn here? That (other way) is way faster.' I shrugged - begrudgingly - and went dawn's way. A minute later, the GPS again offered her directions. dawn again argued that the GPS 'was on crack' and I, frustrated, snapped at her with a 'will you shut the fuck up!' Not a shining moment in our power exchange.

We talked about this later and dawn conveyed (rightly so) she was doing her duty - offering me advice on something. What I should have said instead of STFU was 'although I value your opinion, I don't really want to hear it right now.' And although I can say that in the future, in the moment it felt ponderous.

On a quick aside, I do have the right to say 'STFU' and

on occasion say things like that. But when it is said in anger, then that reflects a self-control issue, and if I can't control myself, what right do I have to control anyone else?

This section of the book is about those conversations or commands that you both have an understanding of, and having an efficient way to convey them. It is the difference between saying 'I am hungry and it is approaching 6pm, which is when we often eat dinner, so let's go to the car and drive to a suitable establishment and fill our mouth holes' versus saying 'let's grab some chow!'

You might find some of these useful for yourself, or come up with your own personal shorthand. Some, like ours, will develop naturally over time.

## Our Shorthand that a Leader Says

### **Da'quil** = *"serve me with silence"*

This word is a command that came about as a result of the story above. It means 'I appreciate your knowledge, skill, and contribution to our relationship, but I'd rather do (this) on my own. Even if it means we get lost, it costs more, or it doesn't go as well, I gain value in making my own mistakes, and sometimes it is fun to be clueless and figure things out on the way. That would be a lot to say! Instead, I say 'Da'quil.' dawn shuts up, and if I want input, I ask for it.

### **I Desire (place) =** *"I'll tell you where we are eating, and you can make the best of it."*

As it happens, dawn - and some of my other partners - have a variety of dietary restrictions. Gluten free, keto, no seeds, no meat, nothing with a face and so on. This leads to many conversations that go something like this. 'Do you want to eat at Pizzaland? Oh, it is all gluten. How about Salad Plaza? Oh, not good for keto. Ok, how about...' Sometimes it isn't about restrictions at all - just preference. Sometimes you're in the mood for Indian food, sometimes not (this by the way is a lie - I am always in the mood for Indian food). Nothing is wrong with this. With a full time partner, you are likely to have a few hundred conversations like this, with some give and take, until you find what suits both people.

Unless I say 'I desire Waffle House' or 'I desire Thai food.' If 'I desire' is spoken, dawn knows that we are not negotiating. We are doing what I want, and she can find something to eat there or can eat when we get home. It is a flex that just reflects we are indeed in a power exchange relationship. dawn by the way expressed appreciation for this, as she knows that her dietary choices and tastes don't match mine, and she doesn't feel like she is serving me when I don't get to experience the joy of yummy gluten because of her preferences.

### **Flex =** *"I am in charge/just because I say so' and sometimes 'nya nya nya!"*

Much like 'I desire,' I don't use flex that often, but it is part of the power exchange aspect that I, as a Leader, get my way sometimes. You'll often find in long term power exchange relationships the Leader ends up being a servant to the relationship (or in other words, 'the follower serves the Leader, the Leader serves the relationship'). But we as Leaders have to remember to claim that seat of power.

We get to 'flex' on occasion and get exactly what we want - and that is the way our followers like it as well. We are giving them a chance to be of service, even when it seems - to us - that we are being selfish. So when I want a blow job without reciprocating; to watch my TV show instead of one of our TV shows; to stay home and read a book instead of whatever plans we might have had, that is a 'flex' and perfectly ok. Now, the challenge is can you flex and not just be an actual selfish ass? We explore that, as well as more on flexing and the seat of power, elsewhere in this book.

### *dawn says*

It seems like everyone in a long term relationship has shorthand words. It happens naturally over time. For us, a 'shoobidoo' is a u-turn in an odd place. We have no idea where the word came from, it's probably because one of us forgot the real word and replaced it with a nonsense word that stuck. "Shit, I missed my turn and no traffic is coming, time to u-turn! Hold on!" gets instead turned into simply saying 'Shoobidoo!' and the other person grabbing the oh-shit bar. By the way, in our world, shoobidoos are a legal driving maneuver if the cop asks. I'm betting they have a different opinion though.

The shorthand words we are talking about in our power exchange world are created on purpose. They aren't necessarily nonsense words, but they could be. Usually, as Dan said, they take the place of a long-winded command.

## **Attend Me =** *"I want you here with me, now."*

When we first designed our contract, one of the shorthand words we found or created (not sure at this point) was 'Attend me.' If Dan said 'attend me' I dropped everything I was doing, quickly and graciously ended conversations, and went to him. It usually meant that I would go to him and kneel, but sometimes he would use this phrase in a more public place and it just meant to come to him.

It was more expedient then, 'hey dawn, I know you are in the middle of something but I need or want your attention now.' And honestly, if I was chatting with other subs when he used that command, I'd wrap up with a super quick, "My apologies, Dan needs me now. We'll pick this up later," and bow out with a smile. It's a gracious way of handling the situation if I'm in the middle of something with others. Hell, even if I was with others that didn't know of our power exchange dynamic, I could still bow out gracefully in this manner.

## **Make it so =** *"We don't need to discuss the whys and hows, do it."*

OK, most of us know where this phrase comes from. Captain Picard of Star Trek stating 'Make it so' to his next in command or crew. If interested, you can look this up on youtube. Someone has put together a compilation of every 'make it so' Picard says during the series.

It's an easy shorthand that brooks no argument from a follower. "I want a peanut butter and banana sandwich. Make it so." Means I don't have to remind him that dinner is coming up or that he wanted to cut down on bread consumption. So when he says, "make it so," he's made a decision and doesn't need any more information. And if he has to pay a price for not being hungry when dinner is served or not sticking to reducing bread, he'll take responsibility for that.

**I don't want options, I want service =** *"Stop telling me all the options. I told you I want something to eat. You know what I like. I trust you to make a decision on your own about what you are going to serve me. Instead of talking, get busy."*

Let's say Dan says, 'dawn, make me a sandwich.' Well, in my head and with my need to impart information so that I make him the 'right' sandwich, I'll start listing things we have available, hoping he'll make a choice. "Well sir, we have peanut butter, deli meat, hummus...' and at this point he'll state, 'I don't want options, I want service.' Then he will either give me that look that brooks no argument, or he'll turn away and go do what he was going to do.

This is actually empowering to me. He knows I'll evaluate what we have, and what he may be in the mood for and enjoy. It's my time to shine. And I know that he won't complain about what I make him. I'm not a brat. He knows that what I serve him is with genuine intent of best service.

## Our Shorthand that a follower Says

There are also shorthand words that I use as a follower. Some of these I cover in the survivor chapter, but will mention here as well.

**I'm just giving you information =** *"I know you are ready to make a decision and I'm not trying to influence that decision. I just want to make sure that you have all the information you might need to make an informed decision."*

This is my way of letting him know that I feel neutral in the information I'm giving him. I just want to give him knowledge that he might not already have. I'm acknowledging that the information I'm sharing with him may seem like I have an opinion one way or the other, or that I'm trying to influence his decision without stating anything outright. That would be manipulation in my book, and I have no interest in communicating that way. So, I say "just giving you information."

He can use that information or not, or even say 'Da'quil' like he mentioned earlier, which tells me he doesn't want any more information. So, instead of giving him more info, which I thought was an act of service, he now wants me to be quiet instead. I'm good with either. But, I need him to let me know if he doesn't want to hear the information. If I have more info and don't share it, and then come to find out that he would have made a different decision later because he didn't have that information, I would feel awful.

**WAM / blip / hiccup =** *"I've just had a trigger reaction to something that I experienced."*

It can be as simple as while watching a movie and an actor says their line, turning to Master and saying, 'wow, that caused a blip/hiccup.' Which means, "I felt a slight trigger response there. I'll need to look at that." Dan uses that word as well. It's easy code for "well, that emotion caught me by surprise. I'll need to look at that." It doesn't mean it needs to be looked at immediately, but that we caught our reaction and know that it's a small trigger response to a story. More about stories in the survivor and mindfulness sections.

WAM moments are bigger reactions. "What About Me" is usually in response to something someone has said or done that caused a significant bodily/emotional reaction to happen. "Dawn, I'm taking Karen on a cruise." WAM! Instant reaction from my gut. "What about me?" used to be a verbal response that I truly needed an answer to. He would feel attacked, and get on the defensive. Happiness was not soon to follow, and this reaction was the core reason for the few times we ended up using porch time in the early years.

Once we figured out that it was a trigger response, I could then verbalize, "Ouch, that was a WAM moment." This way he knows I had a negative response, but it's not based on the current moment. It's about a story from a past experience or a future fear (which is also usually about a past experience).

Dan has used this word as well. I can remember telling him some details of something the boyfriend and I had done. I could feel his reaction and asked him what was wrong. Instead of guessing and assuming I had done something wrong, making up a wrong story in my head, he was able to use the shorthand, "WAM moment, but I've got it." I asked if he wanted to talk about it, and he responded with, "After I give it some thought to see what it was." Great. I don't have to make up a story because I know he'll talk to me about it later, he just needs some time with the feeling - like the internal processor that he is.

These three little shorthand words have been amazing at resolving some of our communication issues. Instead of feeling like we needed to confront a partner for how they made us feel, we can communicate that we had a feeling but it was about us and our reaction, not what they said or did.

dawn: I see that Dan has gotten his own coffee. "Oh, that caused a hiccup, sir."

Dan: "Really? What's that about?"

dawn: "I think it's because I feel like I was being a bad slave and should have realized you needed coffee." (See the story I'm telling myself there?)

Dan: "Nope, I just wanted to get my own coffee." Boom, story erased, and I can go on with my day.

It's actually gotten to the point where I can say, "Well the story in my head tells me… that I should have been a better slave and gotten your coffee." (I dig more into this in the survivor and mindfulness sections.)

## **Hawk and mouse =** *"you and I see things from a different view"*

This is a new shorthand phrase for us which we discuss in greater depth in another section of the book. But in essence, it's a recognition that Dan and I interact with the world differently. As I mentioned before, he's an internal processor while I'm an external processor. Once we figured out our communication styles were different, we were able to understand each other a bit better. Well, the same is true for 'Hawk and mouse.'

Dan is hawk. His view is about the bigger picture. "We need to invest for retirement, let's move this savings account to a better place." My view is of the details… mouse. "Sir, what about the interest rates of different places, and the fact that we have to pay a fee, and that we can see the money in the savings account more easily? And how does that affect taxes?" Mouse can be annoying to hawk. I have to be careful that he doesn't eat me in response… or maybe… nah, that's not what we're talking about here.

Now that we have that phrase, it's easier to respond to the annoyance. I can see the look on his face. I can respond with 'hawk and mouse,' and the expression melts. He sees that I understand that I'm being annoying with the questions, but that it's in my nature to look at all the details. Both views are our individual strengths that complement each other.

I'm surprised how often we've used this phrase during the last year of selling everything, packing up, and moving into an RV. Dan is throwing stuff into a junk drawer. I'm taking it out and bagging everything with labels and putting it back. He looks at me like I've lost my mind. "Hawk and mouse, Sir." He turns away with a shake of his head.

**I am in need of service -** *"I know you've been in a funky space that affects your ability to serve. Are you in a headspace today that allows for service?"*

For some of us, there are days when our mental health just isn't in the best of places, and service becomes an extreme challenge. A Leader that recognizes this, and wants to check in to see where a sub's headspace is, may use a shorthand phrase to show it's their Master asking, not their friend… like, "I am in need of service."

At this point, an acknowledgement phrase that the sub could reply with would be needed. "Sir, it would be a pleasure to serve you," could work as an affirmative. Or "Sir, it would be my pleasure to serve you, but today is challenging," could be the response on a bad day. Whatever you use, make sure you both realize this isn't a judgment of their mental health, just a way of checking in. This can be very powerful for both of you.

# The Language of Our House

### *Dan says*

When we first started in a power exchange relationship, we used the terminology of Dom/sub because that is what we heard. After being involved in the Leather power exchange scene for some time, we earned the title Master/slave, representing the Great Lakes region.

In the years since then, we have retired those titles, as well. This relationship was designed specifically to suit us and the same is so with the language we now use. The titles/honorifics that we currently use for each other come from a variety of sources - bastardized ancient Sumerian, uncommon English, and others.

**Belum** (*benevolent Leader*) - Leads a power exchange relationship, including being responsible for the actions and words of those that follow. There is no title + name format. Instead, the formal term for those in service to use is simply Belum. If part of a name, it is positioned after the name (such as Daniel Belum). Sir is acceptable for simpler or more intimate situations. There is no suggestion of any title of any sort being required, unless you are a follower of Belum.

**belet** (beloved servant, right hand of Belum) - follows Belum in a power exchange relationship. This term is a title (such as belet dawn) and is also hierarchical; there would never be more than one belet within the domain of a Belum. It is an earned title, never granted lighty, and bears the responsibility of not only the servant of Belum, but also a reflection of the relationship itself. No limitations; thus, service is administrative, sexual, and an active extension of Belum's Leadership, and anything else desired by Belum.

**kame** (beloved servant) - follows Belum in a power exchange relationship. This term is a title (such as kame bat). kame is an earned title, never granted lightly, and bears the responsibility of not only the servant of Belum but also a reflection of the relationship itself. Service may include all aspects of service or only some.

**kojon** (servant) - follows Belum in a power exchange relationship. This term is a title (such as kojon grayson). kojon is a lighter responsibility - in service when present, a free agent in many life situations, but still a reflection of the tribe.

**factotum** (servant, craftsman, jack of trades) - follows Belum in a power exchange relationship. This term is a title (such as factotum grayson). factotum will have more specific responsibilities for services such as repair work or maintenance work (these are sometimes described as "side work," "odd jobs," or "fix-up tasks"). The exchange with a factotum is more clear in specifics -

in return for the service, the factotum has a specific return they expect from the Belum (such as power exchange education, support in a specific aspect of their life, or play).

### *dawn says*

I'm really loving how our language has grown. I'm a person that loves labels, mainly because they help me feel like I fit somewhere. It helps with my confusion with how different I am.

At first we used submissive. I was submitting to Dan, so it fit and worked for a while. But, over time I realized I was acting out of more than submission. Somewhere, something had shifted. No more was I making a decision to submit with everything he required or demanded. Instead, I was obeying him without question. This had developed through experience of being able to trust him, which had turned into faith about his intent of right action. Therefore I had nothing to question. When someone asks me when I turned into a slave, this is what I share with them. It hadn't been a goal in particular. It developed through what we had created together.

This was also about the time that someone we respected in the Leather community pointed out to Dan how he was a Master over a slave, and needed to embrace that title. It took a bit of self-reflection and conversations with others before he decided we'd embrace the titles. And it was after that, that we decided to run for a regional Master/slave title, winning the 2010 GLLA contest.

But, even though I find labels beneficial, I also find

them limiting and fodder for online arguments. So Dan came up with the idea of creating our own labels, something that more reflected us and that we could define. That cuts out the drama of others trying to tell you what a title or label 'really' means. We are in our own designer relationship. There is no right or wrong. This is what works for us.

# Being Power Exchange in a Vanilla World

## *Dan says*

belet dawn and I have been in a power exchange relationship for over twenty years. Most of that time, we live in a world that has no clue or understanding of what it is that we do.

In 2011, when a small book called *Fifty Shades of Grey* was published, the general public saw more power exchange and BDSM in the media. Perhaps a dominatrix shows up on a cop show, or a couple plays with some BDSM concepts. But they do not explore anything that accurately reflects the actual day to day of a power exchange couple. If you are familiar with living in a power exchange dynamic, you know that pretty often, it is like any other healthy relationship, with a focus on clear lines of responsibility and great communication as a foundation.

For me, no one at my job knows that my relationship is power exchange based. No one in the hotel I am sitting in right now, writing this chapter, no one at the grocery store last night, could look at the way dawn and I interact and realize we are not like them. dawn does not dress 'like a slave' and I don't have her address me as Sir in public. I do not have her kneeling next to me at a movie theater (and I would not - those floors are nasty). She doesn't ask my permission to buy clothes when she goes shopping; she has her own money and her own decision making ability. She knows my requirements for situations beforehand, and as far as the public can tell, she is a free agent.

So when we think about being a power exchange couple in public, there are two aspects we consider. First, as much as being in a power exchange relationship is a core value for us, another value we prize is consent. And no one in the general public has consented to our displays of power exchange. Now, you might argue that no one has consented to people holding hands or kissing in public, but is there any harm in that? And I'd agree. But as far as power exchange is concerned, most of the world views it as a fetish, with no distinction between what we live, and how we play.

The second aspect is this: why bother? We have no need to make a public statement. We know who we are. dawn knows that if I say 'We've spent enough in the store, let's go,' that it is her Belum speaking. And when she replies 'ok,' I hear her 'yes sir.'

Now, granted, we do have some public displays that are covert. My water cup is always over half full, hand squeezes for attention, shift in tone for attention.

But let's explore some situations and areas you might be thinking about if you *want* your power exchange relationship to be more visible.

## Family

Almost no one in our family knows we are in a power exchange relationship. (This does not include our kids, and one other exception.) There is no value in that knowledge for them, or for us. They may notice the shift in us - they likely do, as being in a PE relationship is less stressful for us, thus we appear (and are) generally healthier and more relaxed. But there has simply never been a situation where dawn has had to say "let me ask my Sir" before making some family decision. They all easily accept "let me ask Dan."

## Children

While the kids were growing up at home, they met many of our friends who were, at the least, unconventional. They met trans folk, poly triads, gay and lesbian couples, as well as a number of more conventional 'boy-appearing human with a girl-appearing human.' We are grateful that they grew up knowing that not all relationships looked like what was portrayed in the media.

But there were no overt symbols or conversations about power exchange. Instead, they saw that we lived in such a way that we were happy, dawn relied on me for guidance and I treated her with respect, and that we often came together to make decisions, while I generally had the last word in them.

Granted, there were occasional 'they know more than we think' moments. We'd return from an event and dawn would let a 'yes sir' slip by when they were there. Or I would ask dawn for a bowl of grapes and one of the kids would bring it, and I would have to make it clear (to dawn) that I required her to deliver it.

Now, as they grew older, we were less reserved about it. And once we published our first power exchange book, with our pictures on it, we figured we'd all sit down at a table and talk. We said "Hey look, we wrote a book, if you want to know more about it and us, read it. But understand, among other things it includes your mom's sex life." You should have seen them shudder and quickly change the topic.

As our kids became adults, and started to poke around the alt and kink scene, they knew who to come to if they had questions. They also knew that no matter what they chose, we would be accepting of their choice.

So as you decide for your own children, ask yourself what is the value or purpose in using the language of power exchange and explaining it to them. And the risk as well - if Junior is overheard telling his friends that "Daddy is Mommy's slave" there are likely to be consequences to that.

## Friends

I don't really have any advice here, as all our friends know we are in a power exchange relationship. We only surround ourselves with people who we can be authentic around. This means that I don't hang out with co-workers or casual acquaintances much. Now, this works great for us as we move a lot and don't have 'I've known Zed since high school' situations. But many people have long term friendships and have to make that decision: do I risk losing that friendship or just let it go? I can tell you that we've heard stories of it going both ways - the friend who reveals they have always been interested… and the friend that now thinks you are sick and avoids you.

## Polyamorous relationships

We've written extensively about the mix of power exchange and polyamory elsewhere in this book. But some parts, directly related to the topic of power exchange in a vanilla world, are presented here.

When dawn and I were about 8 years into our relationship, I started to date someone named Karen. She was not familiar with power exchange, or much of the alt lifestyle at all. So as it started to get serious, we had to have a conversation that not only did I have an existing relationship (which Karen already knew), but I had to explain that it was a power exchange relationship and what that meant. She, by the way, was very accepting of that, as long as I never tried to do the same with her. We had a wonderful vanilla relationship for twelve years.

dawn and I date other people. We also have other long term relationships. Not all of them are power exchange based. But all of them know that she and I are. And this impacts them directly. Because as the Leader in my power exchange relationship, I come first. If I don't want dawn to date Brad, then she cannot. If I think her going on a trip to Vegas is a bad idea, she doesn't get to go.

In the other direction, people I date need to understand I am full time responsible for my follower. Meaning that if I am on a date with someone else, and dawn (or my relationship with dawn) has a need that must be attended to, I will attend to it.

Now although the above scenarios exist, they don't actually come up much. I have respect for dawn and her relationships and have no desire to run them or 'flex' just because I can. dawn has courtesy for me and my relationships, and doesn't contact me during a date unless it is dire.

What we recommend is that you make a decision on how it will work for you. When a slave or Owner is away on a date, are they considered in a 'power exchange pause' so they can give their full attention to that other partner? Or do you just have to have the conversation with the other partner, establishing that 'we are in a relationship that may interrupt us' - the choice is yours.

We used to have orgasm control as part of our dynamic. dawn would have to let me know that she and her partner were likely to have sex, and ask if it would be ok if she came. We don't do that anymore, as I wanted her to have autonomy in this area. But I will have to say… having her ask permission to cum while on a date with someone else is pretty hot. Although this book is about PE as a relationship instead of a fetish, sometimes it hits those spots where it serves as both.

### *dawn says*

At first, it was very important to me that Dan and I kept our power exchange hidden from everyone except those in the Leather community we had found, and some close friends that were aware of what we were creating. In the past, I had mentioned to my ex that I was interested in power exchange when I first found BDSM, and he thought I'd gone off my rocker. I didn't want to be judged by outsiders, especially while we were still trying to figure it all out. So, I wanted to keep this just between Dan and me.

But, I also wanted to be authentic and embrace what we had created and who we were. It was a bit confusing. So, we came up with a way of dealing with that. I can remember Dan realizing how much I liked being on a leash. So, he attached the leash to my day collar, a chain necklace with an engraved heart on it, and had me button up my coat. He had run the leash through the arm of my coat so that the loop came out of the coat arm and he could hold on to it that way. No one could see, yet we both knew what was going on. It was the perfect combination of being in public on a leash with no one else the wiser.

Early on, Dan had me wear my slave ring 24/7. I was terrified to wear it to work. I was a software trainer, and I had it in my head that everyone would know and judge me for being a submissive. I didn't realize at the time that that was a reflection of my lack of self confidence, but I also had an aversion to flashing my kink at work. Granted, power exchange is a relationship style, but it is also my kink. And since some people don't recognize power exchange as a relationship style, they would be thinking kink as well. I didn't want to deal with that. I was a very private person at the time.

What I found out, though, is that no one really had a clue as to what that ring meant, or the chain necklace I've worn daily for over 20 years. It's just a piece of jewelry to them. They may find it odd that I wear the same jewelry every day, but not odd enough to say anything about it. Over time, the ring broke and Dan decided it didn't need replacing. I do still wear my day collar. The only time that comes off is during medical procedures. As you can imagine, I feel very naked without it around my neck.

I've had a lot of people over the years compliment it, ask where I got it from, ask if it has special meaning because of the engraved heart on it. I smile, thank them, tell them yes it's special, but I don't need to explain why. There is no reason to. "Yes, this is a slave collar showing ownership by Master Dan." What purpose does that serve except to shock someone? They truly don't want to know that much detail if they are a stranger. They are just being polite and trying to make a surface connection over an object. So, that's what I do.

If we do anything in public it is oh-so-subtle. Lunch with a respected Master at a place with self-serve drinks. My job was to keep Dan's water glass full. I became so interested in the conversation that I wasn't paying attention to his glass. He pushes the empty glass towards me and tells me to fill it half with ice, no water. I bring it back. He lays it on its side on the table, without a break in conversation, and has me place my hand in the ice. I sat there during the conversation, knowing that I'd disappointed him in front of another Master, and they both knew what was going on. No one else did. It's not like he stood up and announced that he was punishing his slave. It was subtle.

Pinches on the thigh are subtle, or wrapping his fingers around my wrist. No one but us knows what is going on. No one else needs to know.

# Gift or Reward

### *dawn says*

Back when I was first becoming interested in embracing being a submissive, I kept hearing this concept of submission as a gift. And that Dominants should treat it like a gift. I even made sure to add that line into our first contract. I look at it now and cringe.

In all honesty, I never really understood this concept. No one could ever really explain what it meant, except that it was supposed to elicit the emotion and response from the dominant that submission was special, and they'd better tread lightly or it might be taken away.

See, that's one of the parts that never made sense to me. "It's special, so treat it gently or I'm taking it away." Who takes away a gift? A gift should be given with no strings attached. But, most people that submit in a power exchange relationship, or become a follower, want something in return. Which I agree with; the relationship should have mutual benefits.

The gift. Let's say I give someone a gift, and my expectation is that when I give the gift, they shower me with thank yous, or give me a gift in return. Well, it's not really a gift, then, is it? To me, if you have expectations, then it's a form of manipulation. And if they don't meet my expectations, do I take the gift back? Have you ever taken a 'gift' back from someone?

Again, that doesn't make sense to me. So, thinking that submission is a 'gift' just never clicked in my understanding of things.

While we were talking about this during one of our zoom calls, Dan made a comment that submission isn't a gift, it's a reward.

Oh. Click. This makes sense.

I am submissive... to the right person. I am submissive to the person that has earned my trust. My submission is a reward for their ethical dominance over me. I'm submissive to the ones that let out their authentic Dominant selves; the ones that embrace their seat of power; the ones that are confident and not intimidated by me.

Rewards can be earned over and over and over. And if not earned... well, they aren't earned. If my submission is not earned, well... it's not there.

I mean, my submission is still there inside of me. I am a submissive/slave/belet at heart. But, if access to that submission/following hasn't been earned, they don't get rewarded with it.

Dan has definitely earned my submission. He's worked hard.

So have I.

Hell, if I think about it, I've rewarded myself with my submission as well. It's much easier to keep it locked up, fearing letting it out, fearing not being heard, fearing not being understood. But I've done the work. I've built my confidence in myself. I've let my submission bloom. I trust that my submissive side is valid and empowering. So, I've also rewarded myself.

## *Dan says*

As dawn noted above, the 'submission is a gift' is a fine concept for some, but does not resonate with me. As a matter of fact, I developed a class with the tongue-in-cheek title " 'My submission is a gift and I should be treated as the delicate flower I am' and other bullshit Master Hank doesn't tolerate." Master Hank, in this case, is an exaggerated version of me.

And as rewards like submission must be earned, so must the right to lead. Being a Leader is not an inherent right. You earn that right over and over again, with every correct decision you make - and with every recovery from the occasional bone-headed ones.

# The New Porch Time

## *Dan says*

We've discussed Porch Time before in other writings, but after years of sharing it via classes and workshops, and continuing to practice it ourselves, we've realized that some clarification and enhancements are due.

For those new to the concept, Porch Time comes from an understanding that sometimes we humans are emotional beings. And those emotions are loud, up front, overpowering and get in the way of the actual communication. Porch Time says that instead of trying to control those emotions, we let them out. Not only let them out, but let them out in the presence of the person we are trying to talk with. As valuable as tools like 'with all due respect' are, sometimes our roles - either Leader or follower - get in the way.

A personal example of this: I, as a Leader, believe that I should never Lead from a place of anger. If I am angry about something, especially something that dawn did, I need to control the anger first, then address the issue. Uncontrolled or excessive anger undermines my followers' trust in me.

This works for me nearly all of the time. A few deep breaths, reviewing a situation from various angles, remembering not to take things personally, and the fire fades. Except... sometimes it doesn't. Then is when I call Porch Time and can address my anger (or whatever else I'm feeling) there.

If you have ever needed to vent or let off steam and not worry about the listener. If you've had something inside of you that was powerful but you couldn't verbalize it. Or if you were afraid of what it would sound like when it finally came out. Then, you might already be able to imagine the power of this tool.

Specifically, Porch Time works like this. Anyone in the power exchange - follower or Leader - can call porch time. Very literally, say the words: Porch Time. All parties involved will, as immediately as possible, make it happen. They will go to the designated physical location. For us, living in a small apartment at the time with our children, we would use the porch, hence the title of this tool. Any location is fine, although we recommend avoiding your bedroom or play space. That location, at that time, is deemed 'sacred space,' and all roles are dropped.

Now, elsewhere in this book, we recommend that 'stepping outside of your power exchange to resolve a problem' is rarely a good idea. Here is an exception. Not only are you going to step out of your power exchange relationship, but you are also going to step out of any other relationship or constraint that you have. One of the things that makes Porch Time effective is that emotions get to speak before thoughts - so here we can drop away any energy spent trying to consider decorum, protocol, ritual, or appropriate behavior.

There are some rules to a Porch Time encounter. This keeps your Porch Time sacred space, and a tool for growth. The person who has something to say (initiator) and the person who is going to hear them (listener) each have a part.

## Where

When we created this tool, we had a fenced-in porch that worked great. Your "porch" doesn't need to be a specific place, but it does need to have certain features. It needs to be private; you really don't want interruptions while trying to process powerful emotions, and voices might get loud. If that happens, then that is ok. It needs to be accessible; when asking for porch time, you want to be able to get to that place soon, and it needs to be open, or large. See Walk and Breathe next.

Walk and Breathe is both a rule for Porch Time, and a useful concept in itself. If you are the initiator, it can be valuable that as you are processing and sharing (or venting), you keep physical activity as part of this if you are able. In short, pace. Walk as you talk. And if you are waving your arms and other motions, great!

Do your best to avoid walking *at* the other person. Just walk back and forth. Even go as far as to avoid looking at the other person - you don't want to modify your speaking because they are reacting. And as you walk, breathe. Remember, between a sentence or a thought, to take a deep breath. There is an amazing amount of science on the calming and restorative effect of simple full breaths. So let this be part of the process.

## The Role of the Initiator

Start by saying "This is about me," and go from there. Now, you might be thinking "Wait, this isn't about me, this is about the thing they did to make me jealous or angry!" But it isn't; Porch Time is about your view of things, and your emotions around them. So follow 'This is about me' with 'and my anger about the situation...' or 'and my jealousy around...' or 'and my depression regarding…'

The communication advice of using "I statements" is likely something you've heard about before, and it has value here for the initiator as well. For example, instead of "You take me for granted" or ""You don't listen to me," say "I feel taken for granted" or "I don't feel heard." This reinforces the above 'this is about me' as well as helping the listener stay focused on their role. When a listener hears "You don't listen to me!" it is natural to have a defensive response of "But yes I do!" kick in.

## The Role of the Listener

You are a witness. You are there to listen, not provide a conversation. Porch Time may result in a conversation, but it may not! And yes, that is really difficult. But put aside your need to defend yourself, or help the other person. Your place and the best way you can assist them is to simply be there.

Keep in mind these mantras: "This isn't about me"

and "Don't take things personally."

Once the initiator seems to be done speaking, if you are having an emotional reaction and need time, take it. Say "I need a break," and do your own walking and breathing. You might be surprised, though - when I am really in the mindset of the Witness, I don't really take things that are shared personally.

Alternatively, once the initiator seems to be done speaking and you are feeling emotionally balanced, say "Would you like feedback?" If they say yes, then share your truth. If they say "Not now, or no," then if you have something to say, go journal. You might have a strong desire to share your version of things, but the initiator has a right to say they don't want to hear it right now, they just need to vent.

During the process of Porch Time, the initiator is likely to start very high energy, and through walking and breathing and talking, they will start to get to what is really the issue. The walking slows down, the breathing is more regulated, voice drops in volume.

You might come to realize that what you thought was anger was actually fear. That jealousy was actually about our self esteem. Or that frustration really was frustration, but now it is tempered, and less volatile.

The listener may interact at this point or they may not, but chances are, things are ready for more of a 'team approach.' You might end up with solutions and plans to move forward, or you might not. But you've opened the door.

# Our Experience

## *dawn says*

As Dan has said, many people have heard us talk about Porch Time over the years, but we'd like to add some clarification to the process. Dan has spoken his piece above, but I'd like to share my thoughts as well, as there may be a few pieces that he doesn't see from a submissive's point of view.

This tool was invaluable for us in the beginning of our relationship. We were both coming from vanilla relationships that did not involve great communication tools. For me, I grew up with cold shoulders and no communication. In my previous marriage, it seemed to be about who could yell the loudest, the longest, or just not being able to talk and share thoughts in general.

Here, Dan and I are trying to develop a new relationship that we have no role models for. We have fiction books that we've read, and that's about it. And in these books, everything is done respectfully and quietly. Well, we are emotional human beings that are still on a path of growth, and sometimes respectfully and quietly means things aren't said at all. This is not the type of relationship that either of us wanted. To be able to totally trust each other and be transparent, we needed to share all of ourselves and our emotions and our thoughts, especially at the beginning.

But, how to do this? For me, I absolutely wanted to be respectful and not react to situations and emotions like I had in past relationships. The problem was, I didn't know how. And there weren't any books on how to do this in a hierarchical relationship. So, I would bottle stuff up inside. And we know what happens when we bottle stuff up… eventually, we explode. Which is exactly how I didn't want to respond to my emotions.

By trying to be the best follower, and not be high maintenance with my emotions, I was causing damage to our power exchange relationship, and our relationship in general. I didn't know how to communicate.

I also had this fear of not being heard. For my whole life, I didn't feel like I was being heard. There were things I needed to say, and no one was listening. That's why I'd lose my temper as a kid, and in my last relationship. I didn't want to yell in this relationship, especially with the style of relationship we were trying to design. But, I absolutely needed (and still need) to be heard.

I came into this relationship without any healthy communication skills. Then, one day, I just lost it. I'm not proud of that moment. I felt like I had tried the respectful way more than once, but just couldn't get out all the crap that was going through my head. I was ready to give up on the whole idea of a hierarchical relationship.

I wanted to yell and stomp. But, I couldn't. Plus, I didn't want to do that in front of the kids. They had seen this type of 'communication' with their dad and me, and I didn't want them to think it was going to be this way with Dan, as well. So, what to do?

Dan pulled me out to the porch we had in our tiny apartment. Then, he told me to forget that he was my Dominant and to just let it all out. Wow. What a relief! I didn't like having to do it that way. I really didn't. But, if I didn't get it all out, things were going to explode, and they might not be repairable. That was a huge fear of mine, is that the relationship wouldn't be repairable after I spoke up.

Luckily, Dan isn't the type to take things personally, and it was his idea to go out to the porch. I yelled and stomped, and like the external processor that I am… I talked and talked and talked, until I got to the nugget in the middle of all the twisted spaghetti that was in my head. I knew what I was feeling wasn't 'real,' but I still needed it to be spoken. I needed someone to listen and hear me. I needed Dan to listen and hear me. I needed a place where I could speak the unspeakables.

We realized this space was needed as we built our relationship. We wanted to make sure that we'd never have a reason to say, 'But I didn't know how to tell you,' or 'I didn't know if I could share this,' or even, for me, 'I feel broken when I get angry, so I didn't want to show my anger,' or 'I don't want to be seen as high maintenance.' I *really* didn't want to be seen as high maintenance. I had just started my healing path as well, and some of the stuff we were doing was totally tripping my PTSD.

By being allowed Porch Time, I learned to completely trust Dan with my 'unspeakables.' My fears, my hopes, my anger, my frustrations… hell, even my fantasies... everything. And by being able to share all of this, Dan was able to learn those deep dark secrets of mine, and what my triggers were doing to my thought process. By having this information, he was better able to Master me.

Luckily, with Dan's experience in recovery modalities and my experience in different spiritual practices, we also built some rules around this tool. First of all, we agreed that this is sacred space. This space is not about attacking each other, but about unraveling what is going on in our own heads. We came to understand that whatever we brought to the porch was about how we were responding to a situation, not usually the situation itself. We are also to use the well known trick of using 'I' statements. That was really powerful, because as I said, it was usually having issues with how we were reacting to something, not the situation itself, or what someone else had done.

Over time, we learned a couple of things about this process. For one, the first half hour of me ranting is usually bullshit. Whatever the nugget of truth is, it is buried under a pile of spaghetti. I can clearly remember ranting one time and saying that it was like digging through spaghetti trying to get to the truth of the matter. That I had to talk about all the spaghetti to get it out of my head. This was a great thing for us to discover. At first, Dan would hear me start to rant about something and he would then try to fix it. But, whatever I had started the rant about wasn't the real issue, so he'd be trying to fix the wrong thing. And I'd get frustrated because I knew it was the wrong thing, but I hadn't gotten to the right thing yet, and didn't even know what the right thing was.

Boundaries were put into place. We were allowed to rant as long as we needed, so that we could get through the stuff that wasn't real, the stuff our brains had tried to give a story to, based on past experiences. We were to use 'I' statements because these moments usually had to do with our reactions to something and the stories in our heads, not what was really going on. We weren't to offer advice or offer to fix things until the rant and self-processing was done. Then, we could only offer.

Most importantly, we can't punish the initiator of Porch Time. This needs to be sacred space, safe space. It can be hard, because we may feel attacked if we are the one being asked for a Porch Time session. Don't take it that way. Flip your thinking. Don't take things personally. This moment is about how they are processing something through their filters and their experiences, not necessarily what is really going on. Try to feel honored that they are trusting you enough to share this process with you. You are a witness to their stretching for self-growth.

What we discovered after using this tool a few times was powerful. We truly wanted to make this relationship work, and we were willing to be intentional about it. This created a huge foundation of trust that we could build the relationship on. We started to learn new ways of communicating, and I felt really comfortable that I was being heard in the process.

This is not an everyday tool. Dan and I have used it less than 10 times over 20 years. We've built other tools since then, and have built a meditation practice which helps tremendously with our emotions. But, it's there to be used. Either of us can call Porch Time at any point, and the other will grant it as soon as they can. Of course, we don't have that same Porch now, but knowing what we need, we would find a place that is not in our house/RV where we want calm energy.

I do want to mention that Porch Time may not work for everyone. If not, please find another tool that will work for you; the talking stick that I mention elsewhere could be an option. Hopefully, you've read this book before creating your relationship, and realize that you need to be proactive with building your communication tools. If either of you catch yourselves thinking that you don't know how to bring something up or talk about something, then some sort of communication tool needs to be put in place, or you will find your foundation crumbling.

# Ending the Relationship

### *Dan says*

Let's talk about all the power exchange relationships I've had so far that have ended, and why. And try to determine if either I am just not good at this, or if relationships ending is perhaps not the worst thing in the world, and may even be an appropriate result. I hope from this you'll gain perspective if you ever have a relationship that ends, and some guidance on how to end it in a way that aligns with power exchange relationships.

I will note that I am respecting anonymity (the names below are not actual names) and may skip a person or two, as they do not want to be referenced in a book, even under a false name. This is simply courtesy to them, not hiding my dirty laundry. You'll see in the below some less than shining moments.

## People Who Have Worn My Collar

### Carol, long distance

Carol lived in another city and was just starting to explore alternative relationships. We were Dom/sub and it was very much a partial power exchange. She had a lot of areas of her life where she did not need (or want) my input. Which was fine by me. One of our agreements, specifically because we were long distance, was that she could date other people as long as she told me about it beforehand.

This relationship ended because she breached one of our agreements and I was unyielding in taking her back, or allowing resolution. I reflect on this, years later, and have only slight reservations. Would I have been more forgiving nowadays? I don't know. But at that time, that agreement was a hard limit for me and it was over. I demanded my collar back and received it. This caused us both some emotional pain.

### Angie, our slave

Angie came to us with the desire to be not just my slave, but to be in a relationship with both of us. It included service to me and was sexual. And although parts of it worked well, it didn't really click somehow. I was unable to put my finger on it until it ended…

This relationship ended because Angie found someone else who would be fully her partner. When she was with us, it was still a part time relationship, more of a dating level than 'move in together.' She determined that wasn't what she wanted, and moved on. This felt like a healthy and wise thing all around.

She thought she wanted this, tried it, then realized she wanted that. As long as none of us got attached to the idea that we needed to keep this relationship going no matter what, it was a comfortable way to end. We didn't have a great investment in the relationship yet, so it was easy for us all to transition.

## Temp slave

This was pretty straight forward. We had a negotiated part time relationship - that she would provide services (basic stuff, laundry, etc) and I would provide alternative lifestyle training. No sex, no play, just an exchange.

It ended because she got what she wanted from it and said 'ok, I'm done.' I smiled and said thank you, and the collar was returned. That collar, by the way, was made of yarn, signifying to us both that it was indeed a temporary thing.

## Jen, the artist

This started in a Panera bread, talking to someone who was fairly new to the kink and power exchange lifestyle, about her developing a logo for our podcast. We described who we were, what we wanted to represent in power exchange and kink, and right there on the spot she created it, the same logo we use today for the Erotic Awakening podcast. She also later created the logo that you see on this book cover.

We had no intention of having a conversation about the two of us entering a power exchange relationship at all. But as I described what power exchange was and what it felt like, and as dawn described what it gave her, to help get Jen's creative juices going for the logo, well, other juices were turned on as well. It wasn't long after that meeting that I offered her my collar, and she accepted it. This was both full time and partial power exchange - she was mine 24/7, but I also didn't extend any power in many areas of her life, including her education. She was a college student at the time.

For the first six months, we played on occasion and went to events, but we didn't have sex. It was important to me that part of her training was to realize that she was more than just a place for people to stick their dicks. This training went very well, because when we renegotiated our relationship at the six month mark, she took intercourse off the table completely. And that was fine. Although I will admit to occasionally thinking about how it might have gone.

After one full year, she said she was done. She wanted to move on with her life and find her path. We both knew this was the way things were supposed to go, and our relationship ended. I accepted that collar back on a happy note. I was proud of her growth and the progress she had made in her journey of self actualization. She is married with children now, and seems pretty darned happy.

## Patty, young and hot

Patty came along after I turned forty; she was college aged, very attractive, and approached me with a serious desire to be with me. What isn't to like? It fed all my ego buttons, and away we went. And it lasted all of a few months before she dumped me. Even though it has been a number of years, I am still unclear on what her actual motivation or goal was with me.

The relationship was not smooth sailing. I found a number of scratches on her back, which looked to be from sexual interaction with a person, but she steadfastly told me it was her cat. Another time she wanted to come over; I was watching the Super Bowl and my team was actually in the game. She said if I didn't let her come over she was off to a friend's house to jump his bones. I hung up, and that was that. Never heard from or saw her again.

A good lesson for me is that my ego (or my libido) is not a wise decision maker. Give it a voice, but don't give it the final say.

## Sheila

I did have one partner who started off by saying they were only interested in being of sexual service. Nothing wrong with that... actually, it was pretty great. This one ended just as simply - she realized she was developing a desire for more, but not with me, so she moved on.

Sometimes we think we want sex and suddenly the heart kicks in. It can be a surprise to everyone involved. Sometimes it is great and a natural evolution. Sometimes…

not so much.

## Maya/maya

This is one that when I reflect on it, still gives me pleasant feels. Maya was introduced to me as someone who wanted to learn something about kink. This evolved into them being my collared submissive and we made great bounds together. She did a ton of work on herself, facing some old wounds and figuring out her authentic self and what that looked like. And she made a lot of courageous growth decisions.

It wasn't all perfect and it sure wasn't easy. But time went on, growth continued, and she 'grew her wings.' She became Lady Maya, a skilled Dominant in her own rights. And she became both my maya and my peer Maya. Throughout all this she was just a grand polyamory partner, and had a friendship and relationship with dawn.

Our relationship, I come to realize as I write this, isn't actually over, just changed. She outgrew the need for me as her Dom but still wanted me in that role in a partial, flexible way. She moved to another state to pursue her passion, and we stay in touch. It will be interesting the next time I see her. I want to believe she will slip right back into my collar… yet, I also really enjoy who Lady Maya has become.

We have both grown, enjoyed new experiences, and become new humans. Who knows how our energy will dance? Avoid being attached to the 'who we were' and give space to 'who we are/who we can become.' There are deeper aspects of this relationship, but I don't want to share them with you yet, oh reader. I want to hold onto them as mine and ours. Maybe you'll read about them in her book, which I'm already looking forward to.

## kame bat

As much as I have good feelings when I write about Maya, talking about kame bat fills me with a number of different feelings, from happiness with what we had, to something akin to melancholy. I've mentioned kame bat in a few other places in this book; she died just about two years ago, as of this writing.

After she passed, I was invited to her home by her daughter to clear out anything 'scandalous.' Her daughter had a great understanding of our relationship, and I'm proud that when she found her mom dying, she called us. The toys were removed. Two items I kept were her leather vest (one that I, after years of service, gifted to her,) and the collar. I broke my own rule about collars here; that is and forevermore will be, bat's collar. I have kept it with me since then, with the idea that at some point I'll know what to do with it. Maybe keep it, maybe something else.

Of course the way we *don't* want a relationship to end is when we are not ready for it to end, but life has other ideas. This too is the way things go sometimes. There will be more about this in the section that deals with loss and grief.

## Aspects of Ending a Relationship

### *dawn says*

I've seen a few relationships of Dan's that have ended, but I've only had three other relationships end in my life, four if you count kame bat passing. This is more because I haven't had as many relationships as Dan. One was an ex-fiancé, one was an ex-husband. They were not poly, so don't really count in this conversation, but I will say that I still communicate with both of them. My first poly boyfriend is the third person that I broke up with. And it's only because of how I've seen Dan end relationships - honorably - that I was able to do the same with this person. It could have gotten ugly. He cheated on me. Who cheats in polyamory? Well, I guess he does.

### Honor

What do I mean by ending relationships honorably? I'm surprised Dan didn't mention this. From reading his descriptions above, you should be able to tell that some relationships ended on a good note and because it was time for them to end, and others… not so much.

The ones that ended because it was time or because something changed, not because someone did something wrong, ended honorably. Dan wanted to make sure that the community knew that, so he would write a journal entry on his account on Fetlife (fetlife.com), stating that the time had come to part ways, that they were doing so because they both agreed it was time, and that it was being done honorably.

Not only was this to set an example of how relationships could end, without drama... but it also prevented gossip, and closed the information gap so people would be less likely to wonder if there were any red flags with the people involved.

Did you know that kame bat actually wore Dan's collar twice? The first time was for about 4 years. At that point, she decided she had gotten what she wanted from the relationship and wanted to try something else. She and Dan sat down together, both wrote an announcement, and both put it on their fetlife profiles at the same time. Again, showing how relationships can end, without drama.

kame bat used that same technique with a partner she had been with for a couple years. It was time to move on and experience something else, so they both sat down and wrote the announcement together that they were breaking up, would remain friends, and no one had to pick sides. As a matter of fact, they didn't want people taking sides as so often happens in the vanilla world with divorces.

This also left Dan and kame bat's relationship as a friendship. A great friendship, which she decided to change later again by asking for the collar back. She wore this collar until she died unexpectedly.

Because of the 'no drama' and not having to pick sides during the breakups, it made it easy for me to stay friends with the partners that were part of an honorable break up.

## Our Ending

As for Dan and me, we have a dissolution clause in our contract, and a couple of items that would be cause for an instant ending of our relationship. I don't even want to imagine that happening. I've just gotten to the point of being able to talk about it in our workshops without becoming choked up.

I have a lot invested in this relationship, and in Dan, and in myself. It would be a super hard decision to make if it came down to it. But, I would have a goal of an honorable ending. Could you imagine if it was a dramatic breakup? People having to choose sides? I don't want that. I don't want it for me, him, or our friends, family, and community.

But, Dan has also told me that if it's time to end for whatever reason, or if he breaks the clause, it's my duty to leave and take care of myself. His last command would be for me to walk away. Ugh. I argued that one when we put that in the contract. I'm also a fixer, and I'd want to stay and fix things even if it was beyond fixing. But, over the years, it's now part of my understanding that that would be my final command, and I would need to obey it.

# Another Perspective on Grief and Regret

### *Dan says*

I have no experience with being a grief counselor. I point that out so I can remind you that what I am writing is about my experience and what I learned from it, not a playbook to deal with grief. With that out of the way, let's chat about grief and regret.

## Regret

I am very fortunate with regret as I don't have many. I mean, I made some major dumb choices and skipped some great opportunities, but I am just not the kind of person who clings to the past and to regret. Part of the reason for that is a philosophical mixture of Buddhism and Twelve Step programs like Narcotics Anonymous. The short version of it is a clear understanding that the past is done with, and the future hasn't happened yet. Combine that with a meditation practice, and old stories and thoughts don't get to live rent free in my head much.

But there are a few power exchange related exceptions,

the first two related to kame bat. If you have not read it in other parts of the book yet, kame bat was my collared follower for years. She left that collar to find new relationships and did something no one else has ever done; she came back. And it fit and worked very well for both of us. And then she died. It has been two years at the point I am writing this.

The first regret was around cars. Specifically, when dawn and I started to ride motorcycles, bat respectfully said we were being overly risky and worried each time we rode. I accepted this but did nothing to change it (and that is not the regret). bat said she understood the idea of a motorcycle - the freedom of wind in your face, the intimacy with your surroundings - and has always wanted to ride in a convertible. I said "I will take you for a ride in a convertible" and meant it, and every once in a while thought about renting one. I planned to get around to it one day. Never happened. The problem with 'one day' is sometimes it doesn't happen.

The other regret around bat is personal and none of your beeswax, oh reader. But, same thing - I planned to get around to it one day.

I have other relationships where I have thoughts of 'I wish I had done that more skillfully.' But there is a line between 'regret' and 'mistake that I can learn from.' Don't forget about it, but don't use it as a bludgeon on yourself either. That part is important. Don't hold onto regret as a way to punish yourself.

I sometimes find myself thinking 'if only I had done x, they would still be happy.' But that is not going to get me anywhere. Everything that has already happened... has already happened. You can make amends, but you cannot change anything.

Regret also has less purchase on you if you make a habit of always doing your best. Relationship-wise, stick with whatever agreements or commitments you have. If things go sideways, you are less likely to attach to a regret. That 'I did my best,' when it is true, is powerful.

Finally, one more piece of this is to know 'that's the way things go sometimes.' This is a variation of 'the universe doesn't give a crap' or 'God doesn't run things, Loki does.' Shit goes sideways sometimes. That is the way of it. It is foolish to pretend we have ultimate control. A flat tire that causes a car wreck can be a situation where you punish yourself for not rotating your wheels every 20,000 miles… or can be just bad luck.

The funny thing about writing this chapter is the self evaluation part. I have regret over something that I can no longer do anything about. kame bat will never get that car ride from me in a convertible. It is what it is. Can I make amends to her? No. Can I learn anything from that? Yes.

I can embrace the philosophy of 'If not now, when?' Realize that sometimes I will choose to do or not do something - but that choice means I live with the knowledge that I may never get the chance to do it. And that is ok; you can't do everything. But you can set priorities. I realize that I could be checking out a local coffee shop or watching a TV show; I can either be interacting with kinksters on social media or I can write a book. Neither is good or bad. But there is always a choice.

### *dawn says*

During the first few years of my healing work, I

regretted so many things. I would cry over these things, clinging to what could have been, pushing away things that I wish hadn't happened. I was creating so much suffering for myself, and it was hurting those around me that wanted to help, but couldn't. Mainly Dan. As my Master he wanted to be in charge of all of me, but couldn't fix the suffering. He gave me some ideas and tools that had worked for him, but in the end only I could change the stories causing my suffering.

At some point, a few years into our relationship, he found Buddhism and started meditating. I saw how that affected his outlook on life and decided to do some research myself, attend the sangha he created, and started a daily meditation practice myself. Over time the results were amazing. I learned how to see and stop the stories in my head that were causing the suffering. What happened in the past had already happened. If I kept thinking about what could have been different or 'if only' or 'what if' or anything that was not about accepting the past, I was only causing suffering.

After learning to stop the stories, and becoming more focused in the present, many of my regrets disappeared. Sure, I wish some things had happened differently, but I am truly happy in the moment, and everything that ever happened, led me to being where I am today.

Do I wish I wasn't so dramatic and such a victim acting out during the beginning of my healing path? Absolutely. Do I wish I had handled myself a little more quietly at the beginning? Absolutely. Do I wish I had been more confident in myself as a person and a follower at the beginning of our relationship? Oh hell yes. But, I can't change the past, and that is how it played out. There is nothing I can do about it now, and thankfully, it all worked out.

I lost a friend during this dramatic time of my life, the beginning of my healing journey. You can argue whether they were really a friend, if they couldn't stand by my side during hard times, but it doesn't change the fact that I regret losing them. I thought they'd be around forever. Had never thought there would be an end. But everything has an end. I just wish it hadn't been so soon, and I blame my suffering and victim mode at the time. Like I said, it affected people close to me.

This type of emotion can dig under our very foundation. It could have destroyed my and Dan's relationship. And though I can't change how I dealt with it then, I can change how I deal with it now. I can't let an emotion like regret get in the way of my service, submission, and surrender to Dan. These are things that are done in the present. Regret is about the past. I need to make sure not to expend the energy needed for today, in the past.

## Grief

### *dawn says*

Same with grief. It's over; something in the past that can't be changed. But, unlike regret, it's a bit harder to deal with and to give the response of 'just let it go, it's in the past.' Grieving is more emotional, and goes through many stages. Grieving can hit you from out of nowhere even after you think you've gotten over something. A smell, sound, time on the clock… sometimes we have no clue what is going to cause a pang, or something bigger.

From grieving over my childhood trauma, to grieving over parents and family that didn't protect me, and not understanding why they behaved the way the did, to grieving over my divorce, to losing a close friend that just walked away from our relationship with no word, to losing a best friend who died at the beginning of the covid pandemic… so many things to grieve over.

At the beginning, when I was lost in the 'why?, why?, why?' part of the grieving, all Dan could say is 'I don't know.' As a Master, he would use some of the tools that I cover in the survivor section of the book, but sometimes you just have to let someone cry. It's when I spiral that he pulls out the tools. My grief can cause me to trigger myself. The current grief can cause flashbacks of past grief, which is a whole other thing.

Thank goodness for my work on myself. Thank goodness for Dan reminding me of the tools I've learned. Thank goodness for his hugs and making me feel safe. It's definitely made it easier to deal with the grief in current years much less dramatically.

# Power Exchange and Polyamory

## *Dan says*

Power Exchange is a relationship style that is designed to have a hierarchical Leader/follower structure. There is a person who is in charge; anyone else recognizes that the other person is in charge. There are many styles of power exchange and they go by many different names – Dominant/submissive, Master (or Mistress or Ma'am) /slave, Queen/knight, Owner/property, Leader/follower, and plenty of others.

Polyamory is a relationship style that includes multiple loving relationships. It can take many forms, but overall, that is polyamory in a nutshell.

You might be wondering if you can practice both polyamory and power exchange. Well, the answer is yes. As a matter of fact, if you go to a kink-based event, you'll see many people practicing it.

Here are some specific thoughts, tips, and call-outs about this sort of relationship combination.

First off, as you explore the polyamory part, expect some pushback from non-power exchange polyamory people. Some aspects of power exchange, such as rule-based relationships, one person getting final say (including veto power), and at times, one person can have additional partners but the other can't, might be part of a negotiated power exchange. And some of those items are considered poor relationship etiquette by those who practice non-hierarchical polyamory.

That viewpoint is what it is. These aspects actually might be fine and functional in Power Exchange + Polyamory relationships. Sometimes, it is exactly what all parties want. Power Exchange relationships (when they are done ethically) are done with a lot of negotiations before any power is exchanged.

### *dawn says*

When Dan and I first got together, both of us came into our relationship with some idea of what we wanted. Before starting our relationship, Dan had put me through a couple of tries - interviews. This was specifically to see if I could switch our friendship into something that could involve him being in charge, and me obeying him. After both interviews we found that the answer was a resounding 'yes!!'

As we've said in other parts of the book, we took our time building what we wanted with our relationship. We did a lot of talking, and decided to build our power exchange foundation first. We wanted to do this before bringing others into our lives. We didn't have any role models to bounce ideas off of, so we went with what seemed to make sense at the time.

The basics of our power exchange foundation include:

- A clear hierarchy
- Rules, Rituals and Protocols
- Transparency
- Communication Tools, including a contract

Then, we started building our polyamory foundation. Keep in mind that people practicing multiple partnerships at the time were very hard to find. The internet was still new, and not everyone had access to it. Even the word 'polyamory' was new at the time.

What we did have access to was the swinging community. I'm not sure how it is now, but it was very common then for swinging to be about couples looking for other couples and thirds. This made sense to us, since we had just built our power exchange dynamic as a couple. So, this is what we copied.

Plus, in the power exchange community, what we were seeing was that Owners weren't sharing their subs, and subs were not comfortable with sharing their Owners. It was definitely a monogamous community; Dan and I were seen as the weird ones.

So, we'd never met anyone that were a couple but dated separately, or had other relationships that didn't involve our other partner. In the swinging world that wasn't seen, and in the power exchange world that wasn't seen. It made sense for us to date others as a couple. So began our coamorous journey.

With coamory we didn't have to deal much with jealousy, because we were doing everything together. We had a lot of fun with this, and met a lot of people. We had partners that lasted a while, and some submissives under Dan's collar. But, over time, it started to get harder and harder to be a couple dating others.

We figured out that Dan and I have different dating requirements, and different dating and relationship styles. There was also the fact that he's Dominant and I'm submissive. So, people that worked with that dynamic were harder to find. Plus, we always joke that Dan is like hay; light a match and he's on fire. But, I'm like water; light a match and it still takes forever for me to come to a boil. Coamory wasn't working for us.

Over time, and through circumstances with a couple we started dating where Dan and the wife fell in love, but the husband and I realized we were better off friends, things changed. And now that we were officially dating separately, the jealousy on my part came about full swing. Our book 'The Polyamory Toolkit' contains many of the tools we learned to deal with jealousy, because Dan's kicked in later when I started finding long term partners as well. And even though the book is written from a Polyamory point of view, the tools can be used regardless of whether you are in a non-hierarchical relationship or a power exchange dynamic. They may need to be modified a bit to fit your power exchange dynamic, though.

We'll share a bit more about the challenges of power exchange with polyamory further in, but first let's talk about a few challenges that the non-hierarchical polyamorous world has with mixing in power exchange.

## Dan says

When I am on a poly message board, I see a lot of ideas and concepts that are presented as if 'all healthy polyamorous people' should do or believe something that doesn't apply to us. The fact that I am practicing both polyamory and power exchange means that some concepts that are considered common sense - and by some nearly sacrosanct - may or may not be part of our dynamic. Ideas and views around having rules, a one-penis policy, or veto power don't work the same in power exchange with polyamory as they might for polyamorous people who do not also practice power exchange.

When I asked around about this, I got some feedback that some people simply separate the two; my power exchange always excludes my polyamory from our dynamic. I also got some very harsh feedback that, if you mix power exchange relationships and polyamory, you are everything from an abuser to transphobic. I am still not clear how that is related. Now, to be clear, we (dawn and I) do not have a negative opinion on either how non-power exchange people do polyamory, or on nearly any polyamory view. If everyone is happy and growing and things are consent based, then great! You are doing it right. Keep doing polyamory your way.

But there are lots of ways to do polyamory, and those can change when mixing polyamory with power exchange. For example, at the point of writing this book, I have a follower of 20 years (dawn); a girlfriend of 6 years who identifies as a domme/sadistic top; a recently, amicably ended 12 year poly relationship with a non-power exchange, non-kinky woman; a romantic interest in a former follower who grew into a Leader; a follower of 5 years, kame bat, who recently passed away.

Throughout the past twenty years, I have had various other power exchange followers of many types. If you're thinking this sounds like it could be a bit confusing and complex, I would have to say you are totally correct!

## Rules

### *Dan says*

Polyamorous people who are not in power exchange relationships generally seem to have a negative view of the idea of rules. Normally they suggest instead to have agreements. An example might be that you can't have a rule about how long a date can last; instead you should have an agreement that if a date is going to turn into an overnight, you might make an attempt to let your other partners know.

This doesn't work for me and mine. We are in a relationship that has lots of agreed upon exchanges of power, and those translate often into rules.

Now, as with veto power, just because it is my right, it doesn't mean that I have rules to inhibit my followers' polyamory. I not only let dawn have other relationships; I want dawn to explore and enjoy those relationships. So when she goes off with the boyfriend for a date or a weekend, I don't require any service from her, or place anything beyond the most broad restrictions on her. All I require is that she let me know where she is, and when she will be back.

My view is this: I want dawn to grow and experience all the things. In my collar, she is driven to be her best self, explore things that she might be nervous about, and excel in all things, including service to me. And when she is off on a date, she is still mine, but that collar is very loose; I want her to drive her own happiness and experiences. And then I get joy when she comes back and shares her joy with me.

### *dawn says*

I'm glad we have rules. I've mentioned before that I like structure. I like knowing expectations. These are things that feed me as a follower. It can be confusing for new people that I date when I share that I'm in a power exchange relationship, but I'm ok with that. Some are not, and decide not to continue dating. That is ok as well. I need to date people who are ok with what I have with Dan, and take me at my word when I say that Dan isn't a dick about it. He will not show up out of the blue with new rules that will affect the relationships I have with anyone else. Don't get me wrong, he may change some rules. It's his right. But, they won't be out of the blue, and they won't be based on his ego.

## Veto Power

### *Dan says*

The idea of veto power is that one member of the relationship can tell the other member(s) they are not allowed to date someone. This might be due to jealousy, insecurity, or simply that they dislike the other person!

For us, this is a real thing. It is one-sided, and although vanilla polyam people will say this is not fair… well, they are right. But that is also ok; read on.

We are in a power exchange relationship. I am the Leader, and I am responsible for my follower's health and welfare. If I think she is dating someone unhealthy, I will tell her 'no' and she can't date them anymore. My followers, on the other hand, may have an opinion of who I can or should date, and although I will listen to their opinion, they can not say 'nope, don't date that person.' If this seems like a power imbalance, well, it is a power exchange relationship and there you go! But - and this is the key - I need to be the kind of Leader that isn't ruled by fear, jealousy, or other emotions. If I tell a follower they can't date someone, my reason has to be sound, and not ruled by my insecurity.

As it happens, I've never used veto power with any of my followers' relationships. I have once said you can't play with someone, after overhearing the person in question talking about how they negotiate during the scene to get more past boundaries, which is despicable. But I never said 'you can't date or you must break up with' someone. I would do so, but my followers are pretty wise people, and they haven't tried to start a relationship with anyone unsafe.

## *dawn says*

I've talked to other followers about how they feel about veto power, and I can honestly say that I'm not alone in how I feel. I love that Dan has veto power, and I love that I do not. I don't want veto power. I want to be able to speak up if I have concerns, but I have no interest in telling him 'no.' That would totally mess up my sense of surrender, which like with rules, feeds me.

I feel a sense of safety with the fact that Dan has veto power. I also know that he won't use it unless he truly feels the need to, for me. Though I will admit that I had one boyfriend over the years that I should have broken up with long before I did. It would have made my life so much easier if Dan had pulled the veto card. But, he didn't. He knew that I'd never broken up with anyone before, and he wanted to make sure that I'd be willing to do it. It was hard, but the boyfriend finally crossed a line that I couldn't tolerate. Yay me!

With all that said about my and Dan's power exchange relationship, I do not have veto power in my other polyam relationships either. They also do not have that power over me. All my other relationships are non-hierarchical. We have agreements of how we will communicate when we start dating someone else, but no one else gets to tell me 'no.' And I don't get to tell them 'no,' either.

When my current boyfriend started RVing full-time, and then we started RVing full-time, I asked him if he wanted to know if I hooked up with anyone. He said if it was just sex, he didn't need to know, but if it moved on to an emotional relationship, he'd like to be kept in the loop. Then, he asked me the same question. I admitted that I'd like to be in the loop whether he hooked up or it got emotional. Even if he was going out for coffee with someone else, I'd like to know. I didn't need to know details or even their name if he didn't want to give a lot of details. But, I don't like anything that feels like a secret. We agreed, and that's how we've been communicating. We are still learning this long distance stuff.

Each relationship is different, though. Some situations or communication agreements are different with each of my partners. I learned this from Dan. He gets veto power with his power exchange relationships, but not his non-power exchange ones. They may ask his opinion, or they may not.

## One Penis Policy (sometimes referred to as OPP)

### *Dan says*

This term is mostly used in hetero circles, and often begins with the idea of a male- and female-identifying couple adding more people into their relationship.

OPP is the idea that that any female-bodied person in the relationship is only allowed to have one penis in her romantic and sexual life. In power exchange, an example would be a male Leader who says the female follower may only practice polyamory with other females. As someone who was raised in America, I totally understand why some males start off this way. We have been taught some pretty dumb stuff about how important our penises are, and how if our partners experience another one, they will likely leave us.

If you ask about one penis policy on a polyamory message board, be prepared for some aggressive responses. But the practice of OPP alone does not mean your relationship is unhealthy. If you are in a closed relationship, (meaning that the relationship isn't expanding beyond the number of people who are currently in it,) and the male bodied Leader doesn't like dick, then having a OPP makes sense.

With that being said, though, most males who want a practice of OPP seem to feel that way because of a lack of self-confidence or self-worth. I am not saying all - if the Leader can look in the mirror and honestly determine that his decision that his followers can't be around other cocks is not based on fear, then OPP might be totally valid for them. I am not trying to judge - but I am advising a hard self examination, if this is the path you seek.

We do not practice this personally. dawn can have all the cock she wants, mine or others. I am of the mind that life is short and dawn likes dick, so why limit her? The size and use of my penis is not a defining aspect of who we are.

### *dawn says*

I guess I understand why some people think this is an unhealthy relationship choice, but it also feels very judgmental to me. Who is to say this isn't ok? I actually know more than a few 'tribes' or 'families' or whatever you want to call the groupings that include one Dominant male and more than one submissive female. Or a Dominant man and a Dominant woman with other submissive females. Or whatever combination that only includes one male. And they are happy. The male has no interest in other males in the relationship, and neither do the women.

Everyone knows the expectations going in. It's not a surprise that is sprung on the females later. So, I don't see the problem. It's consensual adults in a consensual relationship. Only once have I known a female to have an issue with it after joining the relationship. So, she left to go pursue her new happiness. That's what people do.

Usually you'll hear that a one penis policy must be based on fear. OK. How many relationships do you know that don't have fear involved somewhere? Whether it's decisions about how finances are handled, or how communication will be done, or jealousy over a partner's new relationship. The trick is, have you looked at that fear and worked on it, if it needed to be worked on? Is it causing stress in your life? Or not?

And what about the other side of the fence? I don't know that I've ever heard anyone have problems with the one vagina policy in a relationship. We have interviewed a female Domme that has a couple of male submissive partners. They are not allowed to date other women. They are fine with this, and enjoy providing this type of service to their Mistress. No one seems to have a problem with that. I don't want to yuck on anyone's yum, if it's between consenting adults.

## Coamorous Polyamory and Power Exchange

### *Dan says*

This is where an existing power exchange couple (or group) decides to bring in additional people for the purpose of including them into a power exchange plus a romantic relationship. This could be bringing in an additional follower, or an additional Leader.

People will often refer to this as unicorn hunting. Unicorn hunting is normally considered a situation where one male bodied person and one female bodied person look for another female bodied person to join them - with a preference that the new person be bisexual.

Where this becomes a problem - or predatory or unethical, depending on where it is discussed - is where the original couple has greater rights than the new person. For example, the existing female has veto power, or the original couple excludes the new person from things unfairly or without their consent.

Things get complex here. How do you avoid being a unicorn hunter? How do you treat that person new to the relationship fairly and ethically? The answer is both easy and complex.

The easy part is to head back to that section on contracts. By co-creating a contract, you make it clear to everyone involved what this relationship's boundaries and expectations are. The person joining the relationship has a clear set of agreements on what they can expect, and what they can require. The followers already in the relationship should also be part of this contract process, and have full understanding along the way of what is being built. They may have a direct hand in building it, in a coamorous power exchange polyamorous situation.

### *dawn says*

For me, there is a difference in coamory and unicorn hunting. Unicorn hunting seems to happen in the non-power exchange world, whereas I see coamory more in the the kink and power exchange world. This is just my experience, it doesn't necessarily represent the truth of the situation, or other people's experiences.

As I stated in another part of the book, Dan's and my first foray into the world of dating other people was through the swing world. It's very common for couples to date together, looking for a third or another couple. For some, it's because it's safer to the dynamic of the couple, and for others it's just because it's hot. But, this isn't usually for relationship situations. It's for sexy times.

But, this was what we knew. When we started dating others and then trying to create relationships, this was the style we followed. At the time, co-amory was a word that people used. I don't see it so often now. We used it to mean a couple dating as a unit. Dan and I actually did this for the first 6 years or so. We were very up front with anyone we met that we dated as a unit. The person coming into the relationship might never date us separately. For some, this isn't what they wanted, and they moved on. For others, it was exactly what they were looking for. We would chat and negotiate, set boundaries, and create communication methods that worked for everyone. These were some amazing relationships that we experienced. A couple of these were pretty long term, and we are still friends with them.

Personally, I don't particularly understand the idea of Unicorn Hunting. Again, it's consenting adults that should be speaking up with what works for them, and what doesn't work. If you don't want to date a couple or become part of their relationship, don't. If you need to date them separately and they can't provide that, it's not the relationship for you, and vice-versa.

But, if you are looking for a third (or more) for an existing relationship, I highly recommend not posting so on a polyamory group. You will get roasted for having the audacity to do so. You'll want to try the swinging groups or kink groups where this is more common, and where singles know they can find couples without being judged.

## The Loving Power Exchange Third

### *Dan says*

The reason for bringing another person into a relationship that is heard commonly both in vanilla polyamory as well as power exchange polyamory is love. Either there is a perceived abundance of love, (we have so much to share, we want to spread the wealth) or someone fell in love (we thought Jim was just going to be a play partner, but it developed into much more).

A lot of this section addresses how to do this as skillfully as possible. But for the Leader, there is a specific challenge. You as a Leader have a huge limitation that you have no control over in this. A limitation in your power that can significantly negatively impact both the new relationship and the existing one. That limitation is the heart. Or, in other words, you can't control who is going to love who.

You can seek control of how people will respond to those emotions. You can set a rule that when people get upset, no yelling or screaming is tolerated. But you cannot demand, order, or require anyone to have an emotional bond with anyone else. You can't control love - it will happen, or it will not.

What you can do is create an environment where love can flourish. If it does, great. If not, then we can still require respect and courtesy, and allow things to work out from there.

One of the reasons to bring in that third person is companionship. This one has come up for me more than once and has worked out twice - although once it worked out accidentally. Specifically for us, I wanted dawn to have another person (often called a slave sister) that was a peer of hers in our life. Someone who she understands, and who understands her, in the way only another follower can.

Whenever I bring in an additional follower, I hope that they and dawn will bond. Not as lovers, but as friends. It just brings me happiness to see her having a pal, a confidante. Now to be clear, I get other benefits as well - another follower in the house has lots of positives for me.

This has never worked for me when I either pick someone because I think dawn will like them, or when I push. It happens, or it doesn't.

## Multiple Followers with the Same Leader

This is one dawn and I have had the good fortune to be part of more than once. One time, it was perfect. Other times it was pretty great. Once or twice, not so much.

### *Why do Leaders want multiple followers?*

The reasons a Leader might want multiple followers vary. Some of these reasons are, to be blunt, unskillful. Both harem collecting and chasing the new and shiny should be avoided by responsible power exchange Leaders. But let's assume positive intent, and look at some other reasons.

One reason is *Enjoyment of Training*. Michelangelo's famous words about sculpting explain this well; "The sculpture is already complete within the marble block, before I start my work. It is already there, I just have to chisel away." I really enjoy it when people who are new to the lifestyle want to explore their potential, and I enjoy helping them get there. In more than one situation, I have been a small part of helping someone transform and become not only a skilled follower, but a more complete human. We both gain from this.

Another reason might be *All the Sex*. Maybe the Leader wants more followers to have more cocks and cunts to play with. There is nothing wrong with this, as long as it is clearly negotiated and understood.

I will admit my one foray into this… well, although

the sex was hot and yummy, it didn't really suit my nature.

Multiple followers might be about filling *Roles*. Some followers are great at service, but not so much at administrative tasks. Other followers are non-sexual but excel at protocol service. Sometimes you may need additional followers because you need service in bed, in the office, and at events, and your followers do not have the skills or desires you need. There is nothing wrong with this - I've had more than one non-sexual follower that brought many great things to the table, but for either their preference or mine, sex was not part of it. And when I needed a blow job, I'd turn to dawn. Win-win.

Similar to roles is *Task Management*. Between dawn and I, we are busy enough that we decided we have too much to do for dawn to have a normal job. She instead takes care of me, and runs our hobby (podcast, books, and presenting). We have a lot more projects we'd love to get involved in that we just don't have the time or energy for. For me, additional followers means additional bandwidth to get shit done. Having a follower dedicated to taking care of our household stuff, for example, would free up time to get that audiobook or a YouTube channel going.

But be careful with this one. Power exchange is an exchange. The follower you bring in to help reduce the time it takes to accomplish something requires time as well. It may be in the form of intimacy, training, energy, or something else, but your follower is going to require a feedback mechanism of some sort for the service they provide. Otherwise, you should just hire a butler or personal assistant.

Now, a side effect to adding any new follower is *What About Me?* When slave J joined us, I gave her the job of getting my coffee. Now, this may seem a small thing to you, but this was no small thing to dawn. It was her job for years, and now suddenly she didn't get to do it. I figured I was doing her a favor - one less thing to do - but her view was that I was taking something away from her.

So when I bring in a new follower and give them a task that dawn used to have, I make sure I replace it for dawn with something else. With the coffee, slave J would ask me how I wanted it and I would say 'go see dawn,' giving dawn the job of making sure that slave J knew how I wanted my coffee. Sometimes this isn't that easy. Sometimes it is that easy - some things don't have an obvious replacement - but it is important to give this some energy, and see what I can come up with.

### *dawn says*

It was actually pretty hard for me when Dan would bring in other followers. OK. It was actually difficult when he brought in anyone, but for different reasons.

With another follower, there were a couple of things going on that made it such a challenge at the beginning. For one, it was the split in attention like Dan mentioned. He was excited about training a new person. I was the 'old relationship' and wasn't getting as much attention as I used to. The NRE, New Relationship Energy, was affecting our MRE, Mature Relationship Energy. Dan has had to learn to keep an eye on his energy levels and how much attention he's giving each of his partners. It doesn't have to be equal, but it does need to be fair, whatever that means for each relationship.

There were times that I also felt a lack of self-confidence, and thought he was starting new relationships because I wasn't enough, was lacking something, or was unworthy. These were not my best moments.

The tool I've learned for this that we talk about in our Polyamory book is the tool of 'And not Or.' I finally learned over time… well, I suppose I knew it, but it finally really clicked one day, that he wasn't adding relationships to replace me or to fill in holes. He was adding them because 'AND.' He likes to experience the world, and people, and he loves to love. It really had nothing to do with me, or with either of us experiencing a lack of anything. This was easier for me to understand… really understand and believe… when I started finding and developing other relationships myself.

## Mixing Non-power Exchange and Power Exchange Relationships

### *dawn says*

As I mentioned, I had issues when Dan brought in other followers at first. I don't so much now. Over time, I developed self-confidence in not only our relationship, but with myself. That's pretty powerful stuff, and it resolved a lot of our stumbling blocks.

But then Dan started dating vanilla women. That was hard to watch as well. I don't tend to make anything easy, if you've noticed. With these partnerships, I was seeing power struggles. I didn't understand it. Why? He had the opportunity to design relationships that were specifically about not having power struggles. He and I had put a lot of work into our relationship with that very foundation. Why something different? Didn't he like power exchange anymore? Should I change what I was doing? The idea hurt my stomach. I couldn't change. I am a follower. I need power exchange. That scared me.

Until I fell back into the realization that it's an 'AND.' I've discovered the dynamic I thrive in. Dan likes variety. He likes to be open to fall in love with whom he falls in love with, not placing limitations on the dynamic. Going with the flow. It was hard for me to be around, though. Luckily, I adjusted over time. Especially since one of his relationships lasted 12 years, and we all bought a house together.

## Multiple Leaders with the Same Follower

### *Dan says*

dawn's boyfriend is dominant in the bedroom, but otherwise practices non-power exchange polyamory. This is *not* what this part is about.

This section is the scenario where I am a Leader and dating (let's say) subby sam. When subby sam is with me, he is mine, both for service and sexually. But, subby sam also is dating Leather Linda, who identifies as his Leader as well.

This can get tricky. If I say 'be here at 5 PM' and Linda

says 'be at my house at 5 pm,' subby sam is going to have to say no to one of us.

You can make this work in different ways. If both relationships are 'part time power exchange' as mentioned elsewhere in this book, then it is easy enough to avoid overlap in time and what will or won't be on the table.

For this one, I'd strongly advise time or location limits be part of it. An agreement of 'our relationship is only a power exchange between us when we are physically together' is the best way to avoid conflict. If one Leader says 'Hey, you have a new bruise, only I am allowed to leave marks,' you can remind them that what happens away from them isn't their business. A confident Leader will accept this. Or they will say 'I am looking for something else' and you can negotiate… or not.

The other way to do this is for both Leaders to come together and talk. They create an agreement on what one person is responsible for, and areas they have no control. One example of this is I am dawn's 24/7 Leader. But when she is with Leather Linda, Linda has complete control over her, and can act as such. We create a container (during this time, at this location) where Linda is in charge… but Linda would either have some limits that I include, or I am so confident in Linda that I don't need to include any. I'd have to be pretty damned confident in Linda to let dawn start a total power exchange relationship with anyone other than me, to be honest.

## *dawn says*

I have a hard time imagining myself with two Leaders.

One would have to be the ultimate in charge. I mean, can you imagine having two managers at your job? Both have equal say, but haven't decided which has say over what? How can I surrender? How can I work on my alignment of will? How can I obey either of them, if they aren't working together? I wouldn't be able to sink into my instinctive obedience mode.

They would have to work together and work with me so that we could all design a plan of action. I need a list of expectations, both of me and of them. I want communication tools so that it doesn't feel like I'm being disobedient or topping from the bottom. If this didn't happen, they would both be setting me up for failure, and I wouldn't be able to trust them. And when we designed something to make it work, both of them would have to check their ego at the door.

I have had a bit of this experience, though the second person was a play partner, not a partner partner, and it was kind of hot. The play partner, let's call him Bill, had set up a scene with me at an event. For me, at that stage of my relationship with Dan, I was allowed to set up my own scenes. He knows how picky I am, so scenes can be rare for me.

Well, Bill and I were going to have a scene. Bill has such respect for Dan that after setting up the scene with me, he went and talked to Dan. Dan pretty much gave Bill blanket consent. He respects and trusts Bill that much, and we've known Bill for years. Anyway, a little bit before the scene was to start, Dan clicked a leash onto my collar and handed me off to Bill for the evening. Then, after our scene, Bill didn't click on a leash because he knew that was Dan's thing, but he held my hand and brought me back to Dan.

This is the type of relationship I would want between two Leaders, if I had two. I'd want them to work in tandem. But, like Dan has had trouble finding someone that would work at a 'sister sub' for me, I'm sure I'd have problems finding the perfect match for what I envision. And that's ok. It still boggles my mind a little bit, trying to think about how that dynamic would work in reality.

I know people who do it. I know people who do it successfully. I don't know if I'm wired to be able to make it work. We'll see. Usually when I say something like that, the Universe decides to act on its sense of humor.

## Tools We've Learned

### *dawn says*

Over the last two decades, we've had to learn a lot of skills to help keep this relationship of power exchange and polyamory moving forward. I could try to draw you the straight line we thought it was going to be, point a to point b. But our real path would be a drawing of a lot of squiggles, loops, and backtracking. It's been a lot of work, and a lot of discovery.

We've had to learn communication skills like porch time, and speaking the unspeakables, and writing our contract... and then re-writing it each year for the first six years or so.

We worked hard on tools like 'working from a place of assistance,' 'not taking things personally,' 'and not or,' and 'seeing things from another person's point of view.' We talk about all of these in more depth in another book of ours, The Polyamory Toolkit.

Not only did we work with these tools, but we also realized that to keep our power dynamic healthy in the midst of all these relationships, we needed time together in our dynamic, just the two of us. When there are more followers involved, it's easy to do events with all of us attending. But we, Dan and me, need time together to recharge as Leader and follower.

# Mindfulness in Service

*dawn says*

## What is Mindfulness and Why is it Important?

Mindfulness is one of those tools that I wish I had learned earlier in our relationship and that I want to and try to share with everyone. We have found it to be so important that we make sure to mention it in most of our classes, as well as meditation, which is what led to us learning mindfulness.

So, what is mindfulness? In its most simplest form, mindfulness is "paying attention on purpose." There are a lot of books out there on mindfulness and meditation. Corporations are even providing classes to their employees on these topics, to increase productivity in their workforce. I use it to bump up my service to gracious service. I use it to be totally present in the moment in my service. To me, mindfulness is more important than skill.

Being mindful can be difficult. Many of us multi-task most of the time. There never seems to be enough time to do all that needs to be done, so we layer things on top of each other. It's not unusual for me to have a TV on in the background as I'm working on the laptop, playing a game on my phone, flirting on text, and trying to figure out what the dog wants. When I'm doing so much at once, how can I give anything my complete attention?

When it comes to service, Dan requires my attention. I require my attention. I cannot be present and serve him if I'm thinking about something else at the same time. Sure, I can go through the motions of serving him, but it's not service as his follower. There is a difference.

For example, there was an evening where we were both working. He was at the table working on something with the podcast, and I was on the laptop on the couch working on a workshop. I hear, "Dawn, get me a cup of coffee." Well, I was in the middle of something so I brought my laptop with me in hand like a pizza box and poured his coffee while reading something. I brought him the coffee, set it on the table, and went back to the couch. Service, right? He asked for coffee, and he got coffee. No hard feelings, no brattiness. Just coffee. Done.

But, that's not what he wanted. When I heard after I sat down, 'slave, I would like a cup of coffee,' I knew I had messed up. I closed my laptop, took a breath to focus myself and bring myself into the room. I got up from the couch, went to him and apologized. He handed me the cup. I slowly walked to the kitchen, feeling myself in the moment. I poured that coffee out and poured fresh coffee into his favorite cup. Before, the cup had only been a tool to hold the coffee. I had no clue which cup I had picked. This time, I was fully aware of what I was doing, and who I was doing it for.

I picked up his favorite cup and when I poured the coffee, I could actually feel the weight of the liquid transferring from one vessel to the other. I could feel the temperature, I could smell the aroma. I held the cup the way he likes it handed to him and felt my feet as I crossed the floor to his side. Gently stepping into his presence, I waited for acknowledgement, and set the cup on the table when he nodded for me to do so. I then made eye contact with him and he smiled at me, releasing me to go back to work. This was what he wanted, not just a hot beverage, but for his follower to serve him. I had not picked up on that, and had only heard the words spoken, because I wasn't in the present moment.

After years of meditating, mindfulness comes naturally to me for the most part. I still multitask. It's in my nature. But, I don't allow that to get in the way of my service anymore. When I make the bed, the only thing I think about is how it's for him. When I take his socks off at night, I put aside the project I am working on, and give my complete focus to the game that we play with his socks and toes battling my slow hands, and our laughter.

Since learning the importance of mindfulness, putting on or taking off his boots takes on a whole new atmosphere. Even if we're at an event and have just gotten back to our hotel room, chatting about the way the class went or about the conversation we just had with someone, I don't talk while taking his boots off. This is a reverent time.

I take a breath to calm my brain down, and focus on the moment. I kneel for him and when I lean in to put my hands on his boots, I can actually smell the leather. I feel the leather and what it's like to have his feet in the boots. I can hear his sigh of relief as I loosen the laces on his boots. During that moment, I can feel our connection. And unless he tells me to do it quickly, I take my time pulling off the boots sensually, rubbing his sock-covered feet one at a time after each boot is placed to the side. I focus completely on the moment.

Think of how needed focus is at a High Protocol event. In my experience, you can't be thinking of a hundred things when you are supposed to be focused on service. If someone's glass is getting low, thinking about anything beyond the present moment is going to prevent you from seeing what needs to be done. For me, the point of a high protocol event is service - and not just plain service, but gracious service. Let's make this special for everyone, not a chore, which is what it feels like to others if someone is not focused on what they are doing.

Maybe it's the stories in your head that are preventing you from being in the moment. "I don't look sexy in this outfit." "I'm terrified they will ring the bell for my service." "I can't do this." "What if they ring the bell and I make a fool of myself?" "What if I do something wrong and get called out on it?" I don't know if you've done a High Protocol event before, but I can guarantee you that most of the subs there are thinking these private thoughts. And these stories and thoughts get in the way of our focus on the task at hand. Doubt, Anxiety, Worry. We talk more about that next.

## What Hinders Mindfulness? And How Can We Resolve It?

Mindfulness and its simplicity may sound easy. You just pay attention on purpose... but for me, I struggled with it for a time. In Buddhism, where you can find a lot of information on mindfulness and meditation, they list five hindrances to mindfulness. When I discovered this, my first thought was one of relief. I'm not alone, but now maybe I can understand what's going on.

### *Desire*

#### *dawn says*

Desire in this sense is grasping or clinging to something we want and don't have. Desire is a distraction from the here and now. If we are always thinking about what we'd like to have instead of what we do have, we can't be in the moment.

#### *Dan says*

A quick point of clarity. Desire is not bad, nor are we advising you to avoid it. Sitting at my desk right now, I can bring to my thoughts that I am hungry and desire food. I can turn my attention toward dawn (who at this moment is getting dressed) and desire to grab her and drag her off to the bedroom. These are not bad things. But if we want to be mindful of what we are doing - whether that is serving our Leader, or writing a book - then the desire can become a distraction. When it is time for lunch, I will engage with my desire to satisfy my hunger. When it is time for midday sex, then that desire will be acted on as well. But right now, I will work on the book.

## *Aversion*

***dawn says***

Aversion is wanting things to be different than what they are. Aversion can also contain hatred, anger, and ill-will. We are spending energy and focus on trying to push something away. We can't be in the moment at the same time.

## *Apathy and Laziness*

Apathy and Laziness is literally about having a lack of alertness and not being able to concentrate. This is a major distraction from mindfulness.

## *Anxiety and Worry*

Anxiety and Worry cause a tenseness as we live in fear of something from the past or in the future. This is the very definition of not living in the present.

## *Doubt*

Doubt is a huge hindrance to a submissive. Doubt is when we have a lack of confidence in ourselves or our relationship. It could be we don't understand what we should be doing, or we don't trust that it works, or we think we are not doing it correctly.

When our minds are wandering, how can we bring our focus back? If it's just us working on ourselves, we can do everything from breathing techniques to bring our thoughts into the movement, to splashing water on our face if we are feeling apathetic, to asking questions to try and resolve doubt. We can ground or anchor, which I cover in the survivor chapter.

But, since we are in Power Exchange relationships, there are other tricks available to us. If I'm not paying attention to Dan or to the situation we are in, or at a High Protocol event, Dan has a certain voice he uses to get my attention. That usually snaps me out of whatever funk I'm in that has caused me to drift away. He can snap his fingers or give me a command, such as to kneel or breathe. If it's in our agreements, which it is, he can slam me against a wall to get my attention. I find that super hot, and will instantly come back.

Know yourself as a sub, or know your sub if you are a Dom, before doing this. It's one of those things that will either work great... or blow up as a landmine. The point is, there are tools available to us that others don't have. Use them.

## How Can You Learn Mindfulness?

### *dawn says*

Mindfulness was a side effect of meditating. I wasn't trying to learn mindfulness when I started a meditation practice. I saw Dan start to meditate as he studied Buddhism, and I watched a sense of equanimity fill his spirit. Things that used to bother him didn't bother him anymore. Instead of stressing about the past and future, he was rooted in the present. I wanted that calmness. So, I started meditating with him.

Not only did I practice mindful meditation with him, but I also participated and led guided meditations and shamanic journeys. All of these are helpful in training your mind to concentrate.

The one I practice the most is mindful meditation. I don't have to do much to prep for this style. I don't need to be in a quiet place. All I need to do is to sit still and breathe. As stories happen, and they will, realize you are in a story and come back to the breath. Feel the air on your upper lip and feel your breath expand your lungs. You can only breathe in the moment, so it's a good practice to get into.

Success isn't not having any thoughts during meditation. Success is realizing you are in a story, stopping it, and coming back to the breath (the moment). You are training your brain to come back, and to let the story go faster and faster each time it happens. Developing this skill during a set meditation time will help you do the same when you aren't meditating. When you are standing in that corner watching over the Doms during a High Protocol gathering, and your mind fills with doubt, you'll be able to catch the story, come back to the breath, and realize nothing is as important as the 'right now' that you are supposed to be focusing on.

### *Dan Says*

I feel like dawn has already done a good job of describing how to meditate. I'm going to share below the same thing, but stated in the way that I teach it.

#### *Sit*

You can use a meditation cushion (zafu) or meditator's bench (Seiza Bench) or just use a chair. If using a chair, which I often do, make sure it is a solid one. No desk chairs with wheels. Sit toward the front edge of your chair. Once you are sitting, you'll want to roll your pelvis forward, so you are sitting on the two bones in your bottom, sometimes called the sitting bones. Allow your back to be straight and dip your chin a bit. In your sitting, find a balance. You don't want to be worried about sitting ramrod straight, but don't slouch either. Think of the string of a musical instrument - not too tight or too loose.

#### *Breathe*

Rest your attention on the breath as it travels in and out of the nose. Just allow yourself to feel the breath. You may find it useful to count it – on the in breath, mentally say "in," and on the out breath, mentally count "one." We will come back to the breath in a minute.

## *Hands*

Do something with your hands. You may want to make a steeple, or "lion's paw," or touch your forefinger to your thumb, or prayer hands. Or something else. Regardless of which position (mudra) you pick, it is yours, and you'll want to keep using it when you meditate.

## *Mind*

Here is the part that people find the most challenging, both in getting over their own preconceived views of what meditation is, as well as what they are supposed to be doing… and just sitting still with yourself! As you sit and breathe, with the intent to rest attention on the breath, counting away, you'll find the mind wants to wander.

Stories of the past, the future, what else you could be doing, are you doing this right, I took a right on my way to work when I meant to go left, but I came across a nice little store where I found that vase that had... oh right, meditating. Your mind will wander. It is ok. If your mind wanders ten thousand times during your sitting, it is ok. Come back to the breath.

I use a mantra I heard. When I recognize my mind has wandered, I say to myself, "Recognize, relax, return to the breath." I am acknowledging that my mind has wandered,

I am not allowing myself to be frustrated about it, and I am getting back to sitting with the breath.

## *Simplify*

One thing that will make this practice easier is to be consistent in when and where you meditate. For me, this is every morning, by this bookcase.

Start with a timer set for ten minutes. When you are ready, you may find it beneficial to go to twenty or thirty minutes.

If you find yourself saying "I am not doing a good job at meditation!" then congratulate yourself on sitting in one spot for ten minutes of practice.

When meditation is easy, then practice meditation when it is easy. When meditation is hard, practice meditation when it is hard.

# Conclusion

As with meditation, so it goes with power exchange: when it is easy, practice when it is easy. When power exchange is hard, practice power exchange when it is hard.

If this relationship style appeals to you, the best way to learn about it is to try taking the plunge. Start conversations. Read books. Go to events, when you can. Try drafting a contract on your own, to think through what your own needs and desires are. Get to know yourself, and get to know other people.

The tools we shared in this book are ones that have worked for us over the last two decades. We hope some of them will help you avoid the pitfalls we stumbled into. Some of them may be right for you, or for your partner(s), and some of them may not. You are the expert in what works for you; use that expertise.

If there's one thing we hope you take away from this book, it is this. Whoever you are, whatever you've been through, you have the ability to learn, and grow, and become the person you want to be. And although it does take work and a good deal of self-reflection, it is possible to create relationships that hold you up, and help you thrive. We did it, and so can you.

# About the Authors

**Dan and dawn** have been a power exchange couple since 2001 and have presented at over 200 events around North America. Not only do they enjoy teaching workshops and classes, they also share their insights and experiences via books, specialized events, and fun consent negotiation playing cards.

Dan and dawn also co-host the longest continuous power exchange and kink podcast, **Erotic Awakening**, exploring all things erotic; they were part of the team that created the Columbus Space, an alternative community center; they won the 2016 MAsT International Member's Choice Presenter of the Year Award, and they are Great Lakes title holders (2010). In addition, they have served as co-producers of PXS (Power eXchange Summit) and BTL (Beyond the Love, A Polyamory Summit), have been featured educators on Kink Academy and Creative Sexuality, and their work has been referenced in multiple books, articles, and media. Learn more at **www.eroticawakening.com**.

# Other Works

## Books

*Living M/s*
*Polyamory Toolkit*
*Sex, Stories, and Power Exchange*
*The Polyamory Dating Guide*

## Classes

Find regular updates on our presentation and event schedule at **www.eroticawakening.com/calendar**

## Podcast

Plus, tune in weekly to the Erotic Awakening Podcast: **www.eroticawakening.com/podcast**

## Patreon

Support and get special perks at **Patreon.com/eroticawakening**

Made in the USA
Las Vegas, NV
29 September 2023